I0272218

WHO WILL BELIEVE MY VERSE?

THE CODE IN SHAKESPEARE'S SONNETS

James Leyland studied theatre at the University of New South Wales, and at the Western Australian Academy of Performing Arts. After several years of theatre work, he lectured in acting, theatre history and cyber-media at the University of Ballarat. Since 2010, he has coached collaborative software development teams.

James Goding is Emeritus Professor of Experimental Pathology at Monash University, Melbourne. His research interests are immunology, biochemistry and genetics, and have involved the analysis of DNA and protein sequences, which are related via the Genetic Code.

WHO WILL BELIEVE MY VERSE?

THE CODE IN SHAKESPEARE'S SONNETS

JAMES LEYLAND & JAMES GODING

Australian Scholarly

Published 2018 by
Australian Scholarly Publishing Pty Ltd
7 Lt Lothian St Nth, North Melbourne, Vic 3051
Tel: 03 9329 6963 / Fax: 03 9329 5452
enquiry@scholarly.info / www.scholarly.info

ISBN 978-1-925588-67-5

Cover design: Wayne Saunders

Cover: The image of Sir Henry Neville is overlaid with the Dedication to Shakespeare's Sonnets. *Who will believe my verse?* – see the first line of Sonnet 17, p. 184.

Contents

Acknowledgements

We thank Brenda James for her friendship, guidance and criticism. Her discovery of the hidden identity of Henry Neville has initiated a revolution in Shakespearean scholarship. We would also like to thank John Casson for advice and generosity in sharing information and ideas prior to publication; Satoshi Tomokiyo for allowing us to cite his work on Elizabethan cryptography and the codes used by Henry Neville in his diplomatic correspondence; Rosemary Warner, who allowed us to cite her work on Sonnet 134; Gareth Hughes of English Heritage for his patience and great assistance in allowing us to examine Neville's portrait at Audley End; rare books curator Helen Clish who kindly allowed us to spend a day examining the annotated copy of *Halle's Chronicles* in the Hesketh Collection at the University of Lancaster; Bernard Lane of *The Australian* newspaper for his courage in publishing our first decryptions during the World Shakespeare Congress held in Brisbane, Australia in July 2006; Amanda Smith and Lyn Gallacher of the Australian Broadcasting Corporation for taking the risk of broadcasting a panel discussion on the Authorship Question; Margaret Rees-Jones for drawing to our attention the measures taken by the Ballantyne Press to preserve the anonymity of Sir Walter Scott; Tony Minchin for his ongoing support and editorial scrutiny; and Adrian Kelly and Owen Gingerich for their scholarly advice. We also thank the many friends who have encouraged us along the way – Mark Bradbeer, Robert van Mackelenberg, Juergen Saalmueller, Mark Alderson, Ian Fraser, Collin O'Brien, Bob Atkins, Richard Larkins, Edward Byrne, John Stocker, Jacques Miller and Gustav Nossal. We are very grateful to Anastasia Buryak and Wayne Saunders of Australian Scholarly Publishing for their care, skill and patience. Finally, our most heartfelt thanks go to Lynne Williams and Emanuela Handman for their patience with our obsession.

Preface

The Sonnets of Shakespeare offer us the greatest puzzle in the history of English literature – A.L. Rowse

The small volume of 154 short poems entitled *Shake-speares Sonnets* published in 1609 has mystified readers for centuries.[1] Why are they so cryptic? Some scholars have felt that they are in some way autobiographical, while others have viewed them as abstract poetical exercises. Part of the problem is that we know so little about the life of the writer.

For the last 200 years countless books have been written to address questions and incongruities surrounding the identity of Shakespeare. Historical evidence reveals little about his life, and almost nothing that is admirable. The glimpses that remain primarily concern petty litigation and grain-dealing. Shakespeare's contemporary Ben Jonson is by far the most forthcoming, but his praises are always diluted with ambiguity.

The only document that Shakespeare is certain to have authored is his will, which seems to lack any great generosity. It contains no mention of authorship, manuscripts or books. Indeed, no evidence has ever been found that he owned any books, though a great many people have looked very diligently. His daughters were illiterate and his own formal schooling must have ended by the time he was fourteen at the most – an educational disadvantage in any era. Nevertheless, there is one certain fact; the name William Shakespeare is printed on 40 or so of the 43 works published in his lifetime.

Hundreds of conflicting theories have been proposed to explain the shortcomings in the historical record. Stratfordians believe William Shakespeare of Stratford is the true author, while Anti-Stratfordians or "doubters" do not. The doubters suggest that in those dangerous times there was a writer in hiding who engaged William Shakespeare the actor, theatre manager and script-broker as a front-man. Dozens of candidates have been suggested, each with an inventory of evidence extensive enough to be compared with that supporting Shakespeare of Stratford.

A definitive identification of the author would be of enormous value in unlocking meaning that currently eludes us. The poetic works in particular are full of cryptic references which appear to relate to the biography of the author, but scholars agree that based on our current knowledge this meaning is probably lost forever.

---

[1] For the remainder of this book we will use the modern spelling, *Shakespeare's Sonnets*.

With so little evidence, so much of which is questionable, controversy has been bitter and personal. Doubters are accused of snobbery and ignorance; Stratfordians of authoritarianism and selectivity. There is no “smoking gun” evidence for any candidate. On the other hand, it is hard to imagine what might constitute a “smoking gun”.

Throughout history cryptography has been widely used to protect sensitive information, and from time to time “doubters” have proposed perceived codes as evidence of an alternative candidate. But theories involving codes have provided powerful ammunition for Stratfordians, and until 2005 no code concerning Shakespearean authorship has yielded sufficient evidence to support its authenticity.

In 2005, an independent English researcher Brenda James proposed Sir Henry Neville as the hidden writer. She had assembled his name from fragments of text she had found in the strange and seemingly clumsy Dedication to *Shakespeare’s Sonnets.* Brenda James and William Rubinstein found that Neville’s education, intellect and outlook all aligned very precisely with what might be expected of the author of the works of Shakespeare. Neville’s social network included both Ben Jonson, Shakespeare’s supposed rival, and the Earl of Southampton, Shakespeare’s supposed patron. Supporting her belief that the Dedication is a code, James noted that as Ambassador to France Neville used codes extensively. Above all, the events of his life matched with the generally accepted chronology of the plays.

James did not reveal her methods in her first book, but we were sufficiently intrigued to set about investigating the Dedication to verify her findings independently. By setting the Dedication in a grid and following instructions based on wordplay in the text, we succeeded in assembling the name Sir Henry Neville. Our preliminary results supported her findings and were published in *The Australian* newspaper in 2006. Although many readers were intrigued, most were not convinced. And even if the name Sir Henry Neville were in the Dedication, this would not necessarily mean that he was the author of the works attributed to Shakespeare.

In 2008, we discovered something new. We found what seemed to be connections between the Dedication and the sonnets themselves, and these connections reinforced our assembly of the name Sir Henry Neville. Though striking, at first these connections seemed random and many sonnets did not seem to fit. However, the further we looked, the more examples we found, and the more consistent the pattern. In many instances, the Dedication illuminated hitherto unnoticed wordplay in specific sonnets, suggesting that the author of the Dedication knew the sonnets as intimately as their author. The multiplicity of alignments suggested that they might show definitively that the person who wrote the sonnets was the same person who wrote the Dedication containing the name Sir Henry Neville.

This book presents our findings. We begin by setting out the known biography of William Shakespeare (1564–1616) which has led many to question whether he is the real author of the works that bear his name. In contrast, the biography of his contemporary Sir Henry Neville (1562–1615) seems to align seamlessly with the accepted chronology of the works.

To better understand the references in the Sonnets, we outline the major known events of Neville's life and something of his friends and connections. Of particular note are the Earl of Southampton with whom Neville was imprisoned and who was dedicatee of Shakespeare's *Venus and Adonis* and *Rape of Lucrece*, and Ben Jonson who certainly worked with Shakespeare the actor, and was a friend of Sir Henry Neville.

As our findings depend on decrypting the Dedication to the Sonnets, we touch on the encryption techniques of the Elizabethan period and the specific grid-mapping system used by Sir Henry Neville as Ambassador to France. His techniques seem to draw on the grid-mapping code described by the ancient Greek Polybius in his *Histories*. That Neville was influenced by Polybius's work is certain, as it provided the political model of *Mixed Government* that he advanced for 10 years in his efforts to reconcile the roles of King James, parliament and the people.

In Chapters 4 to 6 we explore the grid-mapping within the Dedication which also seems to draw on Polybius. The relationships to specific sonnets are based on very distinctive Shakespearean wordplay, and especially the signature "half-puns" described by Stephen Booth. These chapters contain a summary of the evidence that we believe verifies the code and so constitutes a definitive identification of Sir Henry Neville as the author of the Sonnets.

In Chapter 7, we conjecture a new candidate for the mysterious identity within the Dedication, *Mr WH*. Our candidate overlaps with Neville's immediate family in many ways. Indeed, his participation in a plot to kill the Queen, his subsequent imprisonment in the Tower and his escape from execution all mirror Neville's biography to an uncanny degree. In addition, this man was Queen Elizabeth's most eminent teacher of drama who operated out of the very building in Blackfriars where Neville was born, and which later became the Blackfriars Theatre.

In the appendices, we provide a catalogue of Sonnets supporting the encrypted message as well as additional words in the Dedication that also map to sonnets but are incidental to the central message.

In Appendix 3, we include an observation of the name *Neville* which occurs in the very intriguing Sonnet 134. This observation was made and brought to our attention by independent researcher Rosemary Warner who at the time had no connection with the discussion of Sir Henry Neville as a candidate in the Shakespeare Authorship Question.

In Appendix 5, we identify sonnets 7, 12, 30, 52 and 60 as examples where the content seems to align with the most familiar units of time – the week, hour, month, year and minute. The theme of *Time* repeating is explored in many of the sonnets.

We have not attempted to answer the question of how a ghost writer might keep his identity a secret. The 23 years from 1593 when *Venus and Adonis* was published until the death of Shakespeare in 1616 is a very long time to sustain such a subterfuge. This may be explained in either of two ways; either that there was no subterfuge and Shakespeare of Stratford is the true author; or the subterfuge was so effective that no evidence remains. We note that the enduring falsehoods of history tend to be *virtuous lies* (Sonnet 72). That is, the custodians hold the secret for a perceived "greater good".

An illustrative contemporary example of subterfuge is that of the London street artist Banksy whose identity has been concealed for more than 20 years to protect him from prosecution. Similarly, the identity of the best-selling Italian novelist Elena Ferrante has been protected within her circle for 24 years. If the identity of a famous person can be kept secret for decades in an age of electronic surveillance, the notion that this could have been achieved 400 years ago may not seem so remarkable.

Moreover, the longer the secret is kept, the greater the investment a custodian may have in holding it. In such cases it does not seem so unlikely that a secret might easily be buried within one or two generations. In *The Truth Will Out* (2005), Brenda James surmises the circumstances and methods that would facilitate such a subterfuge for Sir Henry Neville. In Chapter 7, we conjecture how it may have come about that such a secret could be buried and lost – even within Neville's own family.

Our analysis is limited to the Sonnets; we have not looked deeply at the other works that bear the name of William Shakespeare. Perhaps the clearest evidence in favour of Sir Henry Neville outside of the Sonnets may be found in the history plays. The plethora of allusions to members of the Neville family and the significant events of their lineage is remarkable. For a thorough examination of these congruencies we recommend *Sir Henry Neville, Alias William Shakespeare: Authorship Evidence in the History Plays* (2015) by Mark Bradbeer and John Casson.

Lastly, our discussion of Shakespearean wordplay is limited to what we believe is necessary for the purposes of explicating our decryption. However, our summary does little justice to this immense topic. We refer the reader to the Stratfordian scholar Stephen Booth for a much greater appreciation of the distinctive poetic art of *Shakespeare's Sonnets.* We acknowledge with the greatest admiration our debt to his work which has provided a much deeper understanding of these poetic miracles.

The earliest sketch of “Shakespeare’s Monument” in the Holy Trinity Church in Stratford, drawn by William Dugdale in 1634 and later engraved by Wenceslas Hollar for *Antiquities of Warwickshire* 1656. It shows the greatest English poet neither holding a pen nor in an attitude of writing (see p. 6)

Chapter 1: The Shakespeare Authorship Question

The collection of poems entitled *Shakespeare's Sonnets* has absorbed and mystified generations of readers. There seems to be vastly more meaning locked away in them than has ever been revealed. Each sonnet is multi-layered and seems to reference specific personal events, people, places and ideas. However, nothing among the few known facts of Shakespeare's life seems to relate to them, leading some to question whether Shakespeare really was the author of the works that bear his name.

Over the last 150 years, more than seventy candidates have been proposed as the true writer of the works of William Shakespeare. It is widely accepted that a few plays are collaborations, but almost everyone agrees that there was only one *Shakespeare.*

That there are so many candidates, each with a biography that maps to certain aspects of the works, is an odd phenomenon. It would seem to suggest that the circumstances needed to produce the greatest writer in western literature are not all that unusual. However, the reality may be that candidates proliferate because a "low bar" for admission to this group has been set with reference to the known biography of William Shakespeare himself. The verifiable facts of his life are few. None presages an eternal genius, and several are distinctly unedifying.

Over the centuries biographers have overlaid this faint sketch with the conjectural colour and line that we have become so familiar with, and that most accept today. Many assertions in biographies of Shakespeare have no basis in the historical record. Similarly, each of the seventy candidates has received narrative embellishment, elaborating from a few known facts that might align with the composition of the works. Perhaps it is the universality of Shakespeare's works that allows resonances to be found in the biography of almost any of his contemporaries.

Nor is it difficult to make a case for why any candidate may want to remain anonymous. Although there was a nominal rule of law, the reality was a theocratic dictatorship. All printed works were subject to censorship and many were banned outright. Any criticism of the clergy or royalty risked brutal and summary punishment. Torture was the norm. Execution was an expression of state authority, and was often transformed into a public spectacle and protracted with fire, hanging, evisceration and dismemberment. Severed heads and limbs were displayed prominently in towns and cities. Almost invariably, the ruin of an individual also meant the ruin of the whole family.

Literary anonymity may seem strange today, but at that time it seems to have been almost as common as not. Although the name *William Shakespeare* was included in the printing of the best-selling poem *Venus and Adonis* in 1593, the author's earliest plays were published anonymously.

It was not until 1598 that a play was ever published under that name. These anonymous early plays are mostly histories and some are intensely political. It is hardly surprising that *Richard II* was first published anonymously in 1597, since it traces the justifiable overthrow of a monarch.

Of the dozens of candidates that have been proposed as the true author, several seem to be argued almost as well as the orthodox account. It is understandable that, as each new or revised fiction is promoted as fact, many readers reject the whole blighted question and adhere to the name on the book as the least troublesome option. However, the large number of candidates does not invalidate the authorship question; rather it reflects the depth of doubt and the lack of evidence with which to identify the right person.

Most scholars admit no uncertainty as to whether Shakespeare was the true author. And indeed, there is documentary evidence from the late Tudor and early Jacobean periods that many people did indeed associate William Shakespeare with the plays and poems now attributed to him. The erotic best-seller *Venus and Adonis,* the first work that named William Shakespeare as author, was published in 1593, and as previously noted, it was not until 1598 that the name appeared on the first of the 40 or so plays that followed. It seems odd that the writer did not capitalise on the commercial success of *Venus and Adonis* by including his name on the plays published through 1594–97, especially if William Shakespeare of Stratford were the writer, given his apparent business acumen. Despite this, there is every reason to think that to the Tudor and Stuart public, William Shakespeare of Stratford was the writer.

Of greater interest are the few contemporary references to Shakespeare from individuals who might have known the real author personally. If Shakespeare of Stratford were not the author, each of these personal references must be wrong, either through error or deliberate misrepresentation. Error cannot explain all, and misrepresentation seems unthinkable, as it would rely on some sort of subterfuge, over a period of more than twenty years. Orthodox Shakespeareans favour the term "conspiracy" with its sinister connotations, but it is a fair question. Which is more likely: an extended, perhaps renewing agreement, sinister or virtuous, to conceal the true author; or that the author is indeed William Shakespeare of Stratford?

Personal references to Shakespeare:

1592 – Robert Greene, *Groatsworth of Wit*
1593, 1594 – Shakespeare's two dedications to Southampton
1595, 1599 or later – George Buc, two annotations
1599 – Ben Jonson, *Every Man out of His Humour*
1606–1615 – Francis Beaumont, verse letter to Ben Jonson

1623 – The First Folio
  Ben Jonson, two commendatory poems
  Heminge and Condell, two epistles
  Leonard Digges, James Mabbe, and Hugh Holland, one commendatory poem each
1629 – Ben Jonson, *Ode (to himself)*
1640 – Ben Jonson, *Timber*, published posthumously.
1640 – Leonard Digges, commendatory verse to *Poems: Written by Wil. Shake-speare. Gent.*, published posthumously.

Impersonal references:

1598 – Francis Meres, *Palladis Tamia*
1598 – Richard Barnfield, *Poems in Divers Humours*
1599 – John Weever, one epigram
1598–1601 – Anonymous university play, *Return to Parnassus*
1598–1601 – Gabriel Harvey, one annotation
1610 – John Davies of Hereford, one commendatory verse
1616–1623 – William Basse, one commendatory verse.

For brevity, we have not included analysis of this testimonial evidence other than some discussion of Ben Jonson and Southampton whose apparent associations with William Shakespeare are taken as some of the strongest evidence in favour of his authorship. Jonson is exceptionally noteworthy as he has most to say about Shakespeare. Southampton is also noteworthy because he is the dedicatee of Shakespeare's early poems, and his silence on this matter is widely interpreted as some sort of affirmation of Shakespeare's authorship.[1] As we will see, both men were closely associated with Sir Henry Neville.

In the remainder of this chapter we summarise the biography of William Shakespeare of Stratford and list the four leading alternative authorship candidates, including Sir Henry Neville of Billingbear.

William Shakespeare of Stratford

William Shakespeare was born in 1564 in Stratford-upon-Avon, an agricultural centre of around 2,000 people. As his father was High Bailiff of Stratford, effectively Mayor, William was entitled to attend the local grammar school, though there is no documentary evidence that he did so. At most, Shakespeare's formal schooling may have continued until he was fourteen.

---

[1] There are several excellent analyses of this testimonial evidence. In *Shakespeare's Unorthodox Biography*, Diana Price methodically reviews the evidence in favour of William Shakespeare and finds not only an unusual absence of evidence of his authorship compared with his literary peers, but also a high level of ambiguity in the surviving testimony. Price, D. *Shakespeare's Unorthodox Biography: New Evidence of an Authorship Problem* (Greenwood Press, Westport Connecticut, 2001; revised edition published by shakespeare-authorship.com/Bookmasters USA, 2012).

Both his parents were illiterate, and it is likely that his wife Anne Hathaway, whom he married when he was 18, was illiterate too. Her signature was the simple mark made by those who could not write. Anne was around eight years older than William, and three months pregnant at the time they were married in 1582.

In contrast to the rich celebration of educated women in the plays, the literacy of Shakespeare's daughters is doubtful. One laboured signature of his eldest daughter Susannah survives, from a time at which she had been married to a published doctor for 40 years.

The signature of Shakespeare's eldest daughter, "susanna hall", from a deed dated 2 June 1647

Shakespeare's younger daughter Judith was certainly illiterate as evidenced in her signatures below.

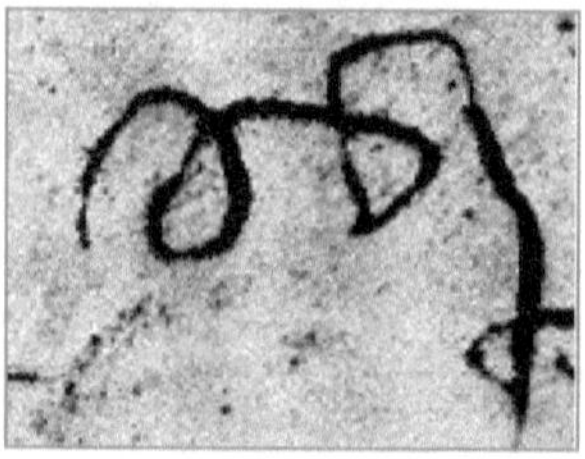

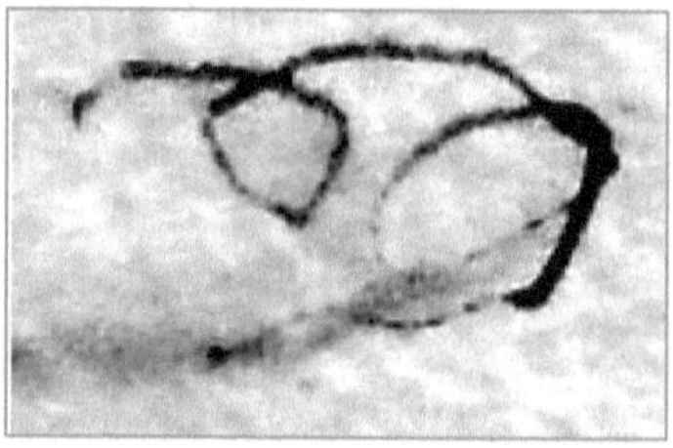

The two "pigtail" signatures of Shakespeare's second daughter Judith, "J", from a deed she witnessed in 1611

At some point before 1592 Shakespeare left his young family in Stratford and went to London where he worked as an actor. Later he appears to have received most of his income as a shareholder in the Globe theatre. He also traded in grain.

The first work now attributed to him dates from about 1590, when he was 26 years old, and the last from about 1612, when he was 48. We know that he travelled between Stratford and London, but there is no evidence that he travelled any further, let alone outside England. Overseas travel required written authorisation and was monitored closely to guard against the movement of Catholic spies.

Even the earliest of Shakespeare's plays shows easy familiarity with the customs and manners of the court and the aristocracy. Moreover, in the history plays, the ancestors of the contemporary Elizabethan nobility are depicted intimately and often very critically. In a highly class-stratified society it seems remarkable that an actor from a small country town could acquire this detailed knowledge and would dare to comment on the lineage of powerful families. The works are generous in depicting all classes, but seem to be written from the perspective of privilege. Specialised references to courtly dress, manners, swordplay and aristocratic sports such as falconry are used with great facility, and with no attempt to explain them to a wider audience.

Shakespeare's only son Hamnet, the fraternal twin of Judith, died in 1596 aged 11. The similarity of this very common name to the character *Hamlet*, which was produced seven years later, is generally regarded as coincidental since *Hamlet* derives from a much older story, *Amleth.* Nevertheless, *Hamlet* seems a most unusual choice for a central character if the writer is also a father grieving for a child with a similar name. It appears that Shakespeare retired to Stratford around 1610, and lived there as one of its wealthiest burghers until his death in 1616, of unknown causes.

Paper artefacts of the middle classes have not survived well over the centuries, but it is a fact that no book has ever been discovered in which he wrote his name (a common practice with books due to their value). And, despite there being no less than 111 letters that appear onstage in the plays, and many more referred to, not one single letter of his own has survived for posterity.[2] Indeed, Diana Price shows that the 24 most famous of Shakespeare's literary contemporaries left documentary evidence of authorship. Shakespeare alone left none.[3]

The most substantial personal document known to have been overseen by Shakespeare is his will. Perhaps significantly, around a third of this document is devoted to protecting his bequest to his younger daughter Judith from her husband Thomas Quiney. Excluding the unsigned manuscript, Hand D of *Sir Thomas More*, the three scrawled signatures on his will amount to half of all Shakespeare's known handwriting. Each signature is spelt differently, with differently formed letters, and none is spelt Shakespeare, or Shake-speare, the variants that were well-established on 40 of the 43 published editions that bear his name.[4] It is conceivable that he was unwell, but there is no evidence in his will that Shakespeare was at all comfortable using a pen.

---

2 Stewart, A. *Shakespeare's Letters* (Oxford University Press, New York, 2008).

3 Price, *Shakespeare's Unorthodox Biography.*

4 The three instances of different spellings on quartos were *Shak-speare, Shakspeare, and Shakespere.*

The will is very detailed, but unlike those of other educated contemporaries it does not include any books or manuscripts, writing materials, paper, furniture associated with writing, desks, bookcases, trunks, chests, cultural objects, paintings, tapestries, or musical instruments. Nothing in it indicates a cultured life. Unlike the unfaltering generosity of his plays, there is no evidence of any community spirit by way of endowments, such as for education. His bequest to the poor is the statutory minimum of ten pounds, and its disbursal is not described.[5]

He was buried in the Holy Trinity Church, with the following epitaph:

GOOD FREND FOR IESUS SAKE FORBEARE,
TO DIGG THE DUST ENCLOASED HEARE.
BLESE BE YE MAN YT SPARE THES STONES,
AND CURST BE HE YT MOVES MY BONES.

It seems most likely that it was Shakespeare of Stratford who composed these lines because they are written in the first person, and because it would be very unusual to misrepresent authorship in such a solemn context. Many commentators have found this curse disappointing.

Conversely, on the two occasions of greatest national grief in his lifetime where we might confidently expect something of eternal quality, Shakespeare does not put his name to any tribute. There is no Shakespearean eulogy for Queen Elizabeth in 1603, nor is anything included under the name William Shakespeare among the eulogies of 32 poets for Prince Henry in 1612.[6] These exceptions are mystifying. However if another author were falsely using the name Shakespeare, these blanks might make more sense.

Nothing is known of the commissioning of the bust of Shakespeare in the Holy Trinity Church in Stratford. Shakespeare's "Stratford Moniment" is referred to in Leonard Digges's prefatory poem in the First Folio of 1623, and is thought to have been sculpted by the eminent Gheerart Janssen. However, the earliest surviving sketch, made in 1634 by William Dugdale, shows the greatest English poet neither holding a pen nor in an attitude of writing (p. xii).

The Leading Authorship Candidates

Four main contenders have emerged as alternatives.

Francis Bacon (1561–1626) was an early candidate, but has few supporters today. Bacon's dates, education, intellect, and many of his interests coincide with what we would expect of Shakespeare. Much of his writing survives, but it is long-winded and very unlike Shakespeare. Although his thoughtful work on codes also survives, the desperate

[5] Bonner Miller Cutting http://www.theshakespeareunderground.com/2011/09/where-theres-a-will-episode-1-with-bonner-miller-cutting/. Accessed 15 September 2013.
[6] Henry Chettle admonishes this neglect in *England's Mourning Garment* (1603).

cryptographic claims of the Baconians have left the whole question of authorship in disrepute and open to ridicule.[7] It should be noted that Bacon was the half-brother of Neville's step-mother, and about the same age as Neville.

Christopher Marlowe (1564–1593) is widely regarded as one of the greatest of Elizabethan poets, but there is a fatal objection to his candidature as the author of Shakespeare. The last of the Shakespeare plays, *Cymbeline, The Winter's Tale, The Tempest* and *Henry VIII,* are generally agreed to date from 1610–1612. In order for Marlowe to be the author of Shakespeare we need to postulate that his well-documented murder and burial in 1593 was a cover-up, and that he lived on for something like twenty years, for which there is no evidence. Because he died so young, Marlowe's art did not achieve its full potential. Nevertheless, it has been observed that this early work outshines the work of Shakespeare at the same age.

Currently, the most popular alternative candidate is Edward de Vere, the Earl of Oxford (1550–1604). The case for him has been argued by many authors, notably Charlton Ogburn, and supported by Oxford's descendants including the current Lord Vere and the De Vere Society.[8] The first half of Ogburn's book presents the anti-Stratfordian case with great clarity, and is worth reading in its own right. The latter half argues for Oxford.

Many *ad hoc* arguments are required to fit Oxford into the authorship of Shakespeare. Oxford died in 1604, but the plays continued until at least 1609, and probably until 1612. Oxfordians counter this by disputing the dates of the plays.

The poetry of Oxford that has survived is mediocre in quality and quite unlike that of Shakespeare. Moreover, it is difficult to accept that he published only his best work under a pseudonym.

And, as has been well documented by Alan Nelson in *Monstrous Adversary*, Oxford's aggressive, violent, and misogynistic personality seems incompatible with the gentle humanism that shines through Shakespeare's works.[9]

The candidate who is the subject of our analysis is the politician, mathematician, and diplomat Sir Henry Neville (1562–1615). Neville's dates align with the accepted production of the works, perhaps even better than Shakespeare's, and Neville's biography matches what we would expect of the biography of the writer of Shakespeare's works.

---

[7] Friedman, W.F., and Friedman, E.S. *The Shakespearean Ciphers Examined: An Analysis of Cryptographic Systems Used as Evidence That Some Author Other Than William Shakespeare Wrote the Plays Attributed to Him* (Cambridge University Press, 1957).

[8] Ogburn, C. *The Mystery of William Shakespeare. Foreword by Lord Vere* (Sphere Books, Penguin, London, 1988).

[9] Nelson, A. *Monstrous Adversary: The Life of Edward De Vere, 17th Earl of Oxford* (Liverpool University Press, 2003).

He has the right breadth of experience, travel, linguistic ability, demonstrated practical intellectual capability, the right literary connections, and the need for discretion. None of these attributes is unique, but no other candidate can claim quite so many.

Most importantly, unlike other candidates, there is a positive claim to his authorship. In 2005, independent literary historian Brenda James published her identification of Sir Henry Neville, a name previously unknown to her, from analysis of the Dedication to *Shakespeare's Sonnets* (1609). She did not publish her cryptographic techniques or detailed results until 2008. In the meantime, we set out to validate independently her discovery of Sir Henry Neville. Our research has yielded evidence that we judge to support her theory as well as a number of reciprocal links between the Dedication and the Sonnets that were previously unknown. This analysis is examined in detail in Chapters 4 to 7. However, first it may be useful to gain a better appreciation of Sir Henry Neville himself.

Personal Testimony relating to Sir Henry Neville

The excesses of Tudor and Stuart courtly manners and the sycophantic tributes to patrons are often repellent to a modern reader. By contrast, the many tributes to the character of Sir Henry Neville consistently express admiration for his greatness of mind and deep affection for his personal qualities. Certainly, Neville had exceptional material and social advantages. But privilege alone does not account for the high regard in which he was held as a thinker, statesman, and person of the most profound integrity and compassion. Moreover, these tributes are often from his social superiors.

In 1578 Henry Savile, one of the foremost intellectuals of the era and one of the compilers of the King James Bible, invited Neville to join his party on a three-year tour of Europe, acquiring books for Oxford University. While on this tour, both Sir Phillip Sidney and his father wrote letters to Philip's brother Robert Sidney commending Neville to him.

From a young age Neville was identified as a potential future statesman. In 1583, Elizabeth's spymaster Francis Walsingham undertook a diplomatic mission to Scotland which included the young Robert Devereux, future Earl of Essex. A contemporary observation of this embassy highlights "Neville" among this company as *distinguished for his book-learning.* The classical scholar Dana Sutton proposes that this Neville is Sir Henry Neville.[10] In the same year Neville was elected to parliament, and throughout the 1580s and 90s he proved himself highly capable in many local government offices.

---

[10] Sutton, Dana. University of Birmingham. http://www.philological.bham.ac.uk/eedes/contents.html. Accessed 31 December 2015. Having just returned from an academic tour of Europe, Neville might well be described in these terms. Walsingham was also a supporter of Neville's mentor Henry Savile. In 1585 Walsingham wrote a letter in support of Savile's application to become Warden of Merton.

In 1599, Queen Elizabeth appointed him as Ambassador to France. His qualifications included demonstrated political effectiveness, fluency in French, Spanish, Italian, Latin and Greek and that both his father and father-in-law were trusted friends of the Queen. Neville's first invidious mission was to recover a substantial debt from the King of France. Elizabeth's Secretary of State Robert Cecil, who was not known for immoderate language, marvelled at Neville's responses to the evasive French king:

I know not how the wit of man could have answered better.[11]

Despite Neville's heroic efforts, the mission failed.

Two years later he became embroiled in the Essex rebellion, probably via his Oxford associate Henry Cuffe who was one of the principal conspirators. Formerly an Oxford Professor of Greek, Cuffe was an unlikely rebel. In his last words, moments before he was to be hung, drawn and quartered, he summoned the determination to beg Neville's forgiveness for having involved him.

Neville *whom no man suspected* was deeply implicated in this plot.[12] That he was spared execution was due to the strenuous efforts of friends at the highest levels of government. However, he could not escape two years of bitter imprisonment in the Tower, together with his life-long friend the Earl of Southampton, Shakespeare's notional patron, who in panic had confirmed Essex's identification of him as a rebel. In happier times, Neville's father-in-law Sir Henry Killigrew had described Neville as *a Christian inwardly.*[13] Characteristically, Neville forgave Southampton, and they remained intimate friends and political allies upon their release. When Elizabeth died in March 1603, the only rebels still imprisoned were Neville and Southampton, and even before James VI left Scotland to ascend the English throne as James I, he sent word ahead to have them released and their titles restored.

Chamberlain gives an indication of Neville's enormous popularity when he writes in April 1603:

The tenth of this month the Earl of Southampton and Sir Henry Neville were delivered out of the Tower by a warrant from the King. These bountiful beginnings raise all men's spirits and put them in great hopes ...[14]

---

[11] Sir Ralph Winwood, *Memorials of Affairs of State in the Reigns of Queen Elizabeth and King James 1*, edited by Edmund Sawyer (London, 1725, I. p. 46).
[12] Spedding, Letters of Bacon, 11, 285, cited in Duncan, O.L. *The Political Career of Sir Henry Neville: An Elizabethan Gentleman in the Court of James I* (PhD Thesis, Ohio State University, 1974), p. 173.
[13] James, B., and Rubinstein, W.D. *The Truth Will Out* (Pearson Longman, Harlow, England, 2005), p. 112.
[14] Chamberlain, J. *The Letters of John Chamberlain.* Edited by N.E. McClure. 2 vols (Philadelphia: American Philosophical Society, 1939).

However, Neville did not share James's absolutist views of monarchy, and did not receive the advancement that he sought. As early as 1605, Neville wrote that he was eager to leave state matters:

> *(to) ... think of my husbandry in the Country, which puts me in mind of that Beatitude which Horace so much commends.*[15]

The *beatitude* commended by the Roman poet Horace, which Neville refers to indirectly, was writing.[16] Indeed, in 1608 King James visited Neville at home:

> *... his head much troubled about an answer to his book.*[17]

We cannot be certain whether this visit was for Neville's assistance with writing. However, writing was clearly important to Neville, and he mixed with the leading poets of the day. He was a member of the Mitre club and of *the Sirenaical Gentlemen.* On this evidence, C.M. Gayley concluded that Neville must have known Shakespeare.[18] But although there is evidence of Neville's association with these groups, there is no evidence of Shakespeare's.[19]

In 1603 the eminent poet John Davies of Hereford wrote the following Shakespearean sonnet to Neville:

To the Noble, discreete, and well beloved Knight Sir Henry Nevill.

There was a Time when, ah that so there was,
Whie not there is? There is and was a Time,
Whẽ Men might cal Gold, Gold; & Brasse, but Brasse,
And saie it, without check, in Prose or Rime.
Yet should I cal thee Gold some (Brasse perchance)
VVould saie I err'd because I nere toucht thee,
And so did cal thee through meere ignorance,
Or (which is worse) through abiect Flatterie.
I am too ignorant (I doe confesse)
To iudge thy woorth, which worthiest Men cõmend,
Yet may I say (I hope) and not transgresse,
Th'art Vertue, Valour, Truth, and Honors friend;
All which presume thou art not gilt by guile
Because thy noble name denies the vile.[20]

---

[15] James and Rubinstein, *The Truth Will Out*, p. 164.
[16] Winwood, *Memorials*, Vol. 2, p. 77.
[17] Chamberlain, *The Letters of John Chamberlain.*
[18] Gayley, C. *Shakespeare and the Founders of Liberty in America* (Macmillan, NY, 1917), p. 17.
[19] Gayley cites Hoskins's *Convivium Philosophicum*, the contemporary poem that lists the members of this group in *Francis Beaumont: Dramatist, With Some Account of His Circle, Elizabethan and Jacobean, and of His Association with John Fletcher* (Duckworth, London, 1911).
[20] The Neville motto is *Ne Vile Velis*, Wish no evil.

The precise meaning is opaque. However, the general sense is that Davies, for some unstated reason, is inhibited from fully crediting Neville with his due *in Prose or Rime.*

Brenda James suggests that Neville collaborated at Gray's Inn with the lawyer Sir Francis Bacon.[21] Gray's Inn was one of the four Inns of Court that to this day provide chambers for barristers and judges. Certainly, some of Bacon's Gray's Inn writings were found in a bundle now known as the *Northumberland Manuscript.* This miscellany, dated to 1596–7, was owned by Neville. The name "Nevell" and the family motto are repeated on the cover. The name Nevell is top-most.[22]

The cover also lists a few contemporary writers and plays - among them *Richard II* and *Richard III.* At this time, no plays at all had been published under the name Shakespeare, so it is most intriguing that among these titles the signature "*Shakespeare*" has been practised five times alongside fragments of the same, a spelling that does not occur in any of the surviving signatures. The annotations on the cover seem to be a list of the original manuscript contents, suggesting that at one time hand-written copies of *Richard II* and *III* were included in this collection.

Around 1610 Ben Jonson wrote an unequivocally admiring epigram to Neville,[23] referring to Neville's *muse* and using language which seems to echo *he that calls on thee* in Shakespeare's Sonnet 38:[24]

To Sir Henry Nevil

Who now calls on thee, Nevil, *is a Muse,*
That serves nor fame, nor titles; but doth chuse
Where vertue makes them both, and that's in thee:
Where all is faire, beside thy pedigree.
Thou art not one, seek'st miseries with hope,
Wrestlest with dignities, or fain'st a scope
Of seruice to the publique, when the end
Is priuate gaine, which hath long guilt to friend.
Thou rather striv'st the matter to possesse,

And elements of honor, then the dresse;
To make thy lent life, good against the Fates:
And first to know thine owne state, then the States.
To be the same in roote, thou art in height;
And that thy soule should give thy flesh her weight.
Goe on, and doubt not, what posteritie,
Now I haue sung thee thus, shall iudge of thee.
Thy deedes, vnto thy name, will prove new wombes,
Whil'st others toyle for titles to their tombes.

---

[21] James and Rubinstein, *The Truth Will Out*, p. 51.
[22] Casson, J. *The Northumberland Manuscript Revisited* (2012).
[23] Jonson, B. 1616. *Epigrams.* Epigram 109.
[24] This sonnet is discussed in Appendix 2, pp. 164–5.

Two of the other leading poets of the day, Francis Beaumont and John Fletcher, seem to have collaborated with Neville. Their political play, *A King and no King* includes a dedication from the publisher which indicates that Neville had, at the very least, an editorial role in its creation:

> *Worthy Knight, Sir Henry Nevill, I present, or rather returne unto your view, that which formerly hath beene received from you, hereby effecting what you did desire.*[25]

A King and no King was first performed in 1611. In 1612–13, Fletcher is believed to have been collaborating with Shakespeare on *Henry VIII, The Two Noble Kinsmen*, and *Cardenio*. In other words, we can confidently say that just prior to Fletcher's theatrical collaboration with Shakespeare he had been having, at the very least, a theatrical communication with Neville.

Finally, in 1603 the eminent theologian George Carleton published a three-page dedication in Latin and Greek in praise of Sir Henry Neville, alongside similar praise for Queen Elizabeth, King James, the Earl of Essex and Sir Philip Sidney.[26] Carleton hails Neville as a poet of both tragedy and of *the slight muse* (comedy and shorter works) who writes of the famous heroes of history, but who hides his own identity.[27] Carleton, a close friend of Neville since they were at Oxford, later became Bishop of Chichester, and ultimately married Neville's widow.

Around the same time, Carleton's assistant, the theologian Thomas Vicars, married Neville's daughter Anne. Vicars is well-known to Shakespeare scholars. In a book published in 1628, Vicars lists the leading English writers of recent history. This list is conventional and unambiguous with the single exception of his reference to Shakespeare who is unnamed, but rather described as:

> ... *a well-known poet who takes his name from shaking and spear.*

For some reason, Shakespeare's name is a topic of interest. There is no evidence that Vicars was personally acquainted with Shakespeare, but he was a member of Sir Henry Neville's immediate family.

---

[25] Lesser, Z. Mixed Government and Mixed Marriage. In: A King and No King: Sir Henry Neville Reads Beaumont and Fletcher. *English Literary History* 69, pp. 947–77 (2002).

[26] Bradbeer, M., and Casson, J. *Sir Henry Neville, Alias William Shakespeare: Authorship Evidence in the History Plays* (McFarland, Jefferson North Carolina, 2015). This dedication prefaces Carleton's first work *Heroici Characteres: Ad illustrissimum Equitem Henricus Nevillum.* Carleton's reference to Neville as a writer is noteworthy since Carleton himself was reputed for his knowledge of literature. Camden, the greatest English antiquary, highlighted just two of Carleton's qualities: *(Carleton) ... that I have loved in regard of* ***his singular knowledge*** *in Divinitie (which he professeth)* ***and in other more delightfull literature*** ... [our bold] (Britannia, Northumberland, 28. Twede).

[27] As with the language in Jonson's Epigram 109, Carleton's *slight muse* also seems to reference Shakespeare's Sonnet 38 (discussed in Appendix 2).

The celebrated contemporary writer John Chamberlain wrote 479 letters covering the period 1597–1626, in which he mentions Sir Henry Neville 43 times, and refers to Southampton as Neville's *great patron* and as his *champion.*[28] Chamberlain also makes many references to the leading poets and artists of the day, including Ben Jonson (35 times), Inigo Jones (35 times), and John Donne (26 times). But, as the editor of the letters comments:

> *... nowhere in the letters is there any indication that Chamberlain so much as knew of the existence of Shakespeare.*[29]

In the following chapter we examine the life of Sir Henry Neville in more detail and the ways in which it coincides with the works of William Shakespeare.

---

28 Chamberlain, *The Letters of John Chamberlain.*

29 Thomson, E., ed., *The Chamberlain Letters* (Capricorn, New York, 1966).

Chapter 2: The Life of Sir Henry Neville

Before Sir Henry Neville

There are many parallels between Sir Henry Neville's family history and the qualities and references found in Shakespeare's works. Although the life of Neville has been described in detail by Brenda James, most particularly in her first book *The Truth Will Out,* it may be helpful to revisit some key events and associations because they are so central to the authorship question.

In the late 1500's several men were named Henry Neville, a potential source of confusion. When we refer to Sir Henry Neville, we mean the man who was born in late 1562 and died in 1615. Where this may be ambiguous, we refer to him as Sir Henry II, and his father as Sir Henry I. The name was also given both to Sir Henry II's eldest son and his famous writer-grandson.

The first Neville in England arrived from France together with William the Conqueror in 1066. Indeed, this Gilbert de Neville was William's admiral and from this time onward the Nevilles sustained a powerful and distinguished dynasty closely associated with kingship. According to James Manning, the family –

> *... stands proudly forth as a pedigree in itself, and is associated with all that is ... distinguished in chivalry, eminent in counsel, and celebrated in the historic annals of Britain.*[1]

Many of Neville's ancestors feature prominently and favourably in the Shakespeare history plays as advisors to kings and occasionally as supporters of their overthrow, but the name Neville is almost always obscured by noble titles.[2]

The history plays began to appear anonymously around 1590. The first was probably *Henry VI,* which is dominated by Richard Neville, the Earl of Warwick, *The Kingmaker.* Also in Henry VI is *valiant Lord Talbot.* The legendary soldier Talbot was raised by the Neville family and then he married into it.

Richard II dates from around 1595. It was re-staged on the eve of the Essex rebellion in 1601, apparently with the aim of inciting support for the overthrow of Elizabeth. This play concerns the deposition of a tyrannical king by Bolingbroke, who becomes Henry IV with the support of Ralph, Baron Neville of Raby.

---

[1] Manning, J.A. *The Lives of the Speakers of the House of Commons* (Myers and Company, 1850).

[2] A fuller account of the references to Neville's family in the history plays can be found in Bradbeer and Casson, *Sir Henry Neville, Alias William Shakespeare.*

The father of Bolingbroke, John of Gaunt was also ancestor to the Nevilles, and is prominent as the wise statesman in *Henry IV* (1597–8). In *Richard III,* Anne Neville is the widow who was *in this humour wooed.*

The Neville family connection with *Henry VIII* is particularly intimate. Sir Edward Neville, the grandfather of Sir Henry II, held several positions very close to the king in the court of Henry VIII. He was knighted in 1513, and in 1516 held the offices of Master of the Hounds, and Gentleman of the Chamber. In 1520, he was present at the *Field of the Cloth of Gold* near Calais, the famously lavish summit meeting between Henry VIII and Francis I of France.

Owen Lowe Duncan notes that Sir Edward Neville was also present at the coronation of Anne Boleyn in 1533, and at the baptism of Prince Edward in 1537:

> *This series of favors, combined with Neville's physical similarity to the King, led to patently false rumors that Sir Edward was Henry VIII's illegitimate son.*[3]

Duncan also notes that Shakespeare includes a reference to this physical similarity in the masque scene in *Henry VIII,* based on a real event described in Holinshed:[4]

> Holinshed:
>
> *The person to whom ...* [Wolsey] *offered the chair was Sir Edward Neville, a comely Knight, that much more resembled the king's person in that mask than any other. The King perceiving ...* [Wolsey] *... so deceived, could not forbear laughing, and pulled down his visor and Master Neville's too.*[5]
>
> Shakespeare's *King Henry VIII*, Act I, Scene iv:

Wolsey	Pray, tell 'em [the masquers] thus much from me: There should be one amongst 'em, by his person, More worthy this place than myself; to whom, If I but knew him, with my love and duty I would surrender it.
Chamberlain	... There is indeed; which they would have your grace Find out, and he will take it.

3 Duncan, *The Political Career of Sir Henry Neville*, p. 5.

4 The second edition of *Holinshed's Chronicles* was the primary source for Shakespeare's history plays (see also p. 27).

5 Boswell-Stone, W.B. *Shakespeare's Holinshed, the Chronicles and the Historical Plays Compared* (*Notes and Queries* (1st series), ii, 307; London, 1896, New York, 1966), p. 445.

Who will believe my verse?

Wolsey	Let me see, then. By all your good leaves, gentlemen; here I'll make My royal choice.
Henry VIII	Ye have found him, cardinal. [Unmasking]

Edward Neville is not named in Shakespeare's re-telling, but the scene is unmistakeably that described in Holinshed.

Like so many others close to Henry VIII, Edward Neville had his highs and lows. On the last of these low ebbs he is reported to have said:

> ... *that the King was a beast, and worse than a beast.*[6]

Edward finally fell from grace, and was beheaded on Tower Hill in 1538 for:

> ... *devising to maintain, promote, and advance one Reginald Pole, late Dean of Exeter, enemy of the King, beyond the sea ...*

Edward Neville's son Sir Henry Neville I (1520–1593) was the godson of Henry VIII. Surprisingly, in view of his father's execution, Sir Henry I and the King were on good terms. When Henry VIII died in 1547, Sir Henry Neville I was witness to his will, in which he was left 100 pounds *in token of special love and favour.*[7]

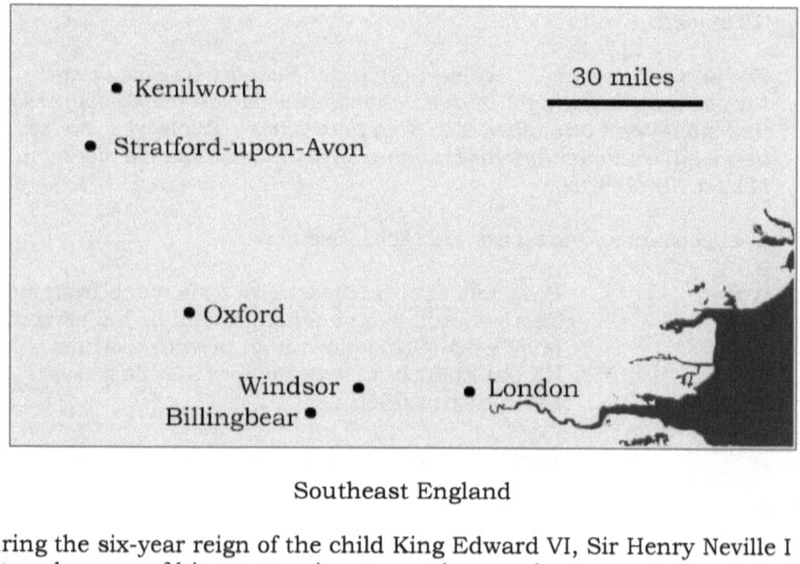

Southeast England

During the six-year reign of the child King Edward VI, Sir Henry Neville I featured as one of his most eminent courtiers, and as a regular participant in the royal entertainments, the *Revels*. He held a variety of high offices, and

[6] Froude, J.A., *History of England from the Fall of Wolsey to the Death of Elizabeth (1856–1870)*, Vol III, p. 334.
[7] Duncan, *The Political Career of Sir Henry Neville*, p. 11.

in 1549 Edward granted him Billingbear, a manor house in Berkshire. In 1551, at the age of about 30, Neville was knighted at Hampton Court together with William Cecil, later Lord Burghley, the most powerful man in England.

The Nevilles, the Revels and the Blackfriars Theatre

The Neville family had a number of connections with royal entertainments. The demand for quality and variety in these performances called upon the skills of the finest artists across all disciplines; from simulated battles to the most refined theatrical and musical works, which were often performed by children. Collectively, these entertainments were known as the Revels, and they required scrupulous management. In the Revels accounts, Sir Henry I is named among four illustrious challengers to a joust in January 1550, and again in a grand Christmas spectacle *Triumph of Horsemen* in 1551–1552.[8]

Henry Neville I was first married in 1551, the year in which he was knighted. His wife Winifred Losse also had a connection with the Revels. Her father Hugh Losse had overseen a major project to survey and build storage facilities for the extensive inventory of the Revels in 1546–1547. These buildings were known as the "Offices and Wardrobe of the King's Revels, Blackfriars", later to become *the Blackfriars Theatre.*

A committed Protestant, Sir Henry Neville I fell out of favour when the Catholic Mary was crowned in 1553. Indeed, his opposition to, or fear of, Queen Mary was so great that in 1554 he abandoned his Berkshire estate and fled to live as an exile in Padua and later in Germany. It is presumed that he left with Winifred. Strangely, there is no further record of her, not even of her death or burial. There were no children from the marriage, and it is not known how it ended; whether as a result of death, divorce, prolonged illness, abandonment, or for some other reason. It is possible that she died overseas. If this is the case, it might explain the gap in the documentary record.

Neville returned to England in 1556. And when Elizabeth came to the throne in 1558 William Cecil assisted him with recovery of his confiscated Berkshire lands.[9]

In 1560 Neville's connection with the genesis of the Blackfriars Theatre resumed when he leased the former Offices of the Revels in Blackfriars. He immediately enlarged the building, created a kitchen, and lived there until 1567–1568.[10] It has been suggested that he may have lived a double-life at Blackfriars, at a distance from Billingbear, with the woman who would

---

[8] Streitberger, W.R. *Court Revels 1495–1559.* Studies in Early English Drama (University of Toronto Press, 1994).
[9] Duncan, *The Political Career of Sir Henry Neville*, p. 14.
[10] http://www.theatredatabase.com/16th_century/first_blackfriars_theatre.html. Accessed 24 October 2015.

become his second wife, Elizabeth Gresham.[11] Elizabeth was the niece and heir of the enormously wealthy merchant Sir Thomas Gresham, who was therefore young Henry Neville's great uncle.

The surmise concerning a double-life derives from the absence of any known marriage record other than an "agreement" which dates from 1568. Arguing against this is a letter that Sir Thomas Gresham sent to William Cecil which has Gresham happily entertaining the young couple in May 1565.[12]

The first child of Sir Henry I and Elizabeth, also named Elizabeth, was born in 1561. Their eldest son, who was to become our Sir Henry II, was also born at Blackfriars and was baptised in 1564.[13]

In 1567, the Nevilles relocated to the newly rebuilt stately home at Billingbear, 3–4 miles from Windsor. For the previous ten years, Sir Henry Neville I had been Steward of Mote Park, a part of Windsor Great Park. Also among the office-holders at Windsor was his friend Richard Farrant, who was Master of the Children of St. George's Chapel.[14] These child singers and actors were highly trained for court performance.[15]

In 1576, when Farrant was looking for a London performance space for his of Children of St George's Chapel, Sir Henry I wrote a letter endorsing him to secure the lease on his former home. Having secured the lease, Farrant then transformed the building into the famous theatre at Blackfriars.[16] At the same time, Farrant merged his ensemble with the Children of the Chapel Royal in London. These children were supervised by the sonneteer, musician dramatist, and former plotter *Master William Hunnis.*[17]

Henry II's mother died in 1573 when he was 10. Five years later Sir Henry I married for the third time. His new wife was Elizabeth Bacon Doyley, the daughter of Sir Nicholas Bacon, and half-sister of Sir Francis Bacon. By all accounts she was a formidable person; highly educated, aristocratic and

---

[11] James, B. *Henry Neville and the Shakespeare Code* (Music for Strings, Bognor Regis, 2008), pp. 200–10.

[12] John William Burgon (1849), *The Life and Times of Sir Thomas Gresham Vol 2*, p. 443.

[13] The precise birth date of Sir Henry II is uncertain. On the 16th of November 1573, a record of his mother's funeral described him as ten and half years old. When he matriculated at Oxford in December 1577, his birth-date was recorded as 1562, and his age as 15. When he died in July 1615, his close friend Sir James Whitelocke gave his age as 52 years. If we allow the age "ten and a half" to mean "not quite 11", the three dates can be triangulated to a birth-date for Sir Henry in late November or, more likely, December 1562.

[14] It is possible that Neville knew Farrant from as far back as 1550 when Farrant was a Gentleman of the Chapel Royal and they were both involved with the Revels.

[15] Stopes, C. *William Hunnis and the Revels of the Chapel Royal* (1910), pp. 19–21; 139.

[16] http://www.theatredatabase.com/16th_century/first_blackfriars_theatre.html.

[17] Hunnis was the pre-eminent royal dramatist at the time when theatre began to flourish early in the reign of Queen Elizabeth. He was involved in an unsuccessful plot against Mary Tudor, for which he was imprisoned in the Tower but ultimately released. In Chapter 7 we consider the case for Hunnis as a possible candidate for *Mr WH* in the Dedication to the Sonnets.

cultured. In a letter to his brother-in-law, Sir Henry I acknowledged that she *wore the britches.*

Elizabeth was the dedicatee of perhaps the most important collection of keyboard music of the Renaissance, *My Ladye Nevells Booke,* composed by William Byrd. Along with Farrant, Byrd was also a Gentleman of the Chapel Royal.[18]

Elizabeth was also the dedicatee Thomas Morley's *First Book of Canzonets.* Morley, who had been Byrd's student, married a servant of Sir Henry Neville I. Accordingly, it seems reasonable to assume he was close to the Neville household at Billingbear. Scholars surmise that Morley worked with Shakespeare, since he composed *It was a lover and his lass* from *As You Like It* (1599–1600), and *O Mistress Mine* from *Twelfth Night* (1599–1600).[19]

Youth and Study

From the age of four Henry II grew up at Billingbear in Berkshire. His father seems to have enjoyed country life, including horsemanship and falconry. Indeed, in his will Sir Henry I left a falcon to a friend of whom the bird was fond.[20] Henry I had ongoing duties as Steward of Mote Park, and it is probable that his eldest son accompanied him on some errands and became familiar with Windsor Great Park and surrounds. Intimate knowledge of Windsor is evident in *The Merry Wives of Windsor,* including the re-enactment of the legend of *Herne the Hunter* and reference to the actual tree that was *Herne's Oak.* Since Stratford-upon-Avon is some 90 miles away, it seems unlikely that Shakespeare would have had any intimate knowledge of Windsor.

It is possible that it is Sir Henry I who is portrayed as the forester teaching the Princess (perhaps Queen Elizabeth) to shoot in *Love's Labours Lost* Act IV Scene i.[21] Owen Lowe Duncan believes it is also Sir Henry I who is referred to by the secretary of the visiting Duke of Wurtemburg in 1592:

> *It had pleased her Majesty to depute an old distinguished lord to attend his highness and she had commissioned and directed him not only to show his highness the splendid royal castle at Windsor, but also to amuse him by the way with shooting and hunting red deer.*[22]

[18] McCarthy, K. *Byrd* (Oxford University Press, 2013), Chapter 9.
[19] Long, J. H. 'Shakespeare and Thomas Morley', *Modern Language Notes,* Vol. 65, No. 1, p. 17 (1950).
[20] *Will of Sir Henry Nevell or Nevile of Waltham Saint Lawrence, Berkshire,* National Archives. PROB 11/81/118.
[21] James and Rubinstein, *The Truth Will Out,* pp. 124–5.
[22] W.B. Rye (ed.), *England as Seen by Foreigners in the days of Elizabeth and James I* (London 1 1865), p. 14. Extract in Duncan, *The Political Career of Sir Henry Neville,* p. 15.

The great majority of the Shakespeare plays are based on historical sources or older works. Other than the *Tempest,*[23] only *Merry Wives of Windsor* and *Love's Labours Lost* are thought to derive from Shakespeare's own invention, which would seem logical if Sir Henry Neville II were the true author.

It is clear that Henry II grew up in a highly intellectual environment. He attended school in the household of William Cecil, Lord Burghley. Also, given the number of family associations, it seems most likely that Henry II witnessed professional theatre and music performed by children of the Chapel who were around his own age at Windsor, elsewhere on other state occasions, and from 1576 at Blackfriars itself.

It has often been surmised that the 11-year old Shakespeare must have seen and had vivid memories of the festivities presented by the Chapel performers at Kenilworth in 1575. One of these works, composed by Master William Hunnis, is referred to in *A Midsummer Night's Dream* and in *Twelfth Night.* While it is not impossible that a youthful Shakespeare was present at this performance, as Kenilworth is around 13 miles from Stratford, the same suggestion may be made for the 12-year old Henry Neville, whose father had such close connections with the directors, performers, and with the courtly audience.

Henry II's mother Elizabeth (nee Gresham) died when he was 10 years old. This had profound consequences for him. Her uncle, the enormously wealthy merchant Sir Thomas Gresham, had nominated her as his heir, but when Sir Thomas died in 1579, she had already been dead six years. Accordingly, the greater part of his enormous estate passed to her eldest son, our Henry II.

Intriguingly, Shakespeare refers to Thomas Gresham's ideas in the last line of the famous Sonnet 144:

> *Till my bad angel fire my good one out.*

Booth notes the pun on *angel* (which also referred to a coin):

> *The pun is activated by the splendidly comic echo of "Gresham's Law", an economic axiom propounded by Sir Thomas Gresham in a letter to Queen Elizabeth in 1558: "Bad money drives out good."* [24]

It is not clear why this economic principle might have had personal significance to Shakespeare.

---

[23] For Neville's connection to *The Tempest* see pp. 39–40.
[24] Booth, S. *Shakespeare's Sonnets* (Yale Nota Bene, New Haven, 2000), p. 500.

Neville matriculated at Oxford in December 1577 when he was 15.[25] At Merton College he studied mathematics, astronomy and classics. A special interest in scientific astronomy, as distinct from the prevalent astrology, is expressed throughout Shakespeare:

Sonnet 14

Not from the stars do I my judgement pluck
And yet methinks I have astronomy
But not to tell of good or evil luck

King Lear

... when we are sick in fortune, often the surfeit of our own behaviour, we make guilty of our disasters the sun, the moon, and the stars;

Julius Caesar

The fault, dear Brutus, is not in our stars,
But in ourselves

The works attributed to Shakespeare demonstrate close familiarity with the *New Astronomy* of Neville's kinsman Thomas Digges, the originator of the enduring theory that space is *infinite* which is referred to in *Hamlet.*[26]

Hamlet:

O God, I could be bounded in a nutshell and count myself a king of infinite space, were it not that I have bad dreams.

Neville's signature is present in a volume on spherical geometry by Theodosius (next page). He donated a similar volume on the celestial geometry of Ptolemy to Merton College Oxford.[27] Both volumes are written in Greek and heavily annotated in Latin and Greek, attesting to his deep involvement in mathematics and his fluency in both languages.

---

[25] http://www.historyofparliamentonline.org/volume/1604-1629/member/neville-sir-henry-i-1564-1615. Accessed 22 June 2015.
[26] Falk, D. *The Science of Shakespeare. A new look at the Playwright's Universe* (Goose Lane Editions, Fredericton, New Brunswick, Canada, 2014).
[27] Casson, J. *Much Ado About Noting* (Dolman Scott, 2010), p. 181.

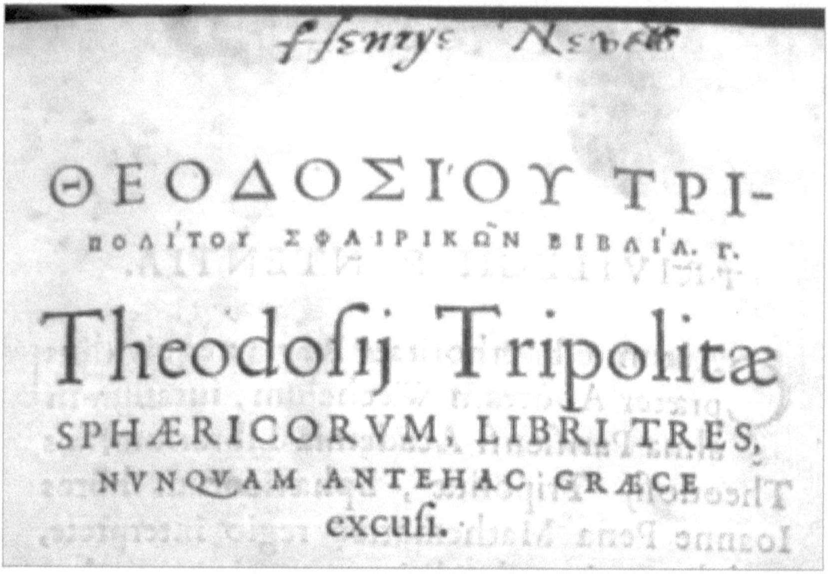

Treatise on spherical geometry by Theodosius, bearing Neville's autograph (private collection)

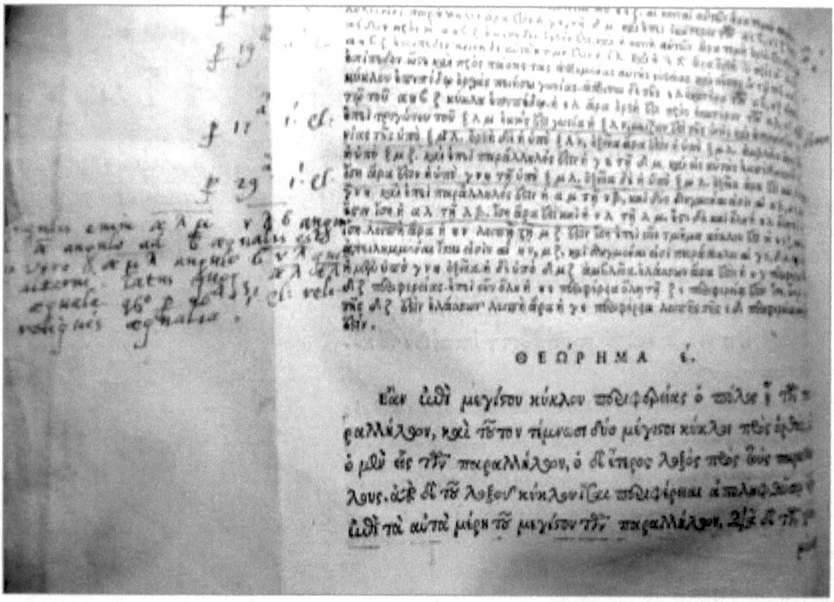

Annotated treatise on spherical geometry by Theodosius (private collection)

Neville's interest in astronomy is eternalised in an astronomical diagram in the upper left-hand region of his portrait at Audley End (below). The Greek inscription has been interpreted as meaning *everywhere without visible symbol.*

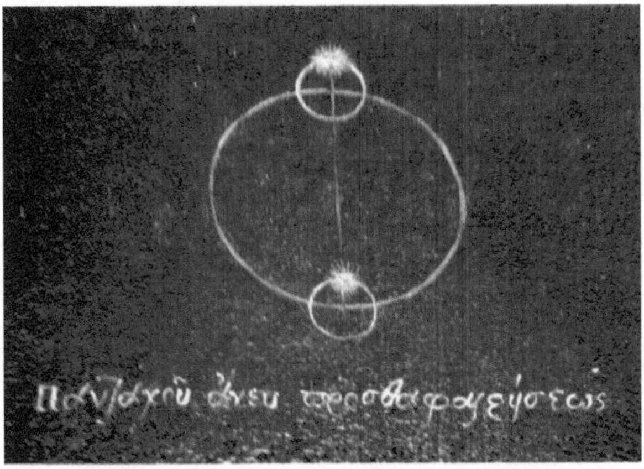

Detail of portrait of Sir Henry Neville. Attributed to Robert Peake (1599)

At Merton, Neville studied under one of the foremost intellectuals of the Elizabethan era, Sir Henry Savile. Savile became Neville's tutor in Greek, Mathematics and Astronomy at Merton and his life-long friend. Savile later became famous for his role in the translation of the *King James Bible.*[28] However, his greatest work is a vast translation of the church father St. John Chrysostom. Chrysostom's exact contemporary was St. Jerome who is famous for the *Vulgate*, the first translation of the Bible into Latin, and a primary source for the later *King James Bible.*

There is an intriguing connection between the towering figure of St. Jerome and Shakespeare. St Jerome is also famous for his *Chronicon*, a huge undertaking to record all the major events in human history. In one entry, Jerome confuses the father of Roman drama *Lucius Livius Andronicus*, with the father of Roman history *Titus Livius* (Livy). The result is the erroneously conflated name *Titus Lucius*. It is thought that the name of the early play *Titus Andronicus* celebrates this obscure but charming saintly blooper. It is uncertain where Shakespeare may have come across a rare copy of *Chronicon* containing this error. However, there was at that time, and there remains today a manuscript copy at Merton College, which might be expected to have been minutely examined by the biblical scholar Henry Savile and by his lively students.[29]

---

[28] Nicolson, A. *God's Secretaries. The Making of the King James Bible* (HarperCollins, New York, 2003).
[29] An image of this page of *Chronicon* is available at: http://image.ox.ac.uk/images/merton/ms315/f111r.jpg. The reference to Titus is in the fifth line of the body text.

Savile also translated Tacitus and from 1596 corresponded with Isaac Casaubon over a period of more than ten years in relation to Casaubon's translation of the Greek historian and cryptographer Polybius.[30] The writings of Polybius are central to Neville's political vision and, as we will see, to his encryption.

A Statesman Prepares

During Elizabeth's reign, university education and international travel came to be regarded as essential preparation for potential statesmen. Owen Lowe Duncan notes:

> *By 1559 a member of Elizabeth's first parliament had become so convinced that humanist education and leadership went together that he moved that an ordinance be made to bind the nobility to bring up their children in learning at some university in England or beyond the sea from the age of twelve to eighteen at least.*

Both A. L. Rowse and J. H. Hexter believe that the proposal was drawn up by William Cecil, the patron of the Nevilles.[31]

Merton College stands out in particular as having been administered toward this end:

> *As an institution for the promotion of academical education under collegiate discipline but* secular *guidance, it was the expression of a conception entirely new in England ...*[32]

As noted, Neville studied in Cecil's household. One can reasonably surmise that Cecil's view loomed large in family discussions concerning Henry's advancement, and that Sir Henry I's choice of Merton for his son was preparation for his becoming a statesman, in accordance with the Cecil model.

From 1578 to 1582 Savile took leave of absence from Oxford and travelled throughout Europe acquiring books and manuscripts. Henry Neville II was among a select group of scholars invited to accompany him. Their travels extended to Poland, France, Austria and Italy, and certainly included Paris, Prague, Vienna, Padua, Venice, and Rome.

Around half of the plays attributed to Shakespeare are set in continental Europe. What we know of the scholars' itinerary aligns neatly with the locations in the plays: *All's Well that Ends Well* – Paris; *Titus Andronicus, Julius Caesar, Coriolanus* – Rome; *Two Gentlemen of Verona* – Verona, Milan;

---

[30] Goulding, R.D. 'Savile, Sir Henry (1549–1622)', Oxford Dictionary of National Biography, OUP, 2004; online ed., Jan. 2008, www.oxforddnb.com/view/article/24737. Accessed 7 October 2014.

[31] Duncan, *The Political Career of Sir Henry Neville,* p. 5.

[32] G.C. Broderick (1885) referenced in Duncan, *The Political Career of Sir Henry Neville.*

Romeo and Juliet – Verona; *The Taming of the Shrew* - Padua; *Merchant of Venice, Othello* - Venice; and, *Measure for Measure* – Vienna. Other plays are set in greater Europe: *Twelfth Night* – Illyria; *The Winter's Tale* – Sicilia, Bohemia; *The Comedy of Errors* – Ephesus; *Love's Labours Lost* – Navarre; *Much Ado about Nothing* – Messina; *Pericles* – Various; *A Midsummer Night's Dream* – Athens; and, *The Tempest* – An island, though the characters are from Milan and Naples. Many commentators have concluded that, given the detailed references to towns, streets, buildings, and even trees, Shakespeare must have visited Europe, and in particular Italy.[33, 34] It is extremely improbable that Shakespeare of Stratford ever left England.

Sadly, Neville left no diary from this time that has survived. Only a very few fragmentary references are available to us. Brenda James notes:

> *Savile left a (near indecipherable) common-place book of his travels for the years 1581–1582 which survives at the Bodleian Library, but nothing in the way of a travel diary by Neville survives ...*[35]

For a time, Sir Robert Sidney joined Neville's group. Robert's brother was Sir Philip Sidney, the best-loved and most distinguished literary aristocrat of the period. In 1580, Sir Philip Sidney wrote to his brother:

> *I have written to Mr. Savile, I wish you kept still together, he is an excellent man: and there may if you list pass good exercises betwixt you and Mr. Neville, there is great expectation of you both ...*

Sir Philip's father, a life-long friend of Sir Henry Neville I, had earlier written to Robert on a similar theme:

> *... I hear well of you and the Company you keep, which is of great comfort to me. To be of noble parentage, usually raises an Emulation to follow their great Examples. There can be no greater Love than of Long time hath been, and yet is, between Sir Harry Neville and me; and so will continue till our lives end. Love you those we have done and do.*[36]

Following their arrival back in England in 1581, the astronomer Tycho Brahe sent an engraving of himself to Henry Savile's brother Thomas, with the request that he distribute copies to his friends. Remarkably, the family crests that surround the central portrait of Brahe include those of *Rosenkrans* and *Guldensteren.*[37] It is generally believed that this engraving is the source of the names in *Hamlet.* It seems most unlikely that William Shakespeare of Stratford would have seen this engraving.

---

[33] Roe, R.P. *The Shakespeare Guide to Italy* (Harper Perennial, New York, 2011).
[34] Bassi, S., and Fei, A.T. *Shakespeare in Venice. Exploring the city with Shylock and Othello* (Editrice Elzeviro, Treviso, Italy, 2007).
[35] James and Rubinstein, *The Truth Will Out*, p. 74.
[36] Collins, A. (ed.) *Sidney Papers* (London, 1746), I, 271. Extract in Duncan, *The Political Career of Sir Henry Neville*, p. 61.
[37] James and Rubinstein, *The Truth Will Out*, p. 151.

1586 engraving of Tycho Brahe featuring the names *Rosenkrans* and *Guldensteren*

In 1583, Neville found himself on an upward path toward statesmanship. As noted in Chapter 1, he is most likely the "Neville" who was sent to Scotland among a diplomatic mission organised by Elizabeth's aging spymaster Sir Francis Walsingham, and which showcased the charismatic young Earl of Essex. The embassy was intended to counter the rising influence of the Earl of Arran over the young King James VI. It may have been hoped that their youthful presence would provide vitality pleasing to the 17-year-old king that was wanting in the decrepit Walsingham. Certainly, the experience for the 20-year-old Neville and 17-year-old Essex would have been of inestimable value.

If Neville were writing poetry and plays, this early responsibility might well have alerted him to the incompatibility of an artistic identity with that of the statesman, for which he was preparing. The artist is concerned with self-expression; the statesman, with self-control. Any personal disclosure by a statesman is a potential vulnerability. From this point, to put his own name to political works – such as the early history plays – would be to compromise irretrievably his value to the state.

In the following year, Neville was elected to the House of Commons, aged about 21. He also married Anne Killigrew, the daughter of the illustrious Sir Henry Killigrew and Catherine Cooke, one of the famous Cooke daughters of Gidea Hall in Essex. The Cooke girls were reputed to be the most educated women in England. Catherine's father, Anthony Cooke, was famous in his lifetime for his devotion to his children's education, and the Cooke household has since become known as the "female university".

It is unknown what influence Anne had over the work of Sir Henry, but the works attributed to Shakespeare are distinguished in their celebration of educated and accomplished women.

Sir Henry Killigrew was one of the editors of the second edition of *Holinshed's Chronicles* (1587), the primary source for Shakespeare's history plays. Killigrew was also greatly admired by Queen Elizabeth, as evidenced by the many embassies, some personal, with which she entrusted him.

At the age of 21, Neville was highly educated, well-travelled, marked for advancement, and very advantageously and intimately connected with several of the most powerful individuals in England.

Neville, Southampton, and the Cecils

Among Neville's lifelong friends was the Earl of Southampton, Henry Wriothesley (1573–1624). *Venus and Adonis* (1593) and *The Rape of Lucrece* (1594) were both dedicated to Southampton. The fact that the dedications bear the printed name *William Shakespeare* is widely cited as the clearest evidence of Shakespeare's authorship. These dedications seem to imply patronage.

However, apart from a 1605 performance of *Love's Labours Lost* by the King's Men in Southampton's London residence, arranged for James's consort, Anne of Denmark, there is no other evidence that Southampton and William Shakespeare were ever associated with each other.[38] By contrast, the intimate lifelong friendship, business association, and political alliance between Southampton and Neville are well-documented.

Like Neville, Southampton's family had suffered episodes of disgrace. His father had been imprisoned twice in the Tower. Southampton was only eight years old when his father died and he succeeded to the title of 3rd Earl of Southampton. Because of his age, in late 1581 the young Henry Wriothesley was made a ward of Sir Henry Neville I's old friend William Cecil, Lord Burghley.

---

[38] Ellis, D. *The Truth About William Shakespeare. Fact, Fiction and Modern Biographies* (Edinburgh University Press, 2012), p. 68.

Henry II first met Southampton in Cecil's household, between 1583 and 1585.[39] As Neville was by then an adult, ten years older than the 10-year old Earl, it seems most likely that the affection would have begun in a somewhat paternal way. However, there is abundant evidence that their friendship grew and endured over the next 30 years until Neville's death in 1615. Like Neville, Southampton was highly educated and deeply interested in the arts.

It has often been proposed that Cecil is parodied in the character of Polonius in *Hamlet*. In Act I Scene iii we have a particularly intimate view of Polonius managing his household – and in particular, his advice to his children. Cecil's advice to his children was eternalised in his *Ten Precepts* of 1586. Neville had just this intimate knowledge of Cecil, by means of his father's close friendship with Cecil, his own attendance at the Cecil household school, his wife being Cecil's niece, and his own friendship with Cecil's ward Southampton.

There are no known personal connections between Cecil's household and William Shakespeare.

Ambassador to France, 1599

In the 1580s and 90s Neville was active in a variety of local government offices: Burgess, Justice of the Peace, Deputy Lieutenant of Sussex, Sheriff, Steward of Royal Manors, Bailiff of Crown Lands, and High Steward of Wokingham. The responsibilities of these offices were onerous. They required leadership and negotiation skills as well as a working knowledge of the law, particularly property law which underlies so many of the sonnets. Having inherited his great uncle Sir Thomas Gresham's fortune, he was also active with iron mining and refinement and export of steel. All this was alongside raising his eldest two daughters and two sons. The last of the eleven children who survived to adulthood was born in 1613.

From 1597, Neville was active in the House of Commons in the faction of Cecil's son Robert. Robert Cecil, Neville's wife's cousin, was one year younger than Neville. In 1598 Robert succeeded his father as Secretary of State. Letters survive from this time in which Neville advises him on foreign policy.

In 1598 Elizabeth requested that Neville take the role of Ambassador to France. Though it would be accompanied by a knighthood, it was not an attractive proposition.[40] Paris was not the exquisite city that it is today. Moreover, he was required to bear most of the expense himself; a burden that had impoverished an earlier incumbent, his friend and neighbour Sir

[39] According to Neville's testimony as a conspirator in the Essex rebellion.
[40] Birch, T. *An Historical View of the Negotiations between the courts of England, France and Brussels, from the year 1592 to 1617* ... (London, 1749), p. 183. Cited in Duncan, *The Political Career of Sir Henry Neville*, p. 89.

Henry Unton.[41] But whether he wished it or not, Neville was wealthy enough to pay his own expenses. He was fluent in French and already had experience with diplomacy, but he accepted the post with great reluctance.

It is generally agreed that *Henry V* was written in 1599, the same year that Neville began his embassy. In the spirit of an ambassador to France, the last scene of the play predicts everlasting peace between England and France. Moreover, half of this scene contrasts Katharine's fluent French with Henry's clumsy efforts:

> Henry: *No, Kate? I will tell thee in French; which I am sure will hang upon my tongue like a new-married wife about her husband's neck, hardly to be shook off. Je quand sur le possession de France, et quand vous avez le possession de moi, (Let me see, what then? Saint Denis be my speed!) Donc votre est France et vous etes mienne. It is as easy for me, Kate, to conquer the kingdom as to speak so much more French: I shall never move thee in French, unless it be to laugh at me.*
>
> Katharine: *Sauf votre honneur, le Francois que vous parlez, il est meilleur que l'Anglois lequel je parle.*

The mission to France was primarily to hasten repayment of a large debt owed by the Protestant Henry IV of Navarre. Elizabeth had long supported his advancement to the throne of France to counter Catholic hostility toward England, particularly from Spain. The preservation of warm relations with France was also critical. At Neville's first audience, King Henry was more than cordial; he even embraced Neville. He confirmed the validity of the English claim, but deferred a direct response.

At the same time that Neville was pressing for repayment, hostility toward Protestants in France was increasing, forcing them to worship in secret. The massacre of more than 30,000 Protestants across France in 1572 was an appalling and vivid memory. Indeed, Neville's mother-in-law, Jael de Peigne, was a French Huguenot refugee. Neville responded to the renewed threat openly, by holding Protestant services at his lodgings. A few commentators have interpreted this as evidence of an emerging Puritanism in Neville. However, his religion seems never to have affected his many close friendships with Catholics, notably Southampton and Ben Jonson. Conducting these services might even be seen as a kind of political demonstration or performance to promote religious tolerance. Given the violent hostility to Protestantism all around him, it was certainly courageous.

The frustrations of Neville's embassy mounted. No matter how articulate his persuasions, the distastefulness of repayment ensured that the king became

[41] James, *Henry Neville and the Shakespeare Code.*

more remote, and the meetings less frequent. However, the expenses that Neville bore for state entertainments were undiminished.

Most of Neville's negotiating was conducted with the most eminent, formidable and longest-serving French Secretary of State, Nicolas IV de Neufville, Seigneur de Villeroy (1543–1617). Coincidentally, they were both Nevilles.

Neville had more to deal with than the obfuscations of the French. Delays in communication with Robert Cecil meant that the French often knew more of English matters than he did himself. As we will detail in Chapter 3, much of this correspondence was written in code. The highly energised Neville found his capabilities lying idle. Moreover, the Queen, although eager for repayment, seemed oblivious to the graver matters of foreign policy that tormented Neville and, maddeningly, more focussed on the gossip of the French court. Neville pleaded with her repeatedly for permission to return home. A brief respite was eventually granted, and he sailed to England in August 1600.

It was around the time of Neville's embassy that *Twelfth Night* was written. The name of the character of Duke Orsino is thought to anticipate the state visit to England of Count Orsino from Italy. Neville was one of the very few who knew of this visit, having been informed by his secretary Ralph Winwood in a letter from France dated 20 November 1600.[42] It seems most unlikely that William Shakespeare would have been privy to this information.

The Essex rebellion

Soon after his return to England, Neville became involved in events which were to all but ruin him.

In 1600, Elizabeth turned 67. Her decision-making was deteriorating and her rule became ever more erratic. Of most concern was that there was no clear successor. As early as 1587, Elizabeth had declared it a treasonous offence even to discuss succession. There was a very real dread that upon her death civil war could erupt, resulting in vulnerability to invasion. These fears, together with potential opportunities for advancement, emboldened factions to prepare to seize power.

It was in this climate that the plans of the Earl of Essex and his advisors evolved. As noted in Chapter 1, it seems probable that as young men Essex and Neville had shared the diplomatic mission to Scotland in 1583. Essex had become the favourite of the Queen from about 1588, but Essex began to lose favour; initially by marrying without Elizabeth's consent in 1591.

A series of military postings followed. His public reputation reached its zenith following his raid on the Spanish at Cadiz in 1596. In reality, the

[42] James and Rubinstein, *The Truth Will Out*, p. 132.

victory was largely good fortune. Nonetheless, his humane treatment of the townspeople won him high praise throughout Europe.

Then, in 1599, having been posted to Ireland to suppress nationalists, Essex angered the Queen by abandoning his post before victory was assured. Further ill-judged actions provoked her to remove his offices and place him under house arrest. She also cancelled his monopoly import tax on sweet wines, depriving him of a huge income which she took for herself.

Early in 1601, banking on real public affection, Essex gathered a leadership group of around 80 followers, principal among whom was Neville's close friend the Earl of Southampton. Essex had arranged that they would march from Essex House to confront the Queen at Whitehall Palace. However, on the morning of February 8, rather than proceeding directly to Whitehall, Essex marched in the opposite direction to connect with 1,000 men he was advised had been promised by Sir Thomas Smith, Sheriff of London. This delay and the non-appearance of the promised support lost Essex the day, and he and his followers surrendered to the Queen's militia late in the evening. Neville, as arranged, had remained at a distance from the rebels at Whitehall throughout the action. Had the rebellion succeeded, Neville would most likely have become Secretary of State.

We know that there had been secret communication between the Essex faction and James VI of Scotland, who seems to have offered them support.[43] However, the specific aims of the rebels, if ever they were coherent, were buried forever in the aftermath of the insurrection. At best, they sought to force Elizabeth to hear their grievances. Most likely, they sought to overthrow her.

The trial of the conspirators is well documented. It began on 19 February 1601, and was punctuated by an incident which seems to have a parallel in *Hamlet,* where Polonius hides behind a curtain. At his trial, Essex alleged that Robert Cecil had made remarks that the only valid successor to Elizabeth was the Catholic Infanta of Spain. Cecil, who had been hiding behind a curtain, revealed himself and successfully denied the charge.

Essex and Southampton were found guilty of treason. At their sentencing, the edge of the executioner's axe was turned slowly and ceremoniously towards them. The sentence prescribed in such cases was:

> *... to be hanged by the neck and taken down alive, your bodies to be opened, and your bowels taken out and burned before your face...*

Essex successfully appealed to be beheaded. His sentence was carried out on 25 February 1601.

---

[43] Rowse, A.L. *Shakespeare's Southampton. Patron of Virginia* (Harper and Row, New York, 1965).

Southampton faced the likelihood of a similar fate. Robert Cecil, who had grown up with Southampton, was sympathetic to his cause. On 26 February 1601, he wrote to Sir George Carew:

> *It remaineth now that I let you know what is like to become of the poor young Earl of Southampton, who merely for the love of the Earl* [of Essex] *hath been drawn into this action ... and yet when I consider how penitent he is, and how merciful the Queen is, and never in thought or deed but in this conspiracy he offended, as I cannot write in despair, so I dare not flatter myself with hope.*[44]

Southampton's defence of ignorance of the law was believed, and his death sentence was commuted to life imprisonment, with confiscation of his lands and wealth, and loss of his titles. He became *Mr Henry Wriothesley.*

Neville's Disgrace

Neville was drawn into the Essex faction by Henry Cuffe, Regius Professor of Greek, who had been a student at Oxford with Neville. He held this office for seven years before resigning to become secretary to Essex.

When Essex made his full disclosure, Neville was immediately sent for. Keenly aware of the danger, Neville had hastened to Dover to return to France. When stopped by the Queen's men, he galloped back to London. The contemporary historian Camden was present when Neville's written statement was read at Cuffe's hearing. Camden wrote:

> *And Sir Henry Neville ingenuously confessed (if my memory fail me not, for I was then present and heard his confession read) that Cuffe had suggested unto him at his, the said Neville's, return out of France, that it would be imputed to him that the treaty at Boulogne failed of success; that he came to him oftentimes afterward and persuaded him to come and see the Earl, which once he did; that after this, when he was even ready to return into France, he entreated him to go to Drury house and hear what should be consulted on, protesting that nothing was to be propounded there which was not for the good of the kingdom and of the Earl, and which he might hear without breach of loyalty to the Queen; and lastly that he prayed him to be present with the Earl when he should invade the Court, and laid open unto him the whole plot; which ... Neville misliked as a matter full of danger, difficulty, and wickedness, and smiling at it, said it was in the number of those things which are never praised till performed.*[45]

---

[44] Green, M. *Wriothesley's Roses in Shakespeare's Sonnets, Poems and Plays* (Clevedon Books, Baltimore, Maryland, 1993).

[45] William Camden, *Annales Rerum Gestarum Angliae et Hiberniae Regnante Elizabetha (1615 and 1625), with the annotations of Sir Francis Bacon* – A hypertext critical edition by Dana F. Sutton, University of California, Irvine. Posted 27 March 2000, revised 1 February 2001.

Several other conspirators were also found guilty of treason and beheaded. As noted, moments before his brutal execution on March 13, Cuffe had the determination to beg Neville's forgiveness for having involved him:

> *But whereas I have brought that noble knight Sir Henry Neville into danger, I am heartily sorry for it, and I earnestly entreat him to forgive me.*

On 27 May 1601, after a period of house arrest for Neville, John Chamberlain wrote to Dudley Carleton:

> *Sir Harry Neville is in the Tower, which at first made many men think he should come to his answer, but this whole term having passed without any arraignment, makes me think there shall be no more blood drawn in this cause ...*

Camden recounts that Neville was summoned again:

> *The 8th of July was Sir Henry Neville called before some of the Queen's Privy Counsel and Judges at York house, and charged that he had been present at the consultations in Drury house, that he had not revealed the designs there propounded, and had imparted to Essex the secrets of his French embassy. He confessed that at the Earl's request he acquainted him with the journal of his French Embassy, that he was present at one consultation only, that he condemned their counsels as a sick man's dreams, but durst not accuse Essex and such great men, shunning the name of an Informer, and hoping they would change such inconsiderate and as yet unresolved counsels, or that he might timely enough and without suspicion reveal them after his return from France. Yet was he, by general voice of them all, sharply reprehended as worthy of heavier punishment, and adjudged to the Tower.*

It is not clear how Neville's life came to be spared; but it is known that Robert Cecil made some efforts on his behalf.[46] Neville now faced an uncertain life as a guest in the Tower, perhaps until his death. He was fined the crippling sum of 10,000 pounds and stripped of his titles and offices, which included Member of Parliament, Ambassador to France, and Joint Teller of the Exchequer. He became *Mr Henry Neville.*

Southampton's physical accommodation in the Tower was reasonably comfortable. He paid a weekly rent of 9 pounds, and was situated next to the Queen's gallery, with a withdrawing chamber and bedchamber. Nonetheless, his initial confinement was very strict. Neville's conditions of imprisonment are less clear. Brenda James records that they were confined in adjacent areas, but that Neville in particular was severely persecuted.[47] [48]

---

[46] Stopes, C.C. *The Life of Henry, Third Earl of Southampton, Shakespeare's Patron* (Cambridge University Press, Cambridge and New York, 1922).
[47] James, *Henry Neville and the Shakespeare Code.*
[48] James and Rubinstein, *The Truth Will Out.*

Burning of the letter *T* on the forehead was usual for convicted traitors, but there is no record of Neville having been branded. Neville's mentor Henry Savile was also briefly imprisoned, perhaps because of his involvement with Essex and his writings on Tacitus.[49]

Not surprisingly, Neville sought to downplay his role in the rebellion. However urgently political circumstances demanded action of the group, and however enthusiastically they were supported by the public, they were clearly plotters and Neville had colluded with them. By association at the very least, he was a plotter too. For a throng of men to march armed on the Queen was not a subtle action. The risks were clearly mortal and Neville, having balanced the risks, had agreed to play his role.[50] He was, unquestionably in legal terms, a traitor. His father-in-law Killigrew disowned him. Although James pardoned him, it is not altogether surprising that Neville never gained the King's trust and he never achieved the high office that he had hoped for.

The convenient fiction that Neville was a bystander allowed him to be restored to a large extent, and it protected succeeding generations of his family from the taint of disgrace. This misrepresentation seems to have been maintained and ultimately the true extent of his role was buried.

Shakespeare and the Essex rebellion

The theme of kingship in crisis is clearly evident throughout the history plays, and becomes a central issue in Shakespeare's later works after the Essex rebellion, in which his supposed patron Southampton was a prime mover.[51] As mentioned earlier, the arras scene in *Hamlet* (written in 1601) seems to recall Cecil's appearance from behind the curtain at Essex's trial.

Moreover, someone among the rebels had sufficient knowledge of Shakespeare's works to commission a new performance of *Richard II* on the eve of the rebellion itself. The play concerns the overthrow of an unworthy monarch, and had not been performed for several years. Presumably, it was intended to encourage public support for the rebellion.

---

[49] *"Savile's friendship with Essex dated back to at least 1591. In that year, he published his translation of* Tacitus's Histories *and* Agricola *under, it seems, Essex's patronage ... [Savile] implicitly supports the view that it is permissible for a military commander, at least, to rebel against a bad monarch – quite against the political orthodoxy of his time, and certainly significant in the light of his association with Essex."* Goulding, '*Savile, Sir Henry (1549–1622)*', ODNB.

[50] It does not seem too great a stretch to surmise that the whole indecision of Hamlet expresses Neville's agony prior to his commitment to this action.

[51] Lesser, Z. 'Mixed Government and Mixed Marriage in a King and No King: Sir Henry Neville Reads Beaumont and Fletcher'. *English Literary History* 69, pp. 947–77 (2002).

Although its authenticity has been disputed, many accounts claim that in response Elizabeth said:

> *I am Richard the second, know ye not that?* [52]

Regardless of the authenticity of this claim, it is clear that the authorities were not pleased. Augustine Phillips, one of the Chamberlain's Men who had performed *Richard II*, was sent to face the court, but no one was charged. Surprisingly, Shakespeare was not questioned, though he was the named author on the title page of the second edition of *Richard II*, published in 1598.[53] Moreover, the status of his company seems to have been entirely undiminished. Indeed, it performed before the Queen on the eve of Essex's execution, just 17 days after *Richard II* had been staged.[54] And even in her understandable rage, neither she nor her advisors associated Shakespeare personally with responsibility for a play that was used to justify a threat to her life little more than two weeks earlier.

The coincidence of the Essex rebellion in 1601 with a change of mood in the works of Shakespeare has often been noted. It is discernible among the Sonnets, published in 1609, but probably written intermittently over the previous 20 years. These express personal shame, together with images of imprisonment and branding (Sonnets 111, 112).

However, the division is most evident in the chronology of the plays. There is an abrupt shift from the last of the early comedies, *Twelfth Night,* noted above in relation to Count Orsino, to the great tragedies and problem plays: *Hamlet, Measure for Measure, Troilus and Cressida, Othello* and *King Lear.* William Shakespeare seems to have escaped any material harm whatsoever in 1601, and there is nothing else in his biography that might explain this profound emotional change.

In contrast, the change of fortune for Sir Henry Neville was catastrophic. For reasons unknown, Elizabeth reserved particular bitterness towards Neville and Southampton. For almost two years, together they shared the same fate – shamed, isolated, impoverished, bored, and in mortal fear that new evidence might come to light. Although Neville's involvement was seemingly peripheral, he was imprisoned for longer, and his fines were greater than any other conspirator save Southampton.

---

52 Ellis, *The Truth About William Shakespeare*, p. 113.

53 In dealing with sedition, *Richard II* was clearly a very risky play. Not surprisingly, it was published anonymously in 1597. It was not until 1598, after the publication of *Loves Labours Lost* which seems to flatteringly depict the Queen herself, and Richard *III* which supported the Tudor monarchy, that *Richard II* was published as by William Shakespeare. Indeed, *Loves Labours Lost* was the very first play published under Shakespeare's name. It may have become necessary to associate Shakespeare's name with *Loves Labours Lost* and *Richard III* to discourage any curiosity around the authorship of the "seditious" *Richard II.*

54 Bate, J. *Soul of the Age* (Penguin, London, 2008), pp. 256–86.

Neville and King James

From the late 1590s, Elizabeth's closest advisor Robert Cecil had been making secret arrangements with James VI of Scotland to prepare for a smooth transition of power. There is some evidence that Neville took part in these arrangements prior to his appointment as Ambassador.[55]

As Elizabeth's death approached, Cecil sent James a draft proclamation of his accession to the English throne. She died on 25 March 1603 and within hours James was proclaimed King in London.

James left Edinburgh on April 5 and travelled slowly, perhaps intending to arrive after Elizabeth's funeral. Even before he left, James had sent an order ahead for the release of Southampton and Neville. They were freed on 10 April 1603, and James ordered a royal pardon and the restoration of their titles and wealth. By this time, all of the other conspirators, many with deeper involvement, had paid smaller fines and been released. When he reached London on May 7, James was greeted with great public enthusiasm. Civil war and invasion had been averted by Cecil's astute statecraft.

Though Neville and Southampton were both presented to James on his arrival in London, the preferment which many had expected did not eventuate. James seems to have perceived Neville's capabilities clearly, but he also feared them, and Neville's popularity. James lived in constant fear of overthrow and, on the basis of an unsubstantiated rumour, briefly imprisoned Neville in 1604. Moreover, James believed in the divine right of kings, that he ruled with God's absolute authority. By contrast, Neville was a moderate, who promoted a new form of government for England with a balance of power between King, the aristocracy and the populace. This was the model of "mixed government" propounded by Polybius.[56]

Though disappointed by his lack of advancement from James, Neville participated expertly in the evolving committee processes in the House of Commons. The grievances of the Commons were aggravated by the King's ever-increasing spending on his favourites, to the exclusion of more deserving subjects, and by his demands on Parliament for additional funds. By 1607, Neville was identified with the faction in the Commons in disagreement with the King. They were known as the Popular Party.

As Lord Treasurer since 1608, Cecil (now Lord Salisbury) had made considerable progress in increasing the King's income. Unfortunately, he could not restrain even greater increases in the King's spending. On 16 November 1610 the Commons flatly refused the King the funds he was now demanding.

---

[55] Lesser, Z. "Mixed Government and Mixed Marriage in a King and No King: Sir Henry Neville Reads Beaumont and Fletcher", *English Literary History* 69, pp. 947–77 (2002).
[56] Lesser, Z. *Renaissance Drama and the Politics of Publication* (Cambridge University Press, 2008), p. 165.

James ordered 30 members to appear before him that afternoon. From among them, Francis Bacon began a florid preamble. James immediately cut him off and pointed to Neville, asking:

> *Am I in want?*

Owen Duncan recounts the frank exchange that followed:

> *Neville, perhaps remembering the days ten years before when he had had to deal with the angry thrusts of Henry IV* [of France], *responded – "Yes, I believe you are in want."*
> *"Ought not my wants to be relieved?" pressed the King.*
> *"To this," said Neville, "I must answer with a distinction. Where your Majesty's expense groweth by the Commonwealth we are bound to maintain it, otherwise not. In this one parliament, we have already given four subsidies and fifteenths, which is more than ever was given by any parliament at any time, upon any occasion; and yet withal that we have had no relief of our grievances."* [57]

The following day, the King rejected the grievances of the Commons, and ever after referred to this group as his *thirty dogs.* His Chancellor of the Exchequer, Sir Julius Caesar, characterised the exchange as *contempt in the inferior towards the superior.* However, Caesar also acknowledged that these men were *held amongst the common people the best patriots that ever were.*

James dissolved his first parliament in 1611 without any agreement having been reached concerning supply. Cecil died in May 1612, leaving the position of Secretary of State vacant. Cecil's best efforts had failed to cement workable relations between the King and Parliament. No one was better qualified, more able, or more widely respected in Parliament to fulfil this role than Neville. And, with the help of Southampton, he set about to win it. Despite Neville's apparent defiance, or perhaps because of his frankness, James was amenable to Neville's advice in 1612. It was through Neville's literary connections that this rapprochement was made possible. The poet Sir Thomas Overbury had influence over James's favourite Robert Carr. Overbury, a friend of Ben Jonson and fellow of Neville's literary circle at the *Mermaid,* persuaded Carr to reason with the King regarding the popular cause, and to recommend Neville to him. Somehow, probably via Overbury and Carr, Neville engineered a serendipitous meeting with the King in his role as Forester at Windsor in July 1612.

From this meeting, James was sufficiently interested to ask Neville to put into writing the ideas of which he had spoken. The letter that Neville produced assured the King of the goodwill of the Commons, and the likelihood of agreement being achieved within another parliament. Although the king would be required to make certain concessions, Neville identified several which would not necessarily be burdensome.

---

[57] Duncan, *The Political Career of Sir Henry Neville,* pp. 222–3.

He also gently counselled the King to avoid pressing the Commons, and to show goodwill and grace. The letter was a tour de force of political wisdom and artful diplomacy.[58]

Duncan writes:

> *These were arguments worthy of a renaissance diplomat who had studied his trade at Oxford and upon the Grand Tour, had tempered it in serving at the Court of Henry IV [of France], had since used it to save his life after the Essex affair, and now sought to achieve his greatest personal and public ambitions through it.*[59]

King James was only slightly influenced by Neville's advice. Ultimately, he was not inclined to compromise, and found suggestions for short-term gratification more palatable. Moreover, excessive lobbying by others on Neville's behalf had back-fired. James was determined to select his own closest advisor personally. As Chamberlain writes:

> *... but the surest card of all, Sir Henry Neville, will never see you wronged where he may help. If he had not been strongly oppugned every way, he had been settled before this in the secretaryship. But it is said too much soliciting hath hindered him. And the flocking of parliament-men about him, and their meeting and consultations with the Earl of Southampton ... hath done him nor them no good, for the King says he will not have a secretary imposed upon him by parliament.*[60]

In 1612, an anonymous letter to King James was tabled in the House of Commons. Given the mistrust of the Commons for James, there was much agitation to discover the author in their midst who had undermined their solidarity. After several days' discussion, Sir Henry revealed that he was the author, the *undertaker.*[61] Such was the trust he had earned in the House, the hostility evaporated immediately and the integrity of Neville's actions was acknowledged.

Finally, in April 1614 James appointed Sir Ralph Winwood, Neville's former secretary when he was Ambassador to France. This was a profound blow to Neville which, together with his deteriorating hearing, effectively extinguished his political aspirations. Characteristically, James's decision did not affect Neville's friendship with Winwood.

---

[58] Appendix 6.
[59] Duncan, *The Political Career of Sir Henry Neville,* p. 241.
[60] Chamberlain, *The Letters of John Chamberlain.*
[61] Jansson, M., ed., *Proceedings in Parliament 1614 (House of Commons)* (American Philosophical Society, Philadelphia), pp. 244–53.

In summary, the central preoccupation of Neville's intensive political activities can be seen to revolve around the issue of government in crisis. The same theme is at the heart of almost all of Shakespeare's work during the reign of James I, most particularly in *Hamlet, Troilus and Cressida, Measure for Measure, King Lear, Timon of Athens, Macbeth, Antony and Cleopatra,* and *Coriolanus.*

Above all, as Zachary Lesser notes, Neville was concerned to realise a Polybian model of "mixed government" in which power is balanced between the monarch, the aristocracy and the common people. King James believed in the Divine Right of Kings, and was strongly opposed to this view. Lesser demonstrates that it is this new model of "mixed government" that is evoked in Beaumont and Fletcher's political play, *A King and no King* which was performed for King James in 1611.[62]

As noted in Chapter 1, the first printing of this play (1619) includes a dedication from the publisher as follows:

> *Worthy Knight, Sir Henry Neville, I present, or rather return unto your view, that which formerly hath been received from you, hereby effecting what you did desire.*

It seems that Neville had some influence over this play, perhaps even direct input as he sought to influence King James. Intriguingly, Lesser notes that the other important play in which the concept of "mixed government" is explored is "Shakespeare's" *Othello.*

The Virginia Company, Neville and Shakespeare

Alongside his parliamentary activities, Neville was intent on recovering his enormous losses as Ambassador to France and debts incurred while in prison. Neville's main venture was as shareholder in the London Virginia Company. The aim of this company was to profit from the English colony at Jamestown, Virginia.

A few days after the registration of *Shakespeare's Sonnets* with the Stationer's Office in 1609, a royal charter was granted to the second London Virginia Company, of which Neville and Southampton were among its 50 directors. These shareholders were known as *Adventurers.* It may be noteworthy that the Dedication to *Shakespeare's Sonnets* is presented as from *the well-wishing adventurer.* Shakespeare was not a shareholder in the company and therefore not an *Adventurer.*[63]

---

62 Lesser, *Renaissance Drama and the Politics of Publication*, Chapter 5. This chapter includes an account of Neville's struggles with King James, his promotion of the Polybian model of "mixed government", and the allegorical promotion of this model in Beaumont and Fletcher's *A King and No King.*

63 James and Rubinstein, *The Truth Will Out.*

Shakespeare's last major play, *The Tempest*, is generally dated to about 1610–1611. There are many parallels between the shipwreck described in the play and the famous shipwreck of the *Sea-Venture* in 1609. The *Sea-Venture*, as the flagship of a supply mission to Virginia, encountered a massive hurricane. At the point when all were exhausted, the captain had it driven aground on a reef at Bermuda to avoid sinking. The survivors built two smaller ships from the wreckage and continued on to Jamestown to find that most of the settlers had died of starvation.[64]

The sensational details of the shipwreck and its aftermath were described in a long confidential letter from Virginia, written by Sir William Strachey to a woman he referred to only as *Noble Lady*, probably Sara Smith, the wife of Sir Thomas Smith of the Virginia Company. Although the point has been disputed, it is widely acknowledged to contain much source material for *The Tempest*.[65] The *Strachey Letter* consists of more than 20,000 words, and was circulated privately among the directors of the Virginia Company, at which time it would certainly have been read by Neville.

By contrast, as noted by James and Rubinstein, William Shakespeare had no involvement with the Virginia Company. Nor is it likely that he would have had access to a sensitive and private document that, if made public, might undermine shareholder confidence in the project.

Neville's Last Days

On 9 February 1615, John Chamberlain wrote to Dudley Carleton concerning Neville:

> *... all his hopes at an end, which is but a bad medicine for a man that hath at this instant three dangerous diseases upon him, that is the jaundice, the scorbut [scurvy] and a dropsy [swelling due to fluid retention], which hath brought him to a very weak case and will utterly overthrow him if he find not present remedy ...*[66]

Neville died on 10 July 1615. His friend and fellow parliamentarian James Whitelocke wrote at the time of Neville's death that:

> *... he was the most sufficient man for understanding of state business that was in this kingdom, and a very good scholar and a stout man, but was as ignobly and unworthily handled as ever gentleman was.*

[64] James and Rubinstein, *The Truth Will Out*.
[65] Ibid.
[66] Chamberlain, *The Letters of John Chamberlain*.

Sir Henry Neville was buried in the family tomb at Waltham St Lawrence. There is a blank space on his tomb where an inscription should have been. This may be entirely appropriate given the humility expressed throughout Shakespeare's writing. This is most apparent in the Sonnets, published late in his life. There are many examples:

Sonnet 71, lines 10–11:

When I (perhaps) compounded am with clay,
Do not so much as my poor name rehearse;

Sonnet 81, lines 6–7:

Though I, once gone, to all the world must die:
The earth can yield me but a common grave,

Sonnet 72, lines 11–12:

My name be buried where my body is,
And live no more to shame nor me nor you.

Chapter 3: Neville's Codes

Throughout history, secret communication has served a central function in state security. If a communication is intercepted, it must only be intelligible by the intended recipient. This usually requires an encryption (cipher) of some sort.

In Chapter 2 we noted that Sir Henry Neville was consulted on sensitive state matters including foreign policy, Elizabeth's succession, and later in negotiating the fractious relationship between King James and Parliament. Neville was entrusted with state secrets over many years and he was well-versed in cryptography.

In the 16th and 17th centuries many forms of encryption were used. The celebrated lawyer and intellectual Francis Bacon, who was related to Neville by marriage, described the various types of ciphers in *Advancement of Learning* (1623):

> *Ciphers are commonly in letters or alphabets, but may be in words. There are many different types. Ciphers may replace the characters of the text with different characters or symbols that are listed in a secret table ...*

Bacon goes on to say that the best ciphers can be constructed such that their very existence is not obvious. We propose this is the case with the Dedication to the sonnets.

Cipher terminology

Two types of encryption are relevant to our examination, *Substitution* and *Transposition.*[1]

Substitution ciphers use agreed lists or tables of letters, symbols or words as *substitutes* to hide letters or words in the original message. The following is an excerpt from Sir Henry Neville himself:

> If *100State* might have any assurance to be *6.*GUKYOSWUG*θ.*NWPH ... she would undoubtedly resolve to continue the ... [War with Spain].

The weakness of these ciphers is that the coded words are conspicuous. By contrast, *transposition* ciphers can be very difficult to detect. In *transposition* ciphers, certain characters are *transposed* – moved or extracted – to assemble and obscure the secret message.

[1] Wrixon, F.B. *Codes, Ciphers and Cryptic Communication* (Black Dog and Leventhal, New York, 1998, 2005), p. 131.

The simplest *transposition* cipher is the *acrostic*, which was very popular among educated Elizabethans, as in this example from Ben Jonson:[2]

To Doctor Empiric

***W**hen men a dangerous disease did 'scape,*
***O**f old, they gave a cock to Aesculape.*
***L**et me give two, that doubly am got free*
***F**rom my disease's danger, and from thee.*

Jonson does not name the real "*Dr Empiric*", but the first letter of each line identifies his target.

The Dedication to *Shakespeare's Sonnets* also contains an acrostic – *TTMAP* which we will examine in Chapter 4. We propose that the Dedication uses a suite of simple acrostics as well as other transpositions directed by wordplay. These decryptions rely on the Dedication being set out in a *table*.

Tables for substitution

A more complex substitution technique requires a table that is referenced by both the sender and the receiver of a coded message. This method can be traced to the Greek Polybius (200–118 BC), who devised what is now known as the *Polybius Square*.[3]

	1	2	3	4	5
1	A	B	C	D	E
2	F	G	H	I	K
3	L	M	N	O	P
4	Q	R	S	T	U
5	V	W	X	Y	Z

The Polybius Square

Using this simple table, the letters "D-O-G" may be expressed as a sequence of numbers or co-ordinates, i.e. 1-4, 3-4, 2-2, or as 4-1, 4-3, 2-2.

Polybius was a major influence on Sir Henry Neville. In 1596 the scholar Isaac Casaubon wrote to Neville's mentor Henry Savile requesting Savile's help in translating Polybius's *The Histories* from the Greek.[4] This work contains Polybius's model of "mixed government" which became so central to Neville's political vision. Moreover, it was also in *The Histories* that Polybius described the encryption method above. We propose that this is the very method that was extended by Neville in his diplomatic codes, and again as the author of the Dedication to the Sonnets.

---

[2] Epigram XIII, Jonson, Ben, *Epigrammes. I. booke. The author B.I.*, London (1616).
[3] Wrixon, *Codes, Ciphers and Cryptic Communication*, pp. 22, 190.
[4] This was the beginning of a steady working relationship that continued until Casaubon's death 18 years later. Casaubon, who was one of the most educated men in Europe, produced his translation of Polybius in 1609, the year the *Sonnets* were published. Goulding, '*Savile, Sir Henry (1549–1622)*', ODNB.

The tables of Sir Henry Neville

It is well-documented that as Ambassador to France Neville used several shared lists and tables to produce *substitution ciphers* in his communications with the English Secretary, Robert Cecil.

a. 100	The Queen
a. 101	England/English
a. 121	Earl of Essex
b. 120	French King
b. 122	Monsieur de Villeroy (Nicolas de Neufville the French secretary)[5]
c. 100	King of Spain
d. 100	Duke of Bouillon
f. 150	King of Scotland
f. 154	Ambassador of Scotland
f. 158	French Ambassador
g. 140	Pope
g. 142	Spanish ambassador
l. 160	Protestants
l. 165	Catholics
m. 173	Spain
m. 175	Scotland
m. 177	Rome
o. 194	Rochell
r. 162	The Chancellor
u. 205	War
u. 206	Peace
w. 200	Treaty of Peace

Extract from an extensive substitution table used by Neville (compiled by S. Tomokiyo)[6]

Simple substitutions as in the table above offer only weak security, because their meaning may be determined from the context and frequency of the substitution. More sensitive communications require much greater security. To this end, Neville applied additional and more sophisticated methods, as summarised by Satoshi Tomokiyo:

> *Individual letters are substituted with a "paired" letter according to four tables, each with different pairing. The letters Q, X, Y and Z were reserved to indicate the appropriate table. Text could jump from one table to another, even in the middle of a word. For example, both of the following sequences read "the patriarch":*

[5] Monsieur de Villeroy (122) is Nicolas de Neufville (1543–1617), the longest serving and most eminent French secretary. There may be significance to the coincidence of the names Neville and Neufville, and the code name 122. Sonnet 122 is a key to decrypting the dedication and is discussed in the following chapters.
[6] Tomokiyo, S. "Ciphers during the Reign of Queen Elizabeth I", *Articles on Historical Cryptography,* http://cryptiana.web.fc2.com/code/elizabeth.htm. Accessed 3 April 2016. Tomokiyo cites Davys, J., *An Essay on the Art of Decyphering* (1737), p. 42.

```
Z.EOTDU Y.HCMSCRT
  THEPA   TRIARCH

X.DOWGM Q.IGTLGOW
  THEPA   TRIARCH
```

Q	A	B	C	D	E	F	G	H	I	K
	L	N	O	S	U	M	R	W	T	P
X	A	B	C	D	E	F	G	H	I	K
	M	U	L	T	W	N	P	O	R	S
Y	A	B	C	D	E	F	G	H	I	K
	S	P	R	N	W	O	U	T	M	L
Z	A	B	C	D	E	F	G	H	I	K
	U	N	W	P	T	S	L	O	M	R

Cipher for Sir Robert Cecil and Sir Henry Neville (1599–1600).
Tabulated by S. Tomokiyo[7]

Neville used a different "paired letter" system to correspond with his secretary, Ralph Winwood.[8]

```
6.GUKYOSWUG θ.NWPH
  REPAIDHER    DEBT
```

χ	A	B	C	D	E	F	G	H	I	K	L	M
	X	Z	Q	T	Y	N	P	O	R	W	S	U
θ	A	B	C	D	E	F	G	H	I	K	L	M
	S	P	R	N	W	Q	U	T	X	Z	Y	O
6	A	B	C	D	E	F	G	H	I	K	L	M
	Y	N	Z	S	U	X	R	W	O	P	T	Q

Cipher for Sir Robert Cecil, Ralph Winwood and Sir Henry Neville (1600–1601).
Tabulated by S. Tomokiyo[9]

In this table, Neville uses the symbols χ, θ and 6 to reference each alphabet, freeing Q, X, Y and Z. This table decrypts our earlier example:

> If *100State* might have any assurance to be *6.*GUKYOSWUG*θ.*NWPH ... she would undoubtedly resolve to continue the ... [War with Spain].

Here, the "word" *6.*GUKYOSWUG*θ.*NWPH, is really a series of co-ordinate references to the table above:

6-G	6-U	6-K	6-Y	6-O	6-S	6-W	6-U	6-G	*θ*-N	*θ*-W	*θ*-P	*θ*-H
R	E	P	A	I	D	H	E	R	D	E	B	T

In Chapter 4, we find that the Dedication to the Sonnets contains its own acrostic, *TTMAP.* We take this to be a direction to lay out the text in 15 columns, since *TT* occurs at the 15th letter of the Dedication. This table layout reveals additional encoded text. In Chapter 5 we find that the Dedication also acts as its own reference table, very like Neville's tables above. Co-ordinate references from the Dedication table point to individual Sonnets, the contents of which both reinforce and extend its message.

---

7 Tomokiyo, "Ciphers during the Reign of Queen Elizabeth I".
8 *Winwood's Memorials*, Vol. 1, p. 249, cited by Brenda James in *Henry Neville and the Shakespeare Code.*
9 Tomokiyo, "Ciphers during the Reign of Queen Elizabeth I".

Neville's Code 1600

Q.I refers to the cell at co-ordinates Q and I (shaded). This cell contains the letter T.

The reference table reveals letters.

Q	A	B	C	D	E	F	G	H	**I**	K
	L	N	O	S	U	M	R	W	**T**	P
X	A	B	C	D	E	F	G	H	I	K
	M	U	L	T	W	N	P	O	R	S
Y	A	B	C	D	E	F	G	H	I	K
	S	P	R	N	W	O	U	T	M	L
Z	A	B	C	D	E	F	G	H	I	K
	U	N	W	P	T	S	L	O	M	R

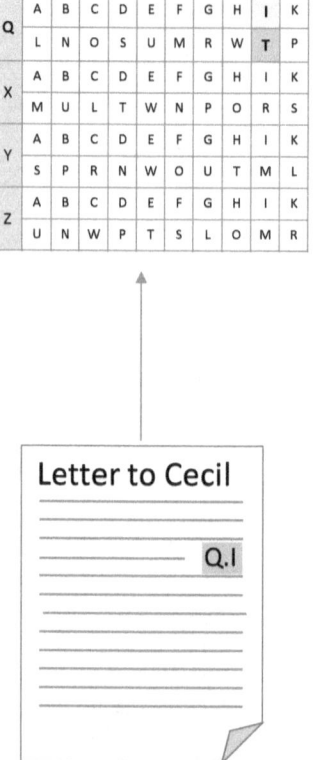

Dedication Code 1609

SONNE occurs at co-ordinates 3-3. We take this to refer to Sonnet 33, in which the word that is conspicuously "missing" is *Sonne.*[10]

The reference table reveals numbers – the numbers of specific Sonnets.

	1	2	**3**	4	5	6	7	8	9	10	11	12	13	14	15
1	T	O	T	H	E	O	N	L	I	E	B	E	G	E	T
2	T	E	R	O	F	T	H	E	S	E	I	N	S	U	I
3	N	G	**S**	O	N	N	E	T	S	Mr	W	H		A	L
4	L	H	A	P	P	I	N	E	S	S	E	A	N	D	T
5	H	A	T	E	T	E	R	N	I	T	I	E	P	R	O
6	M	I	S	E	D	B	Y	O	U	R	E	V	E	R	-
7	L	I	V	I	N	G	P	O	E	T	W	I	S	H	E
8	T	H	T	H	E	W	E	L	L	-	W	I	S	H	I
9	N	G	A	D	V	E	N	T	U	R	E	R	I	N	S
10	E	T	T	I	N	G	F	O	R	T	H	T	T		

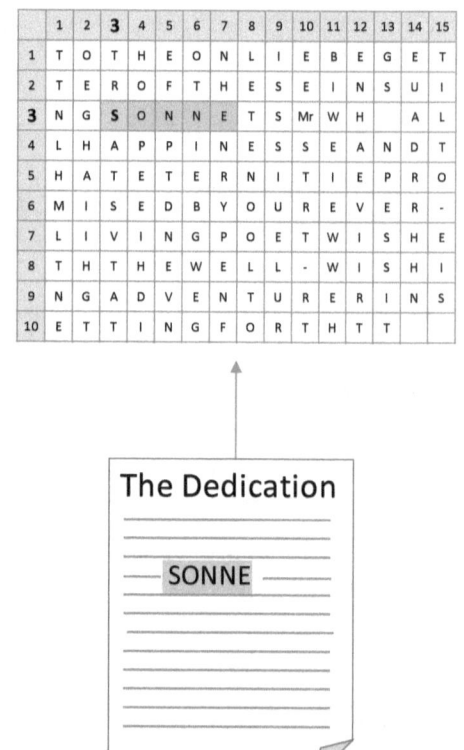

Neville's code (1600) compared with the Dedication to *Shakespeare's Sonnets* (1609). The Dedication is its own reference table, thus overcoming the challenge of including both code and key in one volume

[10] *Sonne* is the usual spelling in the Sonnets.

Chapter 4: The Dedication Contains a Hidden Message

The poems *Venus and Adonis* (1593) and *The Rape of Lucrece* (1594) are among the earliest Shakespearean works. Hugely popular, they were reprinted many times. In contrast, *Shakespeare's Sonnets* is a late work, and seems to have attracted little attention. There is only one record of anyone having bought a copy, and only thirteen copies have survived.

Nevertheless, the Sonnets stand alone in style and content. While a few are easily accessible and renowned for their beauty, many remain mysterious and almost impenetrable. Moreover, the Dedication to the sonnets is famous for its strangeness:

> *... the entire Dedication ... is so syntactically ambiguous as to defeat any possibility of consensus among interpreters.*[1]

In the following chapters we explore a possible resolution in which the Dedication and the Sonnets are closely linked to form one coherent whole.

The quarto of the Sonnets was published in 1609. However, in *Palladis Tamia* (1598) the churchman Francis Meres mentions circulation of at least some of *Shakespeare's sugared Sonnets among his private friends.* In addition, earlier versions of Sonnets 138 and 144 had been published in *The Passionate Pilgrim* in 1599.[2]

Each of the 154 sonnets is numbered, and each has fourteen lines, apart from Sonnet 99 (15 lines), and Sonnet 126 (12 lines). The 329-line narrative poem *A Lovers Complaint* follows in the same volume.

The Sonnets build on and develop the Petrarchan sonnet form, to which sonneteers had adhered for over 200 years. Named after the first humanist poet Francesco Petrarca (1304–1374), the "rules" of the Petrarchan sonnet were formalised by later poets. Highly conventional, these sonnets always concern romantic love in which the beloved is unattainable, often endowed with a higher social status, and cruelly indifferent.

---

[1] Schoenbaum, S. *Shakespeare's Lives* (Clarendon Press, Oxford, 1970).

[2] *The Passionate Pilgrim* was published under the name W. Shakespeare in the small octavo format, and consists of 20 poems. Only five are thought to be by Shakespeare. These are the two sonnets referred to above, plus three poems from *Love's Labour's Lost*. There is no evidence that Shakespeare of Stratford ever challenged the wrongful attribution of the other fifteen poems to him.

In contrast, *Shakespeare's Sonnets* both use and comment on that form; sometimes masquerading as conventional, but playing on double-meanings to redirect or reverse the surface meaning. The majority of Shakespeare's sonnets do deal with love, but the love is seldom idealised, nor solely romantic. Rather, the sonnets encompass love in its many forms; romantic, sexual, fraternal, and paternal. They also explore human suffering and failings, as well as political and artistic achievement.

There are several instances where one sonnet seems to follow on from the preceding sonnet, and many instances where two or more sonnets address very similar topics but are sequentially separate. However, the majority are independent seemingly personal expressions or reflections.

Many themes have been noted – the inevitability of change, the victory of art over time, the permanence of love, the transience of beauty. Some sort of love triangle is discernible, perhaps including a second poet. At least one female identity is addressed as the object of both love and contempt. There are some indications that she may have been one or any of dark-haired, dark-eyed, dark-skinned, darkly-disposed, or that she wore dark make-up. Much of the love expressed seems to be towards a younger man, though the more sexualised sonnets seem to refer to the female identity.

Most commentators observe a logical unity among the first 17 sonnets which can be read as from an older man, urging a younger man to marry and to have children. Casson and Rubinstein argue persuasively that this *fair youth* is Neville's eldest son, whom he is persuading to marry Elizabeth Smyth. Indeed, the younger Henry Neville did marry Elizabeth just prior to the publication of the sonnets; a match which afforded a dowry substantial enough to restore the family's fortune.[3]

Beyond this initial grouping of 17 sonnets, there is little or nothing that can be said with any confidence regarding the sequencing and numbering of the sonnets that would illuminate the themes, characters, or events, much less the biography of the writer.

It is the deeply personal nature of the sonnets that distinguishes them from all of Shakespeare's other works. Unlike the plays and narrative poems, which tell stories, most of the sonnets address the reader directly and personally, like letters. For this reason, many scholars have looked within them for clues with which to assemble a biography. But, although the sonnets seem autobiographical, the identities, places and incidents are never named. The significance of the imagery, symbolism and verbal patterning that distinguish the sonnets is not currently available to us. However, a richer biography of the author might well illuminate a great deal more meaning.

[3] Casson, J., and Rubinstein, W.D. *Sir Henry Neville was Shakespeare: The Evidence* (Amberley, UK, 2016), pp. 200–2.

TO.THE.ONLIE.BEGETTER.OF.
THESE.INSVING.SONNETS.
Mr.W.H. ALL.HAPPINESSE.
AND.THAT.ETERNITIE.
PROMISED.

BY.

OVR.EVER-LIVING.POET.

WISHETH.

THE.WELL-WISHING.
ADVENTVRER.IN.
SETTING.
FORTH.

T. T.

The Dedication to *Shakespeare's Sonnets* (1609)

The Dedication

The title page of *Shakespeare's Sonnets* states "*By G. Eld, for T.T.*" George Eld was a well-known London printer. The initials *T.T.* are generally taken to refer to the London publisher Thomas Thorpe, supported by the Stationers' Register of 20 May 1609:

> *Tho. Thorpe. Entred for his copie under the handes of master Wilson and master Lownes Wardenes a booke called Shakespeares sonnettes vjd.*

Prefacing this monumental but opaque collection of poems is what appears to be a very clumsy or cryptic Dedication, described by Leslie Hotson as ... *perhaps the most famous Dedication in all literature.*[4]

The Dedication also bears the initials *T.T.*, and although it may seem logical to assume that they also refer to Thomas Thorpe, dedications are usually signed by authors to patrons, and not by publishers. In the case of Thorpe, this might not have been so unusual. Thorpe is known to have written at least four dedications. However, unlike the Dedication to the Sonnets, Thorpe's other texts are conventionally obsequious and easily understood.

The ostensible signing of the Dedication by the publisher, together with the apparently random order of the sonnets and the frequent typographical irregularities, have led many commentators to suggest that Thorpe published *Shakespeare's Sonnets* without the author's permission. However, this theory has been convincingly challenged, especially by the Stratfordian scholars Stanley Wells and Gary Taylor.[5] They note that Thorpe was a very reputable publisher and had high standards. Katherine Duncan-Jones has also argued that the negative view is undeserved.[6] She notes that between 1600 and 1625, Thorpe published at least forty-five books by authors of the highest rank, beginning with Christopher Marlowe, and including George Chapman, Thomas Nashe, John Marston and Ben Jonson. Jonson, in particular, had *notoriously exacting standards* and was *an active overseer of his own works in print.*[7] It seems unlikely that writers of such distinction would associate with a dishonest publisher.

The printer of the Sonnets, George Eld, also had a high reputation for quality. As well as printing both *Shakespeare's Sonnets* and *Troylus and Cressida* in 1609, he printed texts for Jonson, Marlowe, Thomas Middleton and numerous others. He and Thorpe produced more than twenty titles together.

---

[4] Hotson, L. *Mr WH* (Rupert Hart-Davis, London, 1964).
[5] Wells, S., and Taylor, G. *William Shakespeare: A Textual Companion* (W.W. Norton, New York, 1997).
[6] Duncan-Jones, K. "Was the 1609 Shake-Speares Sonnets Really Unauthorized?", *Review of English Studies*, New Series. 34, No. 134, 151–71 (1983).
[7] Ibid., p. 162.

Perhaps most tellingly, there is no evidence that Shakespeare ever complained about the publication of this large body of work. Given their highly personal content, the apparently haphazard assembly, and the very odd dedication, if the publication had not been authorised one might have expected some complaint to be voiced by the greatest English writer at the height of his fame.

Who is *Mr WH?*

There have been many candidates for *Mr WH.* The most popular theory is that *W.H.* reverses the initials of Henry Wriothesley, the Earl of Southampton, and Shakespeare's notional patron, to whom the prefaces of *Venus and Adonis* and *The Rape of Lucrece* were addressed. This theory usually links Southampton with the fair youth in Sonnets 1–17 who is unwilling to marry.

Another candidate is William Herbert, Earl of Pembroke. Katherine Duncan-Jones noted that two works published by Thorpe in 1610 bear florid dedications to Pembroke.[8] In 1623, Heminge and Condell dedicated the First Folio of plays attributed to Shakespeare to *the most noble and incomparable pair of brethren*; the Earls of Pembroke and Montgomery.

Both candidates argue against Thorpe being the author of the Dedication. If either Southampton or Pembroke is *Mr WH* it seems highly unlikely that a lowly publisher such as Thorpe would use the belittling honorific *Mr.* In contrast, Thorpe's Dedications to Pembroke a year later are described by Sidney Lee as *extravagantly subservient in tone.*[9] Following this line of logic, either *Mr WH* is not an earl, or Thomas Thorpe did not write the Dedication, or both.

Many other candidates have been proposed. In short, the identities of *Mr WH* and *T.T.* of the Dedication remain uncertain, and since 400 years have passed without revealing either *T.T.* or *Mr WH,* it seems at least possible that the author intended them to remain so. In Chapter 7 we posit a new candidate for *Mr WH,* Master William Hunnis of the Chapel Royal.

---

[8] Ibid., p. 163.
[9] Ibid.

Is the Dedication a cipher?

Many have wondered whether the Dedication has meaning that is hidden.

It is possible that Ben Jonson may have referred to the Dedication in this way. Jonson worked closely with Thomas Thorpe and George Eld, and was clearly involved in the compilation of the 1623 First Folio of Shakespeare's plays. Sir Henry Neville died in 1615, and William Shakespeare died nine months later, in April 1616. This was the year in which Jonson published a volume entitled *Epigrams*. Jonson's dedication of this edition to the Earl of Pembroke might suggest that both men were in on a secret:

> *I here offer to your Lordship: the ripest of my studies, my Epigrams; which though they carry danger in the sound, do not therefore seek your shelter: For, when I made them, I had nothing in my* ***conscience***[10] *of which I did need a* ***cypher*** [our bold].

Prefacing such a significant volume of his work, one would not expect this to be a throw-away line. Jonson's dedication seems to imply that some earlier collection of poems did need a *cipher.*[11]

In his 1964 book entitled *Mr WH*, Leslie Hotson first proposed that the Dedication was indeed a cipher or code.

However, the first real advance in unravelling the Dedication was made by John Rollet in 1997.[12] He noted that although it had often been observed that the uppercase Dedication presented superficial similarities to Roman stone inscriptions, it lacked some key features. The dots (or "points") were on the line, resembling full-stops rather than in the conventional midpoint between lines, and the lines did not begin with points. He reasoned that the "pointing" between words might be a device merely to separate the words so that they could be read easily, and so distract the reader with the surface sense of the text. He suggested that the points should be removed when decrypting the text.

---

[10] We note Jonson's reference to "conscience" in relation to the pair of Sonnets 151–152 that map to *TT* (discussed in Chapter 6).

[11] Jonson's Epigram 109 is discussed in Chapter 1 and Appendix 2. This epigram is addressed to Sir Henry Neville: *"Who calls on thee, Neville is a Muse"*.

[12] Rollet, J.M. "Secrets of the Dedication to Shakespeare's Sonnets", *The Oxfordian* 5, No. 2, 60–75 (1999).

When Rollet set the Dedication in a 15-column table he noticed the vertical or acrostic word *HENRY* in column 7, as below.

	1	2	3	4	5	6	7	8	9	10	11	12	13	14	15
1	T	O	T	H	E	O	N	L	I	E	B	E	G	E	T
2	T	E	R	O	F	T	H	E	S	E	I	N	S	V	I
3	N	G	S	O	N	N	E	T	S	Mr	W	H		A	L
4	L	H	A	P	P	I	N	E	S	S	E	A	N	D	T
5	H	A	T	E	T	E	R	N	I	T	I	E	P	R	O
6	M	I	S	E	D	B	Y	O	V	R	E	V	E	R	L
7	I	V	I	N	G	P	O	E	T	W	I	S	H	E	T
8	H	T	H	E	W	E	L	L	W	I	S	H	I	N	G
9	A	D	V	E	N	T	V	R	E	R	I	N	S	E	T
10	T	I	N	G	F	O	R	T	H	T	T				

Rollet's 15-column setting of the Dedication highlighting the acrostic *HENRY*

Rollet cautioned that it was essential to work from facsimiles of the original quarto edition, of which only 13 copies have survived. Almost all new editions have altered the spelling or layout, rendering decryption impossible.

In 2005, Brenda James and William Rubinstein published *The Truth Will Out.*[13] Through her own analysis of the Dedication, Brenda James had assembled fragments of a name she had never heard before: *Henry Neville.* She went on to discover that his life, education, outlook, social circle and accomplishments seemed to match attributes expected of the true author of Shakespeare. And unlike all previous candidates, there seemed to be no awkward anomalies. However, she gave few details of her decryptions.

At that time, we were not aware of Rollet's work, but when we set the Dedication in a 15-column table, we also found *HENRY* close to the centre. Our setting was slightly different from Rollet's, but the difference is critical. Whereas Rollet had left out the two hyphens from the original text, we included them. We reasoned that if the author had not intended the hyphens to be included, they could have been omitted without sacrificing surface meaning. Like Rollet, we took the pointing to be extraneous. We explored many different tables, but found the 15-column setting that yielded *HENRY* to be by far the most productive. At the time, we had no idea why 15 columns might be significant.[14]

[13] James and Rubinstein, *The Truth Will Out.*
[14] Our results were published in The Australian newspaper in 2006. Leyland, B., and Goding, J.W. "Authors crack the Bard's code", *The Australian,* 19 July 2006.

Over the following two years or so, we made many additional observations which we took to be significant. When Brenda James published her decryptions in 2008, we fully expected that ours would provide an independent confirmation.[15] However, her methods and results were quite different. As much as we were excited by her identification of Sir Henry Neville, and together with Rubinstein, her compelling alignment of his life with the particulars of Shakespeare's works, we found that our separate decryption methodologies did not seem readily compatible.

Guides for decryption

When any text is set in a table and the spaces removed, new words may be formed vertically, diagonally or horizontally. Typically, these words are not intended by the author. When a text is thought to contain a hidden message, a set of criteria might be used to constrain the task of exploring myriad "possible" leads. In the course of examining hundreds of permutations of tables, reversals, and manipulations – not only of the dedication, but of many of the sonnets – we evolved the guidelines below. To merit further exploration, a word or fragment should meet all or most of these:

1. Each word should be unbroken (whether horizontal, vertical, diagonal, forward or reversed).

2. The spelling of each word should be a common contemporary spelling.

3. Each word should have secondary reinforcement.

4. Phrases should be physically grouped (intersecting or contiguous).

5. Phrases should be coherent and grammatical.

6. Any manipulation of the text should be directed from within the text itself.

[15] James, *Henry Neville and the Shakespeare Code.*

A new 15-column setting of the Dedication

As mentioned, the only difference between Rollet's setting of the Dedication and ours is that we retained the hyphens in columns 10 and 15. We believe this to be the most faithful transcription.[16]

	1	2	3	4	5	6	7	8	9	10	11	12	13	14	15
1	T	O	T	H	E	O	N	L	I	E	B	E	G	E	T
2	T	E	R	O	F	T	H	E	S	E	I	N	S	V	I
3	N	G	S	O	N	N	E	T	S	Mr	W	H		A	L
4	L	H	A	P	P	I	N	E	S	S	E	A	N	D	T
5	H	A	T	E	T	E	R	N	I	T	I	E	P	R	O
6	M	I	S	E	D	B	Y	O	V	R	E	V	E	R	-
7	L	I	V	I	N	G	**P**	**O**	**E**	**T**	W	I	S	H	E
8	T	H	T	H	E	W	E	L	L	-	W	I	S	H	I
9	N	G	A	D	V	E	N	T	V	R	E	R	I	N	S
10	E	T	T	I	N	G	F	O	R	T	H	T	T		

HENRY

Having noticed *HENRY*, and perhaps its proximity to *POET*, there did not seem to be any other significant products in the 15-column setting. However, there are two phrases that seem to suggest movement, and so perhaps some sort of transposition; *TERNIT* (row 5) and *IN.SETTING.FORTH* (rows 9 and 10).

TERNIT is conspicuous because it bisects *HENRY*. It may be read together with *OVRE* on the next line. Applying our guidelines, *TERN* does not conform to any common contemporary spelling of *TURN*. It is only a homophone, so it is an unlikely candidate as a decrypted word. However, *TERNIT* is unbroken, coherent, and may have secondary reinforcement (as we explore in Appendix 1). It is not immediately obvious what *IT* might be (the thing that should be *turned over*) unless we take the letters IT themselves to be *IT*. If this is the case, IT becomes TI.

	1	2	3	4	5	6	7	8	9	10	11	12	13	14	15
1	T	O	T	H	E	O	N	L	I	E	B	E	G	E	T
2	T	E	R	O	F	T	H	E	S	E	I	N	S	V	I
3	N	G	S	O	N	N	E	T	S	Mr	W	H		A	L
4	L	H	A	P	P	I	N	E	S	S	E	A	N	D	T
5	H	A	T	E	T	E	R	N	I	T	I	E	P	R	O
6	M	I	S	E	D	B	Y	O	V	R	E	V	E	R	-
7	L	I	V	I	N	G	P	O	E	T	W	I	S	H	E
8	T	H	T	H	E	W	E	L	L	-	W	I	S	H	I
9	N	G	A	D	V	E	N	T	V	R	E	R	I	N	S
10	E	T	T	I	N	G	F	O	R	T	H	T	T		

TERNIT

[16] The conjoined *Mr WH* is followed by a space. This may allow for *Mr* to be read as one character together with the space (as represented above), or as two characters, in which case it seems logical that the space would be ignored. We propose that the space in the Dedication is a necessary inclusion to allow *Mr* to be one character or two.

Who will believe my verse?

When *IT* is reversed, new words take shape in the middle of the table.

	1	2	3	4	5	6	7	8	9	10	11	12	13	14	15
1	T	O	T	H	E	O	N	L	I	E	B	E	G	E	T
2	T	E	R	O	F	T	**H**	E	S	E	I	N	S	V	I
3	N	G	S	O	N	N	**E**	T	S	**Mr**	W	H		A	L
4	L	H	A	P	P	I	**N**	E	S	**S**	E	A	N	D	T
5	H	A	T	E	T	E	**R**	N	T	**I**	I	E	P	R	O
6	M	I	S	E	D	B	**Y**	**O**	**V**	**R**	E	V	E	R	-
7	L	I	V	I	N	G	**P**	**O**	**E**	**T**	W	I	S	H	E
8	T	H	T	H	E	W	E	L	L	-	W	I	S	H	I
9	N	G	A	D	V	E	N	T	V	R	E	R	I	N	S
10	E	T	T	I	N	G	F	O	R	T	H	T	T		

Mr SIR HENRY YOUR POET

MrSIR and *YOUR* become apparent in relation to *HENRY*. The word *POET*, which was previously doubtful, is strengthened in its position directly beneath *YOUR* (U and V were interchangeable in 1609).

At this point, the table might suggest someone who calls himself *Mr Sir Henry*.[17] Since Henry was the most common first-name in Tudor England, the notional *HENRY* in the Dedication could be one of thousands of individuals. A surname is needed to provide a unique identification. If a surname were provided, it is logical that it should be more deeply encrypted. Certainly, no further words or names intersect. Some other direction or transformation is required.

The Encryption of Neville

To this point, the last three lines of the Dedication table have not contributed to the decrypted text *Mr SIR HENRY YOUR POET*.

There are several reasons why the very last phrase *IN.SETTING.FORTH* may be of particular interest. In the first instance, it seems an unnecessary encumbrance to the already over-stretched text, and therefore suspect; it offers a potential numeric pun, where *FORTH* might equal *fourth;*[18] and, most significantly, it is the last phrase in the Dedication. In verse and in wordplay the last word in the line is typically the most significant, and the last line of a poem often holds the key to the whole meaning of the poem. The sonnets themselves are perfect examples of this pattern.

---

[17] We might take a little more encouragement since *Mr SIR HENRY* seems to bear witness to the pivotal events in Neville's life, in which he was stripped of his knighthood by Elizabeth in 1601, and restored by James I in 1603. This crisis was of national significance, and perforce a defining event in his public and private life. Anne Neville sent letters to Elizabeth, pleading for the release of her husband, Mr. Neville.

[18] See pp. 118–23, and James, *Henry Neville and the Shakespeare Code*, in which it is also proposed that *FORTH* means "fourth".

IN.SETTING.FORTH is also ambiguous. The most obvious meaning is that the *WELL-WISHING.ADVENTVRER* or the *ONLIE.BEGETTER* is "*setting forth*", meaning either *leaving* or *putting into writing.*

However, an entirely different possibility is that *IN* refers to a *place*, as we might say "*in bed*". The *place* then would be "*setting forth*", whatever that might mean. The availability of a pun on *forth* and *fourth* seems worth exploring. There may also be a pun on *setting.*

Within the table, there seem to be only two candidates for a *place* that might make sense. One is in a *fourth arrangement* of the table (for example, in *four* columns). We could not find any transformation of the table that yielded significant results. The other candidate is *the fourth* (type-)*setting*, or the *fourth line: L.HAPPINESSE.AND.T.*

No enrichment of the phrase *Mr SIR HENRY* suggests itself. However, consistent with the numeric pun in *FORTH,* the first letter of the fourth line is *L*, which is the Roman numeral 50. In *Loves Labours Lost* the pedant Holofernes puns on the letter *L* as the Roman numeral 50:

Holofernes: *If Sore be sore, then* ***ell*** *to Sore*
Makes ***fifty*** *sores of sorell*
Of one sore I an hundred make
By adding but one more ***L***

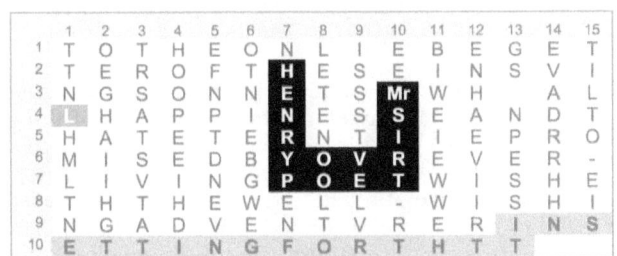

	1	2	3	4	5	6	7	8	9	10	11	12	13	14	15
1	T	O	T	H	E	O	N	L	I	E	B	E	G	E	T
2	T	E	R	O	F	T	H	E	S	E	I	N	S	V	I
3	N	G	S	O	N	N	E	T	S	Mr	W	H		A	L
4	L	H	A	P	P	I	N	E	S	S	E	A	N	D	T
5	H	A	T	E	T	E	R	N	T	I	I	E	P	R	O
6	M	I	S	E	D	B	Y	O	V	R	E	V	E	R	-
7	L	I	V	I	N	G	P	O	E	T	W	I	S	H	E
8	T	H	T	H	E	W	E	L	L	-	W	I	S	H	I
9	N	G	A	D	V	E	N	T	V	R	E	R	I	N	S
10	E	T	T	I	N	G	F	O	R	T	H	T	T		

L

Counting 50 spaces from *L*, we arrive at *NEV.*[19]

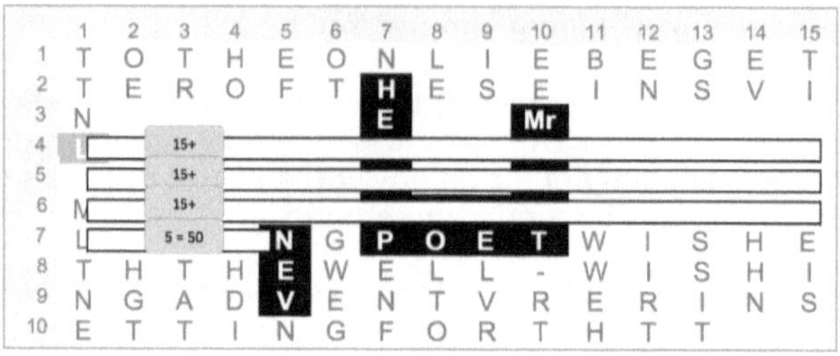

L = 50

This *NEV* intersects with a second *NEV*, and forms the shape of an *L.*

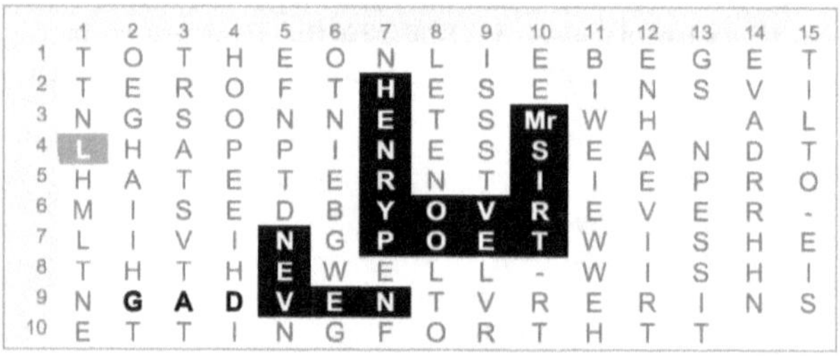

NEV-NEV

Although there is an attractive possibility that this is an *L* made of NEVs (a Nev-Ell), the fragments fail to meet several of our rules of thumb.[20]
The *NEVs* are not connected to the other words, and there is no apparent secondary reinforcement for them, or for any of the other words.
The decrypter seems to arrive at a dead-end. The only faint possibility is the letter *I* at the point of the two *NEVs*, though a diagonal relationship also seems inelegant. Offering a little encouragement is the adjacent word *GAD,* which means a sharp point – a spearhead, or arrowhead. Shakespeare uses this meaning to refer to a writing tool in *Titus Andronicus* Act IV, Scene i:

> Titus: ... *I will go get a leaf of* ***brass,***
> *And with a* ***gad*** *of steel will* ***write*** *these words* [21]

---

[19] For an Elizabethan, the association between L and 50 was much more immediate than for a modern reader. In addition, the proposal that L represents an instruction to move forward 50 places may be reinforced by the content of Sonnet 50.
[20] *Nevell* was the preferred alternative spelling that Sir Henry used as a young man. Neville was baptised *Nevell* and his autograph is spelt *Nevell* in a volume by Theodosius concerning spherical geometry (see Chapter 2).
[21] This may be the reference Jonson recalls in his lines to Shakespeare's engraving in the First Folio which he claims will *surpass/ All, that was ever* ***writ in brass***.

The *words* that Titus writes are the opening lines of Horace's Ode 1.22. It is perhaps significant that Titus intends Ode 1.22 itself as a coded message.[22]

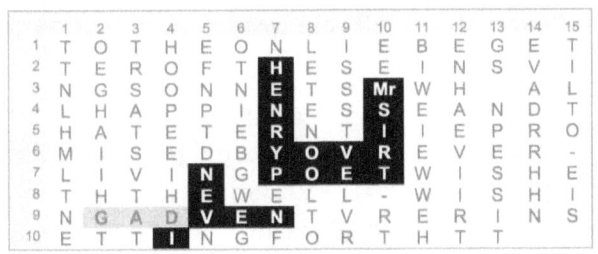

	1	2	3	4	5	6	7	8	9	10	11	12	13	14	15
1	T	O	T	H	E	O	N	L	I	E	B	E	G	E	T
2	T	E	R	O	F	T	H	E	S	E	I	N	S	V	I
3	N	G	S	O	N	N	E	T	S	Mr	W	H		A	L
4	L	H	A	P	P	I	N	E	S	S	E	A	N	D	T
5	H	A	T	E	T	E	R	N	T	I	I	E	P	R	O
6	M	I	S	E	D	B	Y	O	V	R	E	V	E	R	-
7	L	I	V	I	N	G	P	O	E	T	W	I	S	H	E
8	T	H	T	H	E	W	E	L	L	-	W	I	S	H	I
9	N	G	A	D	V	E	N	T	V	R	E	R	I	N	S
10	E	T	T	I	N	G	F	O	R	T	H	T	T		

GAD

	1	2	3	4	5	6	7	8	9	10	11	12	13	14	15
1		O	T	H	E	O	N	L	I	E	B	E	G	E	T
2		E	R	O	F	T	H	E	S	E	I	N	S	V	I
3		G	S	O	N	N	E	T	S	Mr	W	H		A	L
4		H	A	P	P	I	N	E	S	S	E	A	N	D	T
5	H	A	T	E	T	E	R	N	T	I	I	E	P	R	O
6	M	I	S	E	D	B	Y	O	V	R	E	V	E	R	-
7	122	I	V	I	N	G	P	O	E	T	W	I	S	H	E
8	T	H	T	H	E	W	E	L	L	-	W	I	S	H	I
9	N	G	A	D	V	E	N	T	V	R	E	R	I	N	S
10	E	T	T	I	N	G	F	O	R	T	H	T	T		

GAD at sequential letter 122

We notice too, that the G of *GAD* is the 122nd letter in the table. This pairing of GAD and the sequential position 122 in the table seems to mirror the pairing of the "gad of steel" with Horace's Ode 1.22[23] in *Titus Andronicus.*

If, for the moment, we accept that the intersecting *NEVs* do represent an arrowhead pointing to *I*, continuing right-to-left we find *TT*.

	1	2	3	4	5	6	7	8	9	10	11	12	13	14	15
1	T	O	T	H	E	O	N	L	I	E	B	E	G	E	T
2	T	E	R	O	F	T	H	E	S	E	I	N	S	V	I
3	N	G	S	O	N	N	E	T	S	Mr	W	H		A	L
4	L	H	A	P	P	I	N	E	S	S	E	A	N	D	T
5	H	A	T	E	T	E	R	N	T	I	I	E	P	R	O
6	M	I	S	E	D	B	Y	O	V	R	E	V	E	R	-
7	L	I	V	I	N	G	P	O	E	T	W	I	S	H	E
8	T	H	T	H	E	W	E	L	L	-	W	I	S	H	I
9	N	G	A	D	V	E	N	T	V	R	E	R	I	N	S
10	E	T	T	I	N	G	F	O	R	T	H	T	T		

TT

[22] This coded message is to the two brothers who raped and mutilated his daughter.
[23] A photograph of Neville's annotated copy of Horace's Ode is included on p. 162.

To this point, having relied upon three numeric clues, *FORTH* = 4th, *L* = 50, and *GAD* = 122, it does not seem unreasonable that *TT* might also signify a number. Since the Dedication is signed *TT*, it could represent a keyword, particularly as Sonnet 122 begins with what appears to be a typographical error *TT*:[24]

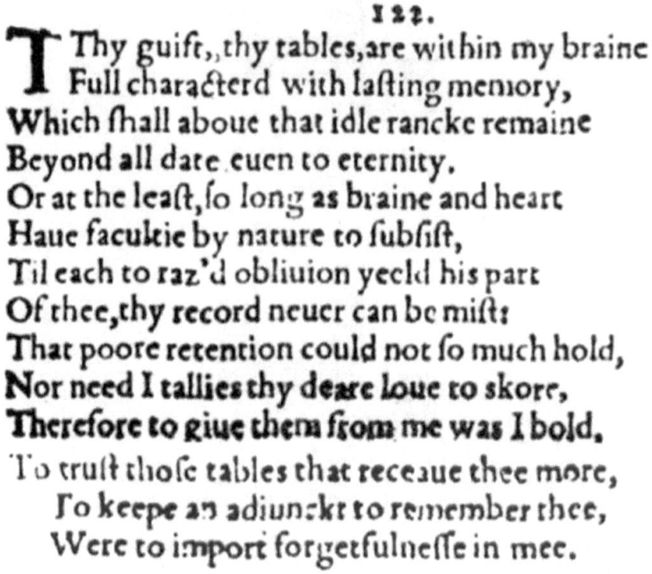

122.

TThy guift,,thy tables,are within my braine
Full characterd with laſting memory,
Which ſhall aboue that idle rancke remaine
Beyond all date euen to eternity.
Or at the leaſt,ſo long as braine and heart
Haue facultie by nature to ſubſiſt,
Til each to raz'd obliuion yeeld his part
Of thee,thy record neuer can be miſt:
That poore retention could not ſo much hold,
Nor need I tallies thy deare loue to skore,
Therefore to giue them from me was I bold,
To truſt thoſe tables that receaue thee more,
To keepe an adiunckt to remember thee,
Were to import forgetfulneſſe in mee.

TT in line 1 of Sonnet 122

The reference to *tables* in this sonnet may also be significant, since they are being used as adjunct to remember someone, comparable with embedding a name in the Dedication table.[25] Further, table books consisted of waxed pages that were marked with a pointed stylus (a gad), rather than an ink pen. These pocket-sized notebooks were for temporary notes only. Once the contents were transferred into a more permanent form, then the pages could be wiped and re-used.[26]

---

[24] *TT* is immediately followed by a second error of duplication, the two commas, which supports the suggestion that *TT* is a deliberate inclusion (see Chapter 6 and p. 132–3).
[25] We note that *gad* is a variant of *goad* which can also be understood as a *reminder.*
[26] Schlueter, J. "Drawing in a Theatre: Peacham, De Witt, and the Table-book", *Theatre Notebook* 68, pp. 69–86 (2014).

If we take to be intentional the links among *GAD* (at cell number 122), Horace's Ode 1.22 (written with a *GAD* in *Titus Andronicus*), and the *TT* in Sonnet 122, the most obvious numerical value to assign to *TT* would seem to be *Twenty-Two.*[27]

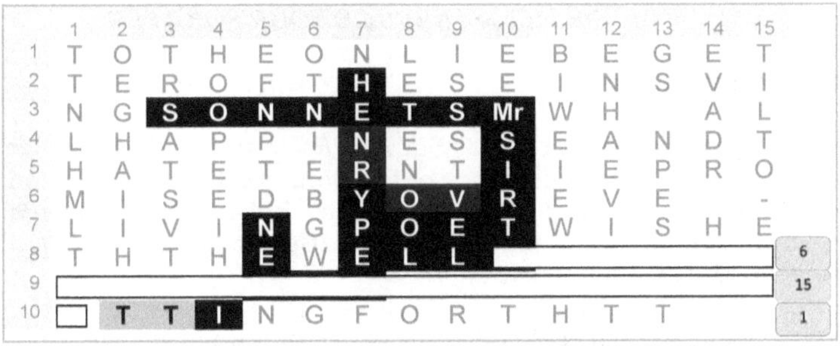

TT = 22. Count 22 spaces

Counting twenty-two letters back from *TT*, *LLE* completes *NEVILLE.*[28]

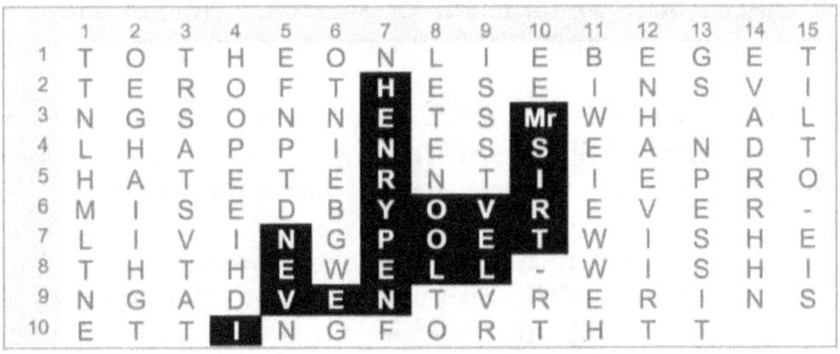

NEVI-LLE is assembled

Although the visual aesthetics of this solution may not be pleasing, one additional guideline has been met, in that all the text is now connected via the new word *PEN* (under *HENRY).* Moreover, the hyphen serves to link the two disconnected fragments NEVI and LLE.[29] This hyphenated name *Nevi-lle* may also offer a pleasing reflection of the hyphenated name *Shake-speare* that graces every second page of the sonnets.[30]

---

27 Supporting the notion that *TT* may be a "key" that represents the number 22 is the fact the *H* of *HENRY* is the 22nd letter of the dedication.

28 Whereas the counting of *L=50* and *GAD=122* includes both the start and end-points, the counting of *TT=22* includes only the end-point (the hyphen) and does not include the start-point "*TT*". This presents a slight inconsistency. However we note that it is not clear on which of the two *T*s the counting should start. With this in mind, it seems more intuitive that the counting should start on the cell back from *TT*, the *E* of *SETTING.* Sonnet 136 maps sequentially to this E and has, *Among a number one is reckon'd none.*

29 In addition to transpositions, contemporary encryptions often used geometric routes including zig-zag, diagonal or spiral to trace a path through columnar matrices (Wrixon, *Codes, Ciphers and Secret Communication*).

30 We thank John Casson for pointing this out.

And although *NEVILLE* is broken, and although there is no secondary reinforcement (with the exception of *GAD*), nevertheless we might now tentatively concatenate a message –

Mr SIR HENRY NEVILLE YOUR POET PEN.

Secondary Reinforcement

Although we have a surname for *Mr SIR HENRY* in the Dedication, we have not identified *NEVILLE* as the author of the Sonnets. Something is missing. The clues assemble in an orderly way, and they have a Shakespearean playfulness, but the solution is unsatisfying. It seems to lack the quality of a work of art worthy of Shakespeare.

There does appear to be a real coded message, and one that identifies Sir Henry Neville, possibly as *YOUR.POET*. However, at this point we can only surmise that he may be the author of the works attributed to Shakespeare. For example, one could imagine a playful Thomas Thorpe having constructed the Dedication, and inserting the *TT* into Sonnet 122. It could be suggested that Thorpe was a friend of Sir Henry Neville and it was some sort of elaborate joke, of which Shakespeare may have approved.

To prove that the *Mr SIR HENRY NEVILLE* in the Dedication was put there by the author of the works of Shakespeare, it would need to be proved that the Dedication and the Sonnets were written by the same person.

One way to demonstrate an indisputable link between the author of the Dedication and the author of the Sonnets relates to the image of the *tally* in line 10 of Sonnet 122. A tally stick was a device to record the number of items owed by a debtor to a creditor. Each item was represented by a notch across the stick. When the stick was split lengthways, both debtor and creditor had a secure record of the debt that could be presented at the time of repayment. After separation, each half proved little, but when matched with each other, there was proof of an agreement.[31] Tally-splitting was effective because it was impossible to falsify either record; the contours and textures of the two split surfaces were far too complex.

---

[31] Tally sticks were used to record debts in England from the Middle Ages even until the 19th century. These sticks were kept by the Exchequer. As we have observed in Chapter 2, until his fall from grace in 1601, Sir Henry Neville was Joint Teller of the Exchequer, and so presumably very familiar with the use of tallies.

Medieval tally sticks held by Winchester City Council Museums[32]

In the next chapter, we explore the possibility that direct and detailed alignments between the Dedication and the Sonnets might constitute a similarly secure pairing which could prove that the name *Sir Henry Neville* was placed in the Dedication by the author of *Shakespeare's Sonnets*. If this is the case, we might logically infer that *Sir Henry Neville* was also the author of the Sonnets.

[32] Flickr, CC BY-SA 2.0 (http://creativecommons.org/licenses/by-sa/2.0), via Wikimedia Commons.

TO.THE.ONLIE.BEGETTER.OF.
THESE.INSVING.SONNETS.
Mr.W.H. ALL.HAPPINESSE.
AND.THAT.ETERNITIE.
PROMISED.

BY.

OVR.EVER-LIVING.POET.

WISHETH.

THE.WELL-WISHING.
ADVENTVRER.IN.
SETTING.
FORTH.

T. T.

We propose that the signature "*TT*" points to the acrostic *TTMAP* (the first letters of lines 1–5). *TT* first occurs at the 15th letter (in *BEGETTER).* In this way, *TTMAP* may be understood as *15MAP*, that is a *15-column map.* Additional evidence that seems to support the 15-column map is detailed in Chapter 6 and on p. 132–3.

Chapter 5: Mapping the Sonnets to the Dedication

In Chapter 4 we examined evidence that the Dedication to the Sonnets may be a cryptogram containing the name Sir Henry Neville. *HENRY* is immediately apparent in the 15-column table but *NEVILLE*, notionally a more sensitive disclosure, is much more deeply encrypted. Indeed, the sequence of steps required to assemble *NEVILLE* is so complex that it might easily be rejected as forced, were it not for the alignment with *TT* in Sonnet 122.

This apparent mapping from a sequentially numbered position in the Dedication, the 122nd character, to the 122nd Sonnet raises the possibility that other mappings might exist. The acrostic *TTMAP* would seem to support this.

If it could be shown that the construction of the Dedication was closely aligned with the construction of the sonnets, this would indicate that the author of the Dedication was, at least, familiar with the sonnets. And if the Dedication were to reveal previously unrecognised attributes of the sonnets, perhaps known only to the author, this would confirm that both were written by the same author. The author of the Dedication would necessarily be the author of the Sonnets.

To this point, the references that might merge the two authors are:

> The arrowhead of *NEVs* in the Dedication code is adjacent to the word *"GAD"*, and the *G* of *"GAD"* is located at cell number 122. The coded message in *Titus Andronicus* is written with a *"gad"* and this is Horace's Ode 1.22.
>
> We take the *TT* in the code table to represent *twenty two,* and *TT* also occurs as a typographical anomaly beginning *Shakespeare's* Sonnet 122.
>
> *TT is* the signature (perhaps the "keyword") of the Dedication.

All of this is suggestive, but not conclusive. We propose that the acrostic *TTMAP* at the opening of the dedication might offer a significant new direction.

Mapping the Dedication

In Chapter 2 we noted the involvement of Neville's mentor Henry Savile in translating Polybius's *The Histories* which includes the *Polybius Square.*[1] We also noted the close alignment between Neville's political vision and *The Histories.*

	1	2	3	4	5
1	A	B	C	D	E
2	F	G	H	I	K
3	L	M	N	O	P
4	Q	R	S	T	U
5	V	W	X	Y	Z

The Polybius Square

Using the Polybius Square, letters may be represented by number pairs, so that *H* would be 3-2, and *HAT* would be 3-2, 1-1, 4-4. The pairs could also be reversed, so that *H* could be represented as 2-3.

Such a system could be used to map a letter or a word in the Dedication table to a specific sonnet number, shedding light on both the word as well as the sonnet to which it maps.

In 1970 Samuel Schoenbaum wrote:

> ... *The Sonnets, the only intimate document connected with the poet, would thus seem to bring the biographer to the threshold of the knowledge – some of it perhaps forbidden – that is the object of his tireless quest ... Clues are scattered throughout the poems in the form of allusions to persons and events...so vague or cryptic that in the end they would simply provide more matter for debate ...*[2]

Wordplay in the sonnets: ideational puns

All readers of poetry are familiar with verbal patterns such as rhyme and alliteration. These techniques exploit particular similarities between words to activate our senses, memory, emotions and thinking. Similarly, punning plays on the close similarity of the sounds of words, typically for comic or ironic effect. A good example is the double entendre on *lie* in sonnet 138:

---

[1] Casaubon wrote to Nevile's mentor Sir Henry Savile and also to the antiquarian William Camden for help with Polybius. As well as being the mentor of Ben Jonson, Camden has at least one close association with Sir Henry Neville. John Casson has discovered a copy of Thomas Milles's *A Catalogue of Honor* (1610). This apparent pre-publication edition has been annotated meticulously as if by a proof-reader. Indeed, Casson notes that some of these same corrections appear printed on pasted-in slips in a copy of *A Catalogue of Honor* in the British Library (BL 608.1.4). Among others, William Camden provided editorial assistance on this volume. Casson also notes that the printer of *A Catalogue of Honor* was William Jaggard who published Shakespeare's works over a period of twenty years. Bradbeer and Casson, *Sir Henry Neville, Alias William Shakespeare.*

[2] Schoenbaum, *Shakespeare's Lives.*

Therefore I lie with her, and she with me,
And in our faults by lies we flattered be.

As well as these more recognisable techniques, the sonnets are engineered upon a dense framework of less obvious verbal patterns, many of which may pass unnoticed. Beneath the surface meaning of each sonnet there are additional layers, and sometimes whole alternative narratives. For example, Sonnet 7 traces the path of the *sun* across the sky, while urging the reader to *get a son*. The word *sun* does not appear in the sonnet, but the simple fact of the sun's movement gives the sonnet a feeling of certainty:

Sonnet 7

Loe in the Orient when the gracious light,
Lifts up his burning head, each under eye
Doth homage to his new-appearing sight,
Serving with lookes his sacred maiesty,
And having climb'd the steepe up heavenly hill,
Resembling strong youth in his middle age,
Yet mortall lookes adore his beauty still,
Attending on his goulden pilgrimage:
But when from high-most pich, with wery car,
Like feeble age he reeleth from the day,
The eyes (fore dutious) now converted are
From his low tract and looke another way:
So thou, thyself out-going in thy noon:
Unlok'd on diest unlesse thou get a ***sonne****.*

Booth cites a more subtle example from Sonnet 56, lines 9–12:

Let this sad interim like the ***ocean be***
Which parts the shore, where two contracted new
Come daily to the banks that when they ***see***
Return of love, more blessed may be the view

The idea that is invoked is *sea*, but the word itself is missing. It is an ideational pun. Booth writes:

> "The word *see* rhymes phonetically with *be* and, through the intermediary of "sea", rhymes ideationally with *ocean*".[3]

These verbal patterns often complement a central idea, sometimes broadening it by adding related meanings, sometimes undermining with mock-logic based on wordplay only. In other instances, the wordplay seems incidental and untethered from any established theme. Booth argues

[3] Booth, *Shakespeare's Sonnets*, p. 231.

strongly that these fleeting “almost puns” provide an intense cognitive stimulation that is at the heart of the works attributed to Shakespeare.[4] It seems the sonnets are crafted to be read very closely and perhaps analytically. They contain meanings that seem to be deliberately obscured. Even when the reader is looking for verbal patterns, the multiplicity of forms and contexts ensures that their presence, meaning, and intention may still remain elusive. In this way, the *Sonnets* have much in common with ciphers.

If it seems fanciful to associate ciphers and encryption with the greatest English writer, we should note that there are at least three explicit references to ciphers in Shakespeare’s works. We have already noted that in *Titus Andronicus*, Titus sends his daughter’s rapists a coded message which is Horace’s Ode 1.22. When Young Lucius presents the poem, he declares (as an aside):

That you are both decipher’d, that’s the news,
For villains mark’d with rape.

In the myth of Philomel upon which *Titus* is based, the imprisoned Philomel frees herself by sending a coded message to her sister using symbols embroidered in fabric.

In *A Lover’s Complaint,* which was published in the same volume as the Sonnets (1609), there is, as in the Philomel myth, a code embroidered on the handkerchief of the wronged maiden in lines 15–19:

Oft did she heave her napkin to her eyne,
Which on it had conceited characters,
Laundering the silken figures in the brine
That season’d woe had pelleted in tears
And often reading what contents it bears ...

In *The Rape of Lucrece* (1593) Lucrece laments in lines 810–812:

Yea, the illiterate, that know not how
To cipher what is writ in learned books,
Will quote my loathsome trespass in my looks ...

In the remainder of this chapter we investigate whether there are instances where the verbal patterning in a sonnet is made coherent when it is mapped to the Dedication.

[4] Booth, *Precious Nonsense: The Gettysburg Address, Ben Jonson’s Epitaphs on His Children, and Twelfth Night* (University of California Press, Berkeley, 1998).

The letter *I*

Perhaps the least convincing of the decryptions is the letter *I* at the point of the arrowhead comprising the two *NEVs*.

	1	2	3	4	5	6	7	8	9	10	11	12	13	14	15
1	T	O	T	H	E	O	N	L	I	E	B	E	G	E	T
2	T	E	R	O	F	T	H	E	S	E	I	N	S	V	I
3	N	G	S	O	N	N	E	T	S	Mr	W	H		A	L
4	L	H	A	P	P	I	N	E	S	S	E	A	N	D	T
5	H	A	T	E	T	E	R	N	T	I	I	E	P	R	O
6	M	I	S	E	D	B	Y	O	V	R	E	V	E	R	-
7	L	I	V	I	N	G	P	O	E	T	W	I	S	H	E
8	T	H	T	H	E	W	E	L	L	-	W	I	S	H	I
9	N	G	A	D	V	E	N	T	V	R	E	R	I	N	S
10	E	T	T	I	N	G	F	O	R	T	H	T	T		

I of *NEVI-LLE*

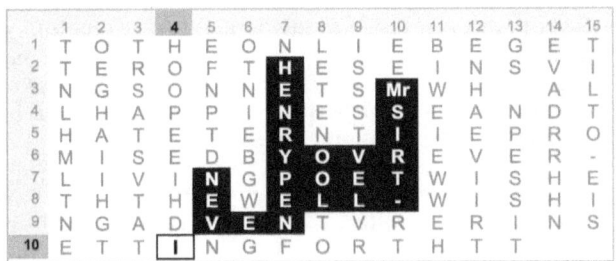

However, using the Polybius method, this *I* maps to two possible number pairings, 10-4 or 4-10. The pair 4-10 cannot map to a sonnet since there is no Sonnet 410. But 10-4 could map to Sonnet 104, and potentially support the intentionality of the letter *I*.

Sonnet 104

To me, faire friend, you never can be olde,
For as you were when first your ***eye I ey'd****,*
Such seemes your beautie still: ***Three*** *Winters Colde,*
Have from the forrests shooke ***three*** *Summer's pride,*
Three *beautious springs to yellow Autumne turn'd,*
In processe of the seasons have I seene,
Three *Aprill perfumes in* ***three*** *hot Iunes burn'd,*
Since first I saw you fresh which yet are greene.
Ah yet doth beauty like a Dyall hand,
Steale from his figure and no pace perceiv'd,
So your sweete hew, which methinks still doth stand,
Hath motion, and mine ***eye*** *may be deceaved.*
For feare of which, heare this thou age unbred,
Ere you were borne was beauties summer dead.

We note in Sonnet 104 the emphatic *eye I ey'd* (line 2). This sonnet has five instances of the number *three*. In Roman numerals, the number *three* is written *III* (*eye I ey'd*). In Chapter 7 we propose that three is particularly significant when we explore the arrowhead as a clock hand. On the 24-hour clocks of that time (see p. 213), *III* is the numeral to which this clock hand is pointing – exactly at 10,4, Sonnet 104 (pp. 134–5).

This example is so elusive that, as far as we know, in the four centuries since this sonnet was published, no commentator has ever associated *eye I ey'd* to the Roman numeral *III* via the word *three*. This alignment of Sonnet 104 to the *I* of the Dedication is very unlikely to be due to chance. It implies a direct connection regarding authorship, because it relies on subtle wordplay and intimate verbal patterning within the sonnet.

Two systems linking the Dedication to individual sonnets

We may now begin to discern two systems which link individual sonnets to the Dedication. We refer to the first system as *sequential mapping* where we count each character in the Dedication and assign this number to the character; so we assign *sequential* position 122 to the *G* of *GAD* because it is the 122nd character in the Dedication.

We refer to the second system as *Polybian* or *co-ordinate (x, y) mapping* as in the previous example which mapped the *I* in row 10 and column 4 of the grid (10,4) to Sonnet 104.[5]

If we accept that this *co-ordinate mapping* of Sonnet 104 is intentional, we might anticipate other *co-ordinate mappings* between code words in the grid and sonnets. Indeed, we propose that all the words in the hidden message may be linked to specific sonnets via *co-ordinate mappings*. In each case the first letter of the word maps to a sonnet that both illuminates the word and is itself illuminated by the mapped word.

Using this *co-ordinate mapping* we can see that the setting of the dedication in 15 columns may not be arbitrary, as it provides co-ordinate mappings to any of the 154 sonnets.

In the remainder of this chapter we examine the clearest examples of this *co-ordinate mapping* of the coded message.

---

[5] This system of (x, y) co-ordinates is commonly known as Cartesian co-ordinates, in honour of Rene Descartes who formalised it in 1637, but as described in Chapter 3, it was known to Polybius some 1700 years earlier.

HENRY

The name ***HENRY*** maps to coordinates 7-2, Sonnet 72.

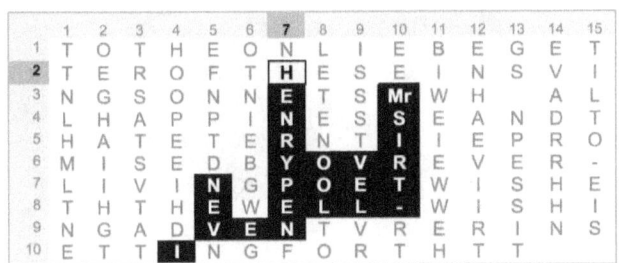

	1	2	3	4	5	6	7	8	9	10	11	12	13	14	15
1	T	O	T	H	E	O	N	L	I	E	B	E	G	E	T
2	T	E	R	O	F	T	**H**	E	S	E	I	N	S	V	I
3	N	G	S	O	N	N	**E**	T	S	**Mr**	W	H		A	L
4	L	H	A	P	P	I	**N**	E	S	**S**	E	A	N	D	T
5	H	A	T	E	T	E	**R**	N	T	**I**	I	E	P	R	O
6	M	I	S	E	D	B	**Y**	**O**	**V**	**R**	E	V	E	R	-
7	L	I	V	I	**N**	G	**P**	**O**	**E**	**T**	W	I	S	H	E
8	T	H	T	H	**E**	W	**E**	**L**	**L**	**-**	W	I	S	H	I
9	N	G	A	D	**V**	**E**	**N**	T	V	R	E	R	I	N	S
10	E	T	T	**I**	N	G	F	O	R	T	H	T	T		

The *H* of *HENRY*

Sonnet 72

O Least the world should taske you to recite,
What merit liv'd in ***me*** *that you should love,*
After ***my*** *death (deare love) for get* ***me*** *quite,*
For you in ***me*** *can nothing worthy prove.*
Unlesse you would devise ***some vertuous lye****,*
To doe more for ***me*** *then* ***mine*** *owne desert,*
And hang more praise upon deceased ***I****,*
Then nigard truth would willingly impart.
Oh least your true love may seeme falce in this,
That you for love speake well of ***me*** *untrue,*
My name be buried *where* ***my*** *body is,*
And live no more *to shame nor* ***me****, nor you.*
For ***I*** *am shamd by that which* ***I*** *bring forth,*
And so should you, to love things nothing worth.

In Sonnet 72, the poet urges the reader to *bury* his *name.*

Sonnet 72 has more instances than any other sonnet of the word "me" as well as a copious sprinkling of the 1st person pronouns *"my"* and *"I"*.[6] In terms of personal pronouns, Sonnet 72 *HENRY* is the most ego-centric of all the sonnets.

[6] We explore this further in Appendix 1.

YOUR

***Y**OUR* maps to 7-6, Sonnet 76.

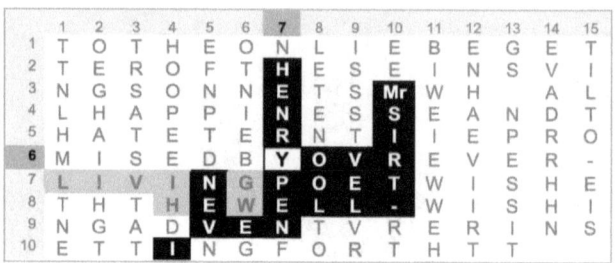

	1	2	3	4	5	6	7	8	9	10	11	12	13	14	15
1	T	O	T	H	E	O	N	L	I	E	B	E	G	E	T
2	T	E	R	O	F	T	H	E	S	E	I	N	S	V	I
3	N	G	S	O	N	N	E	T	S	Mr	W	H		A	L
4	L	H	A	P	P	I	N	E	S	S	E	A	N	D	T
5	H	A	T	E	T	E	R	N	T	I	I	E	P	R	O
6	M	I	S	E	D	B	Y	O	V	R	E	V	E	R	-
7	L	I	V	I	N	G	P	O	E	T	W	I	S	H	E
8	T	H	T	H	E	W	E	L	L	-	W	I	S	H	I
9	N	G	A	D	V	E	N	T	V	R	E	R	I	N	S
10	E	T	T	I	N	G	F	O	R	T	H	T	T		

The *Y* of *YOUR*

Sonnet 76

***Why** is my verse so barren of new pride?*
So far from variation or quicke change?
***Why** with the time do I not glance aside*
To new found methods, and to compounds strange?
***Why** write I still all one, ever the same*
And keepe invention in a noted weed,
*That **every word doth almost tel my name,***
Shewing their birth, and where they did proceed?
*O know sweet love **I alwaies write of you,***
And you and love are still my argument:
So all my best is dressing old words new,
Spending againe what is already spent:
For as the Sun is daily new and old,
So is my love still telling what is told.

The three questions that are being asked in Sonnet 76 all begin with *Why*, offering a possible pun on the letter *Y*. The questions are answered in line 9:

*O know sweet love **I alwaies write of you,***

Alwaies presents a possible summary pun on "all whys". More importantly, the one answer to the three *Why* questions is that the poet always writes "*of you*". The words "*of you"* may be read as a possessive form of "you". The more familiar possessive form is "your", which is our decrypted word – *YOUR*.

There is one other sonnet that has three lines beginning with *Why*, and its first line begins with the synonym *Wherefore*. This would seem to weaken the observation of *Why* in Sonnet 76 but, remarkably, this sonnet is Sonnet 67, which also maps (6-7) to the *Y* of *YOUR*. There is only one letter *Y* in the Dedication, and only Sonnets 76 and 67 have multiple lines beginning with *Why*.

Sonnet 67

Ah ***wherefore*** *with infection should he live,*
And with his presence grace impietie,
That sinne by him advantage should atchive,
And lace it selfe with his societie?
Why *should false painting immitate his cheeke,*
And steale dead seeing of his ***living hew?*** [7]
Why *should poore beautie indirectly seeke,*
Roses of shaddow, since his Rose is true?
Why *should he live, now nature banckrout is,*
Beggerd of blood to blush through lively vaines,
For she hath no exchecker now but his,
And proud of many, lives upon his gaines?
O him she ***stores****, to show what welth she had,*
In ***daies long since****, before these last so bad.*

We suggest that *days long since* in the last line is also an ideational pun on *days of yore.* Following on from Sonnet 67, Sonnet 68 can be read as the second half of a larger poem beginning with Sonnet 67. Sonnet 68 concludes with the phrase *of yore*, echoing both "*of you*" and *YOUR.*

Sonnet 68

Thus is his cheeke ***the map*** *of daies out-worne,*
When beauty liv'd and dy'ed as flowers do now,
Before these bastard signes of faire were borne,
Or durst inhabit on a living brow:
Before the golden tresses of the dead,
The right of sepulchers, were shorne away,
To live a scond life on second head,
Ere beauties dead fleece made another gay:
In him those holy antique howers are seene,
Without all ornament, it selfe and true,
Making no summer of an others greene,
Robbing no ould to dresse his beauty new,
And him as for ***a map*** *doth Nature* ***store****,*
To shew faulce Art what beauty was ***of yore****.*

We note too, the emphasis on *map* in the first line, and its repetition in the couplet.

[7] The unusual phrase *living hew* in line 6 is present in the Dedication adjacent to *Y* (highlighted in the grid on the previous page).

NEVI-LLE

Following a possible direction to read *L* in row four as the Roman numeral L = 50, and so to count 50 spaces, we arrive at ***N****EV*. ***N****EV* maps to 5-7, Sonnet 57.

	1	2	3	4	5	6	7	8	9	10	11	12	13	14	15
1	T	O	T	H	E	O	N	L	I	E	B	E	G	E	T
2	T	E	R	O	F	T	**H**	E	S	E	I	N	S	V	I
3	N	G	S	O	N	N	**E**	T	S	**Mr**	W	H		A	L
4	L	H	A	P	P	I	**N**	E	S	**S**	E	A	N	D	T
5	H	A	T	E	T	E	**R**	N	T	**I**	I	E	P	R	O
6	M	I	S	E	D	B	**Y**	**O**	**V**	**R**	E	V	E	R	-
7	L	I	V	I	**N**	G	**P**	**O**	**E**	**T**	W	I	S	H	E
8	T	H	T	H	**E**	W	**E**	**L**	**L**	**-**	W	I	S	H	I
9	N	G	A	D	**V**	**E**	**N**	T	V	R	E	R	I	N	S
10	E	T	T	**I**	N	G	F	O	R	T	H	T	T		

NEV

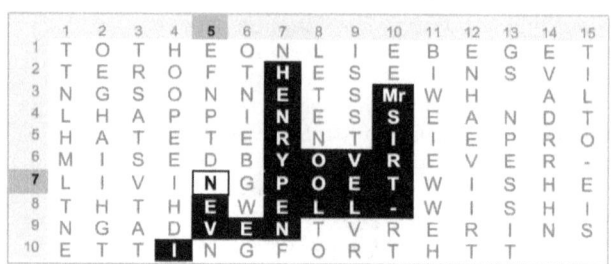

The association between NEV and Sonnet 57 seems to exhibit wordplay similar to the earlier example in Sonnet 7, where Booth notes the "missing" ideational word, is *sun*. In sonnet 57 the ideational word seems to be *knave*. *Knave* is not a word that occurs often in modern English, but it is a close homophone for the fragment *NEV*. In Jacobean times *knave* was synonymous with *servant, fool,* and *slave*, as in King Lear Act 1, Scene 4:

LEAR: Dinner, ho, dinner! Where's my **knave**? My **fool**?

...

LEAR: My lady's father! My lord's **knave**: you whoreson dog! You **slave**!

Sonnet 57 is wholly built on the image of a menial *servant, fool,* and *slave,* possibly evoking the idea "knave" and so *NEV*.

Sonnet 57

Being your ***slave*** *what should I doe but tend,*
Upon the houres, and times of your desire?
I have no precious time at al to spend;
Nor services to doe, til you require.
Nor dare I chide the world without end houre,
Whilst I (my soverain) watch the clock for you,
Nor thinke the bitternesse of absence sowre,
When you have bid your ***servant*** *once adieue.*
Nor dare I question with my iealious thought
Where you may be, or your affaires suppose,
But like a sad ***slave*** *stay and think of nought*
Save *where you are, how happy you make those.*
So true a ***foole*** *is love, that in your* ***Will,***
(Though you doe anything) he ***thinks no ill.***

The all-important couplet capitalises *Will* and so raises the possibility that it could be read as the name *Will* (as in Will Shakespeare). The last line both rhymes and equates *Will* with *think no ill,* which is a fair translation of the Neville motto *Ne vile velis* – effectively Neville's name.[8]

In the same way that Sonnet 67 extends into Sonnet 68 to form a larger poem evoking *YOUR*, Sonnet 57 seems to extend into Sonnet 58 to amplify the idea of a *KNAVE.*

Sonnet 58

That God forbid, that made me first your ***slave****,*
I should in thought controule your times of pleasure,
Or at your hand th'account of houres to ***crave****,*
Being your ***vassail****, bound to staie your leisure.*
Oh let me suffer (being at your beck)
*Th'****imprison'd*** *absence of your libertie,*
And patience tame, to sufferance, bide each check,
Without accusing you of iniury.
Be where you list, your charter is so strong,
That you your selfe may priviledge your time
To what you will, to you it doth belong,
Your selfe to pardon of selfe-doing crime.
I am to ***waite****, though* ***waiting*** *so be hell,*
Not blame your pleasure be it ill or well.

Sonnet 58 develops the imagery of 57. As well as synonyms *slave* and *vassal*, it also introduces the notion of *imprisonment* which is so central to Neville's biography. One might then conjecture the identity of the jailer to be Queen Elizabeth herself. Sonnets 57 and 58 seem to contain at least three possible references to the Queen. In addition to the servility of the relationship, Sonnet 57 has *my sovereign,* and Sonnet 58 has *your vassal* (a menial to a lord or king), and *your charter* (a royal right).

[8] *Ne vile velis* translates word for word as *Wish no ill,* but the meaning is broader and extends to *Incline to no ill.* The all-encompassing *think no ill* seems a reasonable and succinct transliteration.

SONNETS

Consistent with this mapping approach the word *SONNETS* might be added to the decrypted message.

	1	2	3	4	5	6	7	8	9	10	11	12	13	14	15
1	T	O	T	H	E	O	N	L	I	E	B	E	G	E	T
2	T	E	R	O	F	T	**H**	E	S	E	I	N	S	V	I
3	N	G	**S**	**O**	**N**	**N**	**E**	**T**	**S**	**Mr**	W	H		A	L
4	L	H	A	P	P	I	**N**	E	S	**S**	E	A	N	D	T
5	H	A	T	E	T	E	**R**	N	T	**I**	I	E	P	R	O
6	M	I	S	E	D	B	**Y**	**O**	**V**	**R**	E	V	E	R	-
7	L	I	V	I	**N**	G	**P**	**O**	**E**	**T**	W	I	S	H	E
8	T	H	T	H	**E**	W	**E**	**L**	**L**	**-**	W	I	S	H	I
9	N	G	A	D	**V**	**E**	**N**	T	V	R	E	R	I	N	S
10	E	T	T	**I**	N	G	F	O	R	T	H	T	T		

SONNE

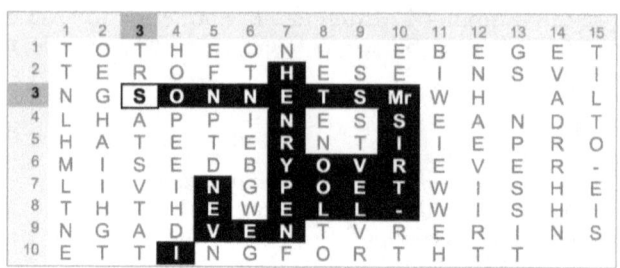

***S**ONNETS* maps to 3-3, and so to Sonnet 33.

Sonnet 33

Full many a glorious morning have I seene,
Flatter the mountaine tops with soveraine eie,
Kissing with ***golden face*** *the meddowes greene;*
Guilding pale streams with heavenly alcumy:
Anon permit the basest cloudes to ride,
With ougly rack on his ***celestiall face****,*
And from the for-lorne world his visage hide
Stealing unseene to west with this disgrace:
Even so my ***Sunne*** *one early morne did shine,*
With all triumphant splendour on my brow,
But out alack, he was but one hour mine,
The region cloude hath mask'd him from me now,
Yet him for this, my love no whit disdaineth,
Suns *of the world may staine, when heavens* ***sun*** *staineth.*

This sonnet deals with the idea of a *son*, but the word "son" is never used. Again, there is an ideational pun, this time on the word "son", or "sonne".[9] In two of the three instances of "son" in the sonnets, it is spelt "sonne". Sonnet 33 invokes the loss of the warmth and beauty of the *sun* as a metaphor for the loss of a living *son*. The word "son" is evoked by its homophone *sun*.

In 1599, Neville apologised for the brevity of his diplomatic dispatch: ... *by reason of some domestical misfortune in the loss of my Son lately borne.*

[9] In Sonnets 7 and 41 it is spelt "sonne". In Sonnet 13 it is spelt "son".

The message in the Dedication

At this point we might tentatively assemble the interconnected text.

	1	2	3	4	5	6	7	8	9	10	11	12	13	14	15
1	T	O	T	H	E	O	N	L	I	E	B	E	G	E	T
2	T	E	R	O	F	T	H	E	S	E	I	N	S	V	I
3	N	G	S	O	N	N	E	T	S	Mr	W	H		A	L
4	L	H	A	P	P	I	N	E	S	S	E	A	N	D	T
5	H	A	T	E	T	E	R	N	T	I	I	E	P	R	O
6	M	I	S	E	D	B	Y	O	V	R	E	V	E	R	-
7	L	I	V	I	N	G	P	O	E	T	W	I	S	H	E
8	T	H	T	H	E	W	E	L	L	-	W	I	S	H	I
9	N	G	A	D	V	E	N	T	V	R	E	R	I	N	S
10	E	T	T	I	N	G	F	O	R	T	H	T	T		

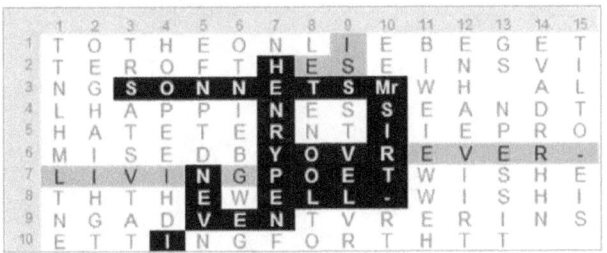

MrSIR HENRY NEVILLE YOUR SONNETS (EVER-LIVING) POET

The message may also be intended to include the intersecting *EVER-LIVING.* Both Sonnet 116 (*EVER*) and Sonnet 17 (*LIVING*) address the idea of eternity, and both sonnets offer persuasive mappings to *EVER-LIVING* (see Appendix 2, pp. 182–5).[10]

Corroborating evidence

The previous examples pair a decrypted word or letter with the number of a sonnet. Each pairing is supported by a precise alignment between decoded words in the Dedication and the cryptic patterning within individual sonnets.

Whether this alignment is meaningful, and therefore likely to be intentional, is always open to subjective and therefore imprecise evaluation. To prove intentionality, there would need to be *many* meaningful alignments, analogous to the aligned contours and textures of the split tally stick invoked in Sonnet 122.

Applying the *Polybian* mapping to other words in the Dedication suggests many more pairings that we regard as significant. Similarly, many *sequential* mappings such as we have seen with GAD also seem to align. Both the *Polybian* and the *sequential* mappings are included in Appendices 1 and 2.

[10] Similarly, the words *HE IS* intersecting with *HENRY* could be taken to complement the message. However, neither *HE* nor *IS* offers a discernible mapping to a sonnet in the way that all the other decrypted words do. Not surprisingly, as they are very short words composed of common letters, there are several instances of *HE* and *IS* in the grid.

Polybius (c.140 CE)

From original stele in Kleitor (Kato Klitoría), Greece. Plaster cast: MCR 164.
© Rome, Museum of Roman Civilization.
Photograph by Sabina Tariverdieva, 2009

Chapter 6: *TT*

Underneath the Dedication, set apart in larger typeface, is the "signature" *TT*. With no evidence to the contrary, most commentators have accepted the conjecture that *TT* stands for the publisher Thomas Thorpe, and that the Dedication was written by him. However, a few commentators have noted that dedications are usually written by authors rather than publishers.

An acrostic *TTMAP* spans the first five lines.

TO.THE.ONLIE.BEGETTER.OF.
THESE.INSVING.SONNETS.
Mr.W.H. ALL.HAPPINESSE.
AND.THAT.ETERNITIE.
PROMISED.

BY.

OVR.EVER-LIVING.POET.

WISHETH.

THE.WELL-WISHING.
ADVENTVRER.IN.
SETTING.
FORTH.

T. T.

Given the importance of *TT* as a direction to count 22 spaces and thereby join *NEVI* with *LLE* in the grid, we would expect to find reinforcement of *TT* as *Twenty-Two* within the sonnets themselves.

As noted, several observations concerning Sonnet 122 support the identification of *TT* as 22. Sonnet 122 begins with an "erroneous" *TT* followed by a duplicated comma (,,) which seems to confirm *TT* as deliberate (see image below). Also, Sonnet 122 maps sequentially to *GAD* and refers to table books in which text was engraved on waxed sheets with a *gad*. Indeed, in *Titus Andronicus*, Titus engraves a coded message with a *gad*. Titus's message is Horace's ode number 1.22, perhaps echoed by the author in the numbering of Sonnet 122.

Notwithstanding these observations, up to this point we have not identified an explicit mapping between *TT* and a sonnet that refers to Twenty-Two. This would seem to be essential to confirm the predictable pattern that constitutes our grid-based decryption. Indeed, we have not yet identified a direction to set the original Dedication text in a grid of 15 columns.

However, before considering the setting the Dedication in columns, another *TT* remains to be investigated. This is the very first *TT*; the *TT* of *BEGETTER* occurring at the 15th letter. If, based on this numbering, we take the "signature" *TT* to signify 15, it would make sense that the acrostic *TTMAP* could signify *15MAP* – a *MAP* of *15* columns.[1] We propose that this is the case, and that *TT* stands for *both* 22 and 15.

To confirm that *TT* is both 22 and 15, we need to return to Sonnet 122 and the two commas. Could they relate to the number 15? We propose that the two commas are a miniature 99. In *Shakespeare's Sonnets*, 99 is immediately associated with 15 because, unlike every other sonnet, Sonnet 99 has 15 lines. In this way, the commas in Sonnet 122, together with *TT* occurring at the 15th letter in the Dedication, may be seen to confirm that *TT* can be both 22 and 15. Accordingly, *TTMAP* can be confirmed as *15MAP* – the primary direction to set the Dedication in a grid of 15 columns. At the same time, the anomaly of the 15-line Sonnet 99 is also finally explained.

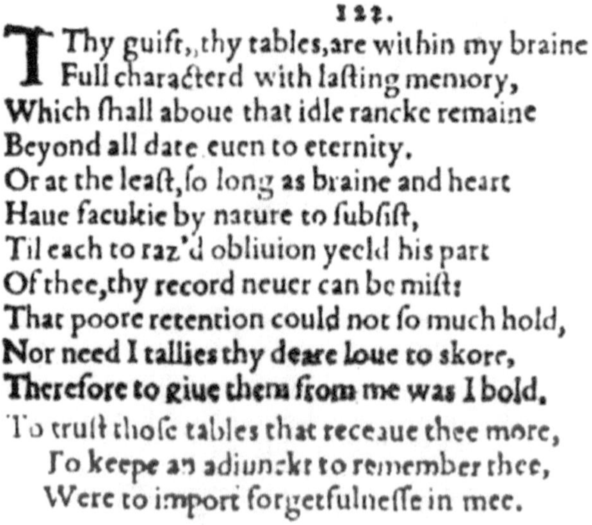
122.
THy guiſt,,thy tables,are within my braine
Full characterd with laſting memory,
Which ſhall aboue that idle rancke remaine
Beyond all date euen to eternity.
Or at the leaſt,ſo long as braine and heart
Haue facultie by nature to ſubſiſt,
Til each to raz'd obliuion yeeld his part
Of thee,thy record neuer can be miſt:
That poore retention could not ſo much hold,
Nor need I tallies thy deare loue to skore,
Therefore to giue them from me was I bold,
To truſt thoſe tables that receaue thee more,
To keepe an adiunckt to remember thee,
Were to import forgetfulneſſe in mee.

Sonnet 122. Note *TT* and the two commas in line 1

[1] It makes no sense for this number (15) to refer to rows because another number would be required to limit the length of the rows. Without the number of columns, no precise mapping is possible. By contrast, if the number (15) refers to columns, there is no need to specify rows since the 148 characters will consume as many rows as required.

But where is the sonnet that explicitly evokes *Twenty-Two*? The logical candidate for a mapping of *TT* can now be identified as the *TT* at the 15th sequential space. The coordinates of this *TT* are 15–1 (see grid below).[2] Disconcertingly, Sonnet 151 does not refer to 22, but as noted previously, there are many instances where two sonnets form a longer poem of 28 lines – Sonnets 57–58, 59–60, 67–68, 77–78, 97–98, 104–105, 113–114 and 133–134. The mapping of these longer poems uses the number of the first sonnet in the pair. In this case, Sonnet 151 clearly forms a pair with Sonnet 152. This 28-line poem is concerned with falsehoods in love, specifically a *double-falsehood*, and refers very explicitly to the *sexual act*. The unusual and graphic reference to sex may be the most obvious, but it is not the only link that directs us to read them as two halves of a longer poem.[3]

Importantly, the second half of this poem (Sonnet 152) presents the only reference in *Shakespeare's Sonnets* to the number *Twenty-Two*:

> *But why of* ***two*** *othes breach doe I accuse thee,*
>
> *When I breake* ***twenty****:*

With the primary direction to set the Dedication in a grid of 15 columns (*TTMAP*), and the mapping of *TT* confirmed, the rules for decrypting *Shakespeare's Sonnets* are complete.

Sonnets 151–152 - *TT*

TT occurs at co-ordinates 15-1, Sonnets 151–152.

	1	2	3	4	5	6	7	8	9	10	11	12	13	14	15
1	T	O	T	H	E	O	N	L	I	E	B	E	G	E	T
2	T	E	R	O	F	T	H	E	S	E	I	N	S	V	I
3	N	G	S	O	N	N	E	T	S	Mr	W	H		A	L
4	L	H	A	P	P	I	N	E	S	S	E	A	N	D	T
5	H	A	T	E	T	E	R	N	I	T	I	E	P	R	O
6	M	I	S	E	D	B	Y	O	V	R	E	V	E	R	-
7	L	I	V	I	N	G	P	O	E	T	W	I	S	H	E
8	T	H	T	H	E	W	E	L	L	-	W	I	S	H	I
9	N	G	A	D	V	E	N	T	V	R	E	R	I	N	S
10	E	T	T	I	N	G	F	O	R	T	H	T	T		

Two and twenty *OTHES* are broken[4]

[2] We might also look to the signature *TT* itself for these coordinates. However, the placement of this *TT* in the grid is uncertain. We have appended it directly to the text but it is not clear that this is intended. Intriguingly, if *TT* were placed – not illogically – at the start of a new row (row 11), it would map sequentially to 151, thus also referencing Sonnet 151.

[3] Neither the sonnet preceding (Sonnet 150), nor the sonnet following (Sonnet 153) has any direct connection to Sonnets 151–152. The 28-line poem 151 stands in isolation.

[4] We note OTHE adjacent to *TT*. The mapping of *OTHE* is discussed in Appendix 2.

Sonnets 151–152

Love is too young *to know what* ***conscience*** *is,*
Yet who knowes not ***conscience*** *is born of love;*
Then gentle cheater ***urge not my amisse****,*
Least guilty of my faults thy sweet selfe prove.
For thou betraying me, I doe betray
My nobler part *to my* ***grose bodies treason****,*
My soule doth tell my body that he may
Triumph in love, ***flesh*** *staies no farther reason,*
But ***rysing*** *at thy name doth point out thee,*
As his triumphant prize, proud of this pride,
He is contented thy poore drudge to be
To stand in thy affaires, fall by thy side*.*
No want of ***conscience*** *hold it that I call,*
Her love, for whose deare love ***I rise and fall.***

In loving thee thou know'st I am forsworne,
But thou art ***twice forsworne*** *to me love swearing,*
In act thy bed-vow broake *and new faith torne,*
In vowing new hate after new love bearing:
But why of ***two othes*** *breach doe I accuse thee,*
When ***I breake twenty****: I am perjur'd most,*
For all my vowes are ***othes*** *but to misuse thee:*
And all my honest faith in thee is lost.
For I have sworne deepe ***othes*** *of thy deepe kindnesse,*
Othes *of thy love, thy truth, thy constancie,*
And to inlighten thee ***gave eyes to blindnesse****,*
Or made them swere against the thing they see.
For I have sworne thee faire: more perjurde eye,
To swere against the truth so foule a lie.

Booth's comments below in are quotes and italics;[5] ours are in non-italics.

1 ***Love is too young*** refers to **Cupid**. This motif is reprised in line 25 (note below).
1 **Conscience** lines 1, 2, 14 (Jonson refers to *conscience* and *cipher.* See page 52).
3 Lines 3-4 refer to the double-falsehood that is reprised in line 16 below.
6 *"...playing on* ***part*** meaning *"bodily part" and specifically the male member,"*
9 ***rising*** *"...The overt reference is to sexual erection..."*
12 *"...the overt reference is sexual;"*
14 *"'rising and falling' is singularly appropriate to [the poem's] theme of involuntary lust; the point is that* ***it is not a metaphor.****"* (Our bold).
16 ***Twice forsworn*** reprises the *double falsehood* referred to in line 3-4 above.
17 ***In act thy bed-vow broke*** *"performing the sexual act".*
19 ***Two***
20 ***Twenty*** Two and Twenty oaths are broken; *TT = 22.*
21 Lines 21-28 detail the broken ***othes*** (see *OTHE* in grid on previous page).
25 ***Eyes to blindness*** This reference to blind **Cupid** returns to the image of baby Cupid from line 1 *Love is too young...* thus cementing the two sonnets as one.

---

[5] Booth, *Shakespeare's Sonnets*, pp. 524–9.

Chapter 7: The Onlie Begetter Mr WH

A key part of the puzzle remains. Who is *Mr WH*, the dedicatee of the Sonnets? Although the evidence is far from conclusive, perhaps a new candidate can be identified: William Hunnis, Master of the Children of the Chapel Royal.

In Chapter 2 we outlined connections among Sir Henry Neville II's immediate family, the Revels, the Blackfriars Theatre, the Children of the Chapel Royal and the Children of the Chapel at Windsor. Sir Henry Neville I's father-in-law Hugh Losse had overseen the establishment of the Offices of the Revels at Blackfriars from around 1548, and Sir Henry Neville I participated in the Revels in the 1550s.

In 1560 Sir Henry Neville I renovated the building that was to become the first Blackfriars theatre, and lived in it for seven years. He also worked at Windsor with his friend Richard Farrant, the Master of the Children of the Chapel at Windsor. In 1575, he wrote a letter of recommendation for Farrant to become lessee of the same building. Together, Master Richard Farrant and Master William Hunnis transformed this space into the original Blackfriars Theatre for the combined ensembles of the Children of the Chapel at Windsor and of the Chapel Royal.[1]

Although we have no direct evidence of any relationship between Sir Henry Neville II and Master William Hunnis, nevertheless there does seem to be a body of circumstantial evidence that might justify consideration. Hunnis was a theatre educator who was active throughout the time Neville was a child. We speculate that the young Henry Neville may have learnt theatre craft from Hunnis either as a Child of the Chapel Royal or alongside these children. If Hunnis were Neville's teacher, this would explain Neville's pedigree as a dramatist and the debt to Hunnis that he might acknowledge in the Dedication to the Sonnets.[2]

Hunnis was a *Master* (Mr) and he signed his published verse with his initials *W.H.* Moreover, as the author most identified with translating into verse the *Book of Genesis* with its two interminable lists of *begats*, he might also be termed affectionately as *the onlie begetter Mr WH.*[3]

---

[1] The famous Gentleman of the Chapel Royal, William Byrd, and his student Thomas Morley whose songs appear in Shakespeare, both dedicated volumes to the first Sir Henry Neville I's third wife, Elizabeth Bacon. Long, J.H. "Shakespeare and Thomas Morley", *Modern Language Notes* 65, 17–22 (1950). Johns Hopkins University Press.

[2] The Children of the Chapel are referred to in Hamlet in Act II Scene ii. Rosenkrantz explains to Hamlet why the adult actors have fallen on hard times: ... *there is, sir, an eyrie of children, little eyases, that cry out on the top of question and are most tyrannically clapped for't.*

[3] There are no less than 54 instances of *begat* in Chapters 5 and 11 of *Genesis*. Hunnis produced three works based on *Genesis*, *A Hyve Full of Hunnye*, *Hunnies Recreations* and a play *Jacob and Esau*.

Hunnis was an early sonneteer[4] and effectively Queen Elizabeth's playwright laureate throughout the first decades of the golden age of English theatre.

There are also many circumstances that suggest close familiarity with the Neville family. Holding the same religious beliefs as the Nevilles, for over 30 years Hunnis was a close colleague of Henry Neville I's friend Richard Farrant. In 1554, the Protestant Neville family abandoned their estates and fled to Europe where they waited out most of the reign of the Catholic Queen Mary. Hunnis was involved in two failed assassination attempts on Queen Mary. It seems possible that the Neville family would have regarded Hunnis's actions as heroic.

However, perhaps most striking are the several facets of his biography that foreshadow the singular and extreme events in the life of Sir Henry Neville II. There cannot be many others whose biographies parallel Neville's so closely. As noted, like Neville, Hunnis took part in a plot to overthrow the monarch and was then convicted for treason. Against the odds, like Neville, he escaped the axe and was imprisoned in the Tower; he too was released and restored to his former position by the succeeding monarch.

We propose that Hunnis, one of the greatest teachers of poetry and drama, is also the *only begetter* to the greatest English poet and dramatist.

If the identity of *Mr WH* is indeed central to the Dedication, we should expect to find similar confirmatory alignments with the Sonnets. Before we begin this investigation, it may be useful to review the life of Master William Hunnis.

[4] Thomas Newton identifies Hunnis as a writer of sonnets in his commendation to *A Hyve Full of Hunnye* (1578). Newton is famous as the English translator of the plays of Seneca. Stopes, C.C. *William Hunnis and the Revels of the Chapel Royal: a study of his period and the influences which affected Shakespeare* (A. Uystpruyst, Louvain, 1910).

The Early life of William Hunnis

The account of William Hunnis that follows draws heavily on what remains his most comprehensive biography, written by Charlotte Stopes in 1910.[5] Stopes's study is especially useful because she identifies linkages between Hunnis and the works of Shakespeare. However, despite the apparent proximity of their respective London operations and their shared interests, she never conjectures any meeting of the two.[6]

Hunnis was born around or most likely before 1530.[7] Based on an analysis of records of people with similar names and interests, Stopes surmises that the original family seat of Hunnis was Berkshire, the same county in which King Edward granted Sir Henry Neville I the estate of Billingbear.[8]

It is probable that like Sir Henry Neville I and II, Hunnis was the son of a knight, because as a youth he was a page to William Herbert, First Earl of Pembroke. Somehow, within or alongside this role, or as a Child of the Chapel himself, he acquired education consistent with that provided by the universities of the time.[9]

William Hunnis and Richard Farrant were both Gentlemen of the Chapel Royal during the brief reign of King Edward from around 1550. As Gentlemen of the Chapel they were required to have achieved the highest skills in both literature and music. It seems possible that both were known to Sir Henry Neville I from this early time when he was active in the Revels and a trusted advisor to the young King Edward.

At Queen Mary's coronation in 1553, Hunnis is listed as one of the Gentlemen of the Chapel who performed an "interlude", a dramatic as distinct from a purely musical performance.

The Catholic Queen Mary proceeded to a most unpopular and unsuccessful marriage with Philip of Spain, whom she styled "King" of England. As an avowed Protestant and opponent of Spain, Sir Henry Neville I moved into exile in Europe. Around the same time, Hunnis became a key player in a complex and wide-ranging conspiracy to depose Mary. The plot involved stealing 50,000 pounds worth of gold from Mary's treasury and smuggling it to France. Having some knowledge of metallurgy, Hunnis was to have re-minted obsolete gold coins to be used to raise forces to remove the Queen.[10]

---

[5] Stopes, *William Hunnis and the Revels of the Chapel Royal*, p. 195.
[6] Stopes rejects William Hunnis as a candidate for *Mr WH*, in favour of Sir William Hervey (stepfather of the Earl of Southampton). Ibid., p. 261.
[7] Hunnis's first publication *Certayne Psalms* was printed in 1550. Ibid., p. 6.
[8] The difficulty of tracing ancestors is exacerbated due to the multiple spellings of Hunnis and their similarity to many other common surnames.
[9] It was common for Children of the Chapel Royal to be the younger sons of knights. They were closely schooled in music and literature. When their voices broke they were often supported in university study. A logical progression would be to resume service as a Gentleman of the Chapel. It is not known if Hunnis took this path. Ibid., p. 13.
[10] Ibid., p. 58. Hunnis also seems to have been a participant in an aborted and undetected attempt to assassinate both Mary and Philip a year earlier. Stopes surmises that Hunnis

Hunnis was tried and imprisoned in the Tower. Despite his frank confession, it seems that there was an error in transcribing his name and he escaped the list of those most seriously attainted, and thereby likely execution.[11] It is probable that he spent two and a half years in the Tower. A key conspirator, John Dethick described Hunnis as *a very handsome man,* but imprisonment aged Hunnis prematurely and his hair turned white.[12]

The Chapel Royal under Elizabeth

Shortly after Elizabeth's coronation in 1558 she released Mary's political prisoners; Hunnis was most likely among them.

Hunnis was soon reappointed as a Gentleman of the Chapel, and his close association with Richard Farrant resumed. Farrant left the Chapel Royal in 1564 to take the role of Master of the Children of the Chapel at Windsor, although he resumed his role as a Gentleman of the Chapel Royal with Hunnis in 1569, seemingly without relinquishing the role at Windsor.

From 1561, as a Gentleman of the Chapel, Hunnis served under the famous poet and dramatist Master Richard Edwards. Edwards and Hunnis were the two main contributors to the most popular poetical miscellany of the sixteenth century, *The Paradise of Dainty Devices.*[13] Along with Edwards, Hunnis is credited with being one of the two fathers of Elizabethan song.[14] Perhaps even more significantly, in response to the appreciative encouragement of Elizabeth herself, theatre flourished under Edwards.

When Edwards died in 1566, Hunnis was elected by the other 31 Gentlemen to become Master of the Children of the Chapel Royal. Stopes surmises that the election of Hunnis and his patent from the Queen were recognition of his skill in theatre more so than in music, as theatre had become the central concern of the Children of the Chapel:

> *Elizabeth's increasing taste for the Drama of itself would suggest that histrionic power was his essential talent, and that he must have given evidence of some special capability in this direction before the death of Richard Edwards, or he would not have been selected to fill his place.*[15]

Hunnis held this position that was so central to the life of Elizabeth's court until his death in 1597, over 30 years later. There is no record of his first year as Master of the Children, but there is a detailed account for services in his second year:

---

may have been personally disaffected due to the burning at the stake of his friend John Rogers, Prebendary at St Pauls, earlier in the month.

[11] Ibid., p. 62.

[12] Ibid., p. 109. Also, see Hunnis's poem *Being asked the occasion of his white hairs.*

[13] Ibid., p. 181. Eight editions were printed before 1600.

[14] Rollins, H.E. (ed.), *The Paradise of Dainty Devices (1576–1606)* (Harvard University Press Cambridge, 1927).

[15] Stopes, *William Hunnis and the Revels of the Chapel Royal,* p. 152.

> *... for seven plays, one tragedy and six masques. Six hundred four and thirty pounds nine shillings and five pence, employed upon these plays, tragedies, and masques following, namely, Imprimis for seven plays, the first named* As plain as can be, *the second* The Painful Pilgrimage *the third* Jack and Jill, *the fourth* Six Fools, *the fifth called* Wit and Will; *the sixth called* Prodigality, *the seventh of* Oreste, *and a tragedy of the* King of Scots.

The sheer volume of work produced in one year gives some indication of the intensity of theatrical production. Stopes also conjectures that the tragedy of the *King of Scots* may have provided the plot for *Macbeth.*[16]

Queen Elizabeth was not universally applauded for her love of drama. An anonymous puritanical pamphlet of 1569 is entitled *The Children of the Chapel Stript and Whipt*:

> *Plays will never be suppressed, while her Majesty's unfledged minions flaunt it in silks and satins. They had as well be at their Popish Service, in the devil's garments ... Even in her Majesty's Chapel these pretty upstart youths profane the Lord's Day, by the lascivious writhing of their tender limbs, and gorgeous decking of their apparel in feigning bawdy fables gathered from the idolatrous heathen poets.*

However, the Queen answered to no-one. In 1575, she was entertained at the Kenilworth festivities; lavish pageantry, dancing, performance, feasts, hunting parties and fireworks that lasted for 19 days by which the Earl of Leicester sought to move her to marriage.[17] Leicester invested heavily in this lavish enterprise to win a Queen. It was the grandest performance festival of the century, and Leicester entrusted Master William Hunnis as the chief artist. Clearly Hunnis was supremely highly regarded.

George Gascoigne, a poet who also contributed to the event, recounts that as Elizabeth arrived at Kenilworth, Hunnis himself greeted her in the role of the *Prophetess Sybil* with verses he had written. Following this, *The Lady of the Lake* was presented. In this monumental production, Elizabeth observed from a bridge while she was addressed by a mermaid on the back of a huge dolphin who calmed the waters of the lake. Later she was serenaded by Arion (whom Gascoigne mistakenly calls Proteus) from an even larger dolphin. Its fins served as oars and it concealed six musicians. This production was also devised by Hunnis.

Many scholars have surmised that Shakespeare might have been present at this performance, since Oberon in *A Midsummer Night's Dream* recalls identical events:

> *... once I sat upon a promontory,*
> *And heard a mermaid on a dolphin's back*

---

[16] Stopes, *William Hunnis and the Revels of the Chapel Royal*, p. 224.
[17] Waldman, M. *Elizabeth and Leicester* (Collins Clear-type Press, London, 1946), pp. 52–62.

Uttering such dulcet and harmonious breath
That the rude sea grew civil at her song
And certain stars shot madly from their spheres,[18]
To hear the sea-maid's music.

And, in *Twelfth Night*, the Captain recounts to Viola:

Where like Arion on the Dolphin's back
I saw him hold acquaintance with the waves.

We speculate that as a child of the Chapel Royal, or alongside these children under Hunnis, the young Henry Neville may have seen or even participated in the festivities. He would have been between 12 and 13 years old at the time. Sonnet 59 seems to support this idea with its reference to "a former child" as we will explore later.

Stopes notes that it was prohibited for plays that had been printed to be performed before the Queen. It is perhaps for this reason that, other than the anonymous *Jacob and Esau*, none of Hunnis's dramatic works have been preserved. However, Stopes states:

> *I strongly believe that he* [Hunnis] *was the author of the anonymous Comedy or Interlude of* Jacob and Esau.[19]

This play exhibits unusual subtlety of motivation and gives prominence to the servant characters to enliven the action. Stopes dates the play to the early reign of Queen Mary:

> *It is the first drama of its kind that eschews all allegorical treatment ... The most striking feature of the play perhaps, is the modernness of its style, a sign that the writer was one of the leaders in the literary developments of the Metropolis. The Dialogue is well-sustained; except for two lively soliloquies there are no long speeches, as were then too common. It is permeated with quiet humour that never approaches either coarseness or profanity.*[20]

---

[18] This line may refer to the fireworks of Kenilworth. Gascoigne describes fireworks in *The princely pleasures of the Courte at Kenelworthe*: *On the next day (being Sunday) there was nothing done until the evening, at which time there were fireworks shewed upon the water, which were both strange and well executed ...*
[19] Stopes, *William Hunnis and the Revels of the Chapel Royal*, p. 265.
[20] Ibid., p. 268.

Unlike Hunnis's dramas, several of his poetic works were published in his lifetime. *Certayne Psalmes chosen out of the Psalter of David* was published in 1550. In the extended title, he described himself as servant to Sir William Herbert. This Sir William Herbert was grandfather to the Earl of Pembroke to whom the *First Folio* is dedicated.

Perhaps significantly in the context of encryption, Stopes notes that in William Webbe's 1586 *Discourse on English Poetry*, Hunnis was praised for his innovative use of *acrostics* in two poems:

> *These two verses by W. Hunnis are now as it were resolved into divers other, every two words or syllables being the beginning of another like verse of the sort.*[21]

In addition, Hunnis used acrostics extensively in his prefatory material to other works.

Perhaps most relevant to the Dedication to the Sonnets are *A Hyve Fvll of Hunnye: Contayning the Firste Booke of Moses, called Genesis* (1578), and *Hunnies Recreations* (1595), both of which deal with the Book of *Genesis* and so may qualify Hunnis as *the onlie begetter.* It may be noteworthy that the publisher of *Hunnies Recreations* was William Jaggard, who published many of the works attributed to Shakespeare. The book was dedicated to Sir Thomas Henneage, stepfather to the Earl of Southampton.

A Hyve Full of Hunnye

A Hyve Fvll of Hunnye is particularly intriguing. In addition to the commendation from his eminent literary friend Thomas Newton, it includes a print of Hunnis's remarkable crest. Both the crest with its bee hives and the title of the book play on the similarity of the name *Hunnis* and *honey.*[22]

However, most startling is that Hunnis himself is depicted, with a diagonal arrow or dart piercing his cheek. As we have noted, Hunnis was reputed to be an unusually handsome young man who aged prematurely as result of his ordeal in the Tower.

---

[21] Stopes, *William Hunnis and the Revels of the Chapel Royal*, p. 161.

[22] It may be noteworthy that at least three of Shakespeare's contemporaries liken his poetry to honey:

Meres:	*mellifluous and **honey-tongued**... sugared sonnets ...*
Barnfield:	***hony-flowing** Vaine ...*
Weever:	***Honie-tong'd*** Shakespeare ... *sugred tongues ...*

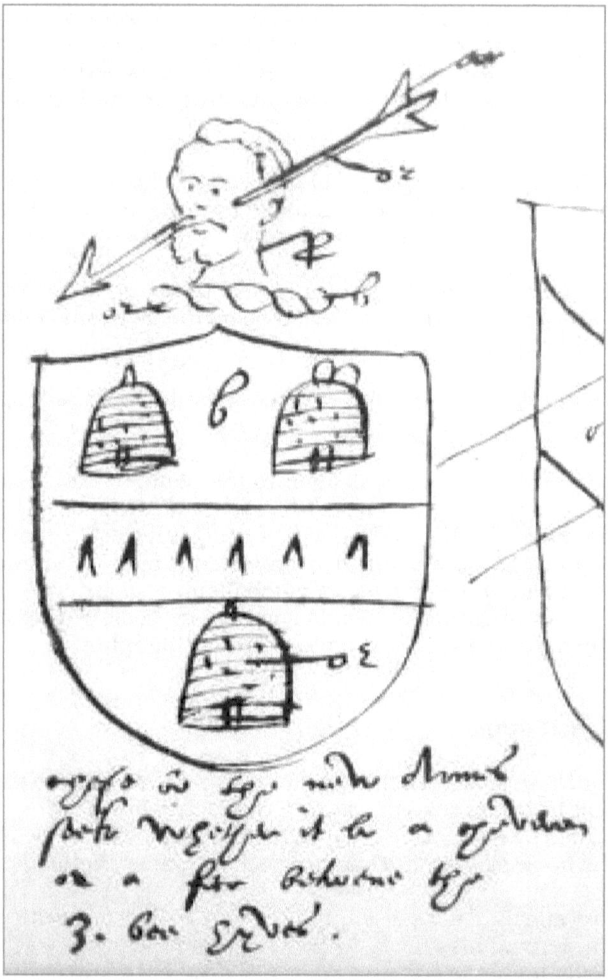

Herald's sketch of Hunnis's crest 1568[23]

In the Herald's sketch of this crest, there are bees around the hives and the object piercing Hunnis's cheek is clearly a dart with a feathered tail. Stopes takes the arrow to be a reminder of his earlier hardships.[24] However, 8 years later, in *A Hyveful of Hunnye* the tail of the arrow is oddly ambiguous. We propose that the arrow piercing Hunnis's aged cheek may also represent the hand of a clock, being the *hand of time.*

[23] Image courtesy of Internet Archive, https://archive.org/.

[24] Stopes, *William Hunnis and the Revels of the Chapel Royal*, Frontispiece.

Hunnis's crest from *A Hyve Full of Hunnye* (1578)[25]

Beneath Hunnis's crest a verse concerning the "Bee" is set out, as below. We note the gentle pun on the final word ***bee***.

The Hyve doth House the harmelesse Bee,
That Hony sweete doth make:
Whose little limmes wyth Laboures longe,
Still streyneth for our sake.
Let us likewise learne of this Beast,
Each one in his Degree,
To sucke the Sappe of Sacred Woorde,
That Heaven oure Hyve may bee.

[25] Image courtesy of Internet Archive, https://archive.org/.

The hand of time

When we began to explore the possibility that Hunnis was *Mr WH*, we were surprised to see a certain symmetry between the motifs of the down and left-pointing arrowhead in the Dedication matrix and the down and left pointing dart in Hunnis' crest. In particular, Sonnets 59 and 60 seem to have identifiable allusions to Hunnis, and 104 and possibly 122 also.

We suggest that it is not just an "arrow" in the Dedication, nor in Hunnis's crest. It is also the hand of a clock, the *hand of time* that disfigures the face of Hunnis, who was so handsome in his youth, according to his co-conspirator Dethick.

	1	2	3	4	5	6	7	8	9	10	11	12	13	14	15
1	T	O	T	H	E	O	N	L	I	E	B	E	G	E	T
2	T	E	R	O	F	T	H	E	S	E	I	**N**	S	V	I
3	N	G	S	O	N	N	E	T	S	Mr	**W**	H		A	L
4	L	H	A	P	P	I	N	E	S	**S**	E	A	N	D	T
5	H	A	T	E	T	E	R	N	**I**	T	I	E	P	R	O
6	M	I	S	E	D	B	Y	**O**	V	R	E	V	E	R	-
7	L	I	V	I	**N**	G	**P**	O	E	T	W	I	S	H	E
8	T	H	T	H	**E**	**W**	E	L	L	-	W	I	S	H	I
9	N	G	A	D	**V**	**E**	**N**	T	V	R	E	R	I	N	S
10	E	T	T	I	N	G	F	O	R	T	H	T	T		

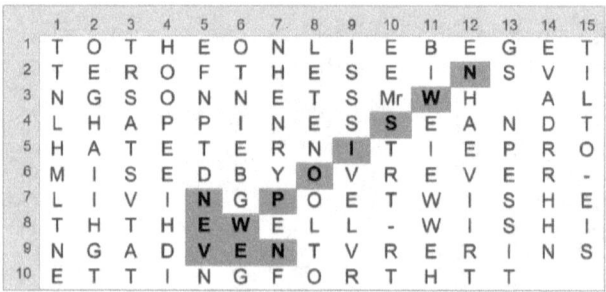

The arrow or clock-hand in the Dedication grid

Overlay of Hunnis's crest on the arrow/clock-hand

A former child

In our pictogram, the tip of the arrowhead maps to 5-9, Sonnet 59. But Sonnet 59 also maps to the *I* of *TERNIT* (y, x). If our "arrow" is in fact a clock hand, it would seem logical to take the *I* of *TERNIT* to be the axis of this hand, since it is the thing that is *turned.*

	1	2	3	4	**5**	6	7	8	**9**	10	11	12	13	14	15
1	T	O	T	H	E	O	N	L	I	E	B	E	G	E	T
2	T	E	R	O	F	T	H	E	S	E	I	**N**	S	V	I
3	N	G	S	O	N	N	E	T	S	Mr	**W**	H		A	L
4	L	H	A	P	P	I	N	E	S	**S**	E	A	N	D	T
5	H	A	T	E	**T**	**E**	**R**	**N**	**I**	**T**	I	E	P	R	O
6	M	I	S	E	D	B	Y	**O**	V	R	E	V	E	R	-
7	L	I	V	I	**N**	G	**P**	O	E	T	W	I	S	H	E
8	T	H	T	H	**E**	**W**	E	L	L	-	W	I	S	H	I
9	N	G	A	D	**V**	**E**	**N**	T	V	R	E	R	I	N	S
10	E	T	T	I	N	G	F	O	R	T	H	T	T		

The point and the axis of arrow/clock-hand

Sonnet 59 seems to highlight significant commonalities between the biographies of the two men and to reference Hunnis's crest.[26] Sonnet 60 follows on from 59. Both sonnets present a cyclical view of time. The image of a child repeating the life of a forebear in Sonnet 59 finds its echo in Sonnet 60 which has *waves ... each changing place with that which goes before,* and the couplets refer to judgements of the poets of the past and the future respectively (see notes below).

Most strikingly, Sonnet 60 presents the vivid image of *Time* piercing the face of youth, precisely mirroring the image on Hunnis's crest. Booth's comments on this phrase are worth presenting *in extenso*:

> ***transfix the flourish*** In context the meaning of this phrase is clear (destroy the beauty), but *transfix* and *flourish* – each of which pertains to what precedes and follows this line – do not obviously pertain to one another and give no immediately apparent literal sense: ***transfix* pierce through** (see *fight* in line 7 and the suggestions of digging, pecking, and cutting in lines 10–12); *flourish* (1) blossoming, state of being in blossom ... (2) highest degree of prosperity, perfection, prime [our bold].[27]

The longer poem concludes with the image of the *cruel* hand of time.[28]

---

[26] We note that the letters along the diagonal spell out the near-word POISWN. Although we regard it as uncertain, nevertheless there are a few points worth noting. These are considered in Appendix 4.

[27] Booth, *Shakespeare's Sonnets*, p. 240.

[28] *The Oxford Shakespeare Complete Sonnets and Poems,* C. Burrow (ed.) (Cambridge, 2002), p. 116.

Sonnets 59–60

If their ***bee*** *nothing new, but that which is,*
Hath ***beene before****, how are our braines* ***beguild****,*
Which ***laboring*** *for invention beare amisse*
The second ***burthen*** *of* ***a former child*** *?*
Oh that record could with a back-ward looke,
Show me ***your image in some antique booke****,*
Since minde at first in ***carrecter*** *was done.*
That I might see what the old world could say,
To this composed wonder of your frame,
Whether we are mended, or where better they,
Or whether ***revolution be the same****.*
Oh sure I am the wits of former daies,
To ***subjects worse*** *have given admiring praise.*

Like as the waves make towards the pibled shore,
So do our ***minuites*** *hasten to their end,*
Each changing place with that which goes before,
In sequent toile all forwards do contend.
Nativity once in the maine of light,
Crawles to maturity, wherewith being crown'd,
Crooked eclipses gainst his glory fight,
And ***time*** *that gave, doth now his gift confound.*
Time doth transfixe the florish set on youth*,*
And ***delves the paralels*** *in beauties brow,*
Feedes on the rarities of natures truth,
And nothing stands but for his sieth to mow.
And yet to times in ***hope****, my verse shall stand*
Praising thy worth, dispight ***his cruell hand****.*

1 The concentration of ***bee, been, before*** and ***beguiled*** and continuing alliteration on *"B"* may recall the beehives of William Hunnis's crest and his ***bee*** verse.

3 ***Spe et Labore*** is the motto on Hunnis's crest – *by hope and by work.* ***Labouring*** occurs in Sonnet 59: ***Hope*** occurs in Sonnet 60 (following).

4 A ***burthen*** is both a musical drone and the sound associated with ***bees***. Stopes notes that nothing is known of Hunnis's childhood, but that given that he became a Gentleman of the Chapel Royal, it is entirely possible that he was a ***former Child*** of the Chapel.[29] We noted earlier that, as a child, Neville may also have been associated with the Chapel.

7 ***Your image*** may refer to the ***image*** of Hunnis in his ***antique book***, published 30 years earlier, in 1578.

8 This use of ***character*** also occurs in Sonnet 122 (discussed below).

12 ***Revolution be the same*** may refer both to the revolving of a hand around the face of a clock, as well as the fact that both men were involved in ***revolutions***; that is, their ***revolutions*** were the ***same***. Perhaps there is a quiet reprise of ***bee*** here too, as in Hunnis's verse.

13 The couplet refers to ***praise given by poets of the past*** (compare with couplet of Sonnet 60 below).

14 ***Subjects worse*** may refer to the status of the two men as rebels.

16 ***Minutes*** This sonnet is discussed in relation to the minute as a unit of time in Appendix 5.

17 Time repeats.

23 ***Time***

24 ***Time doth transfix the flourish set on youth***
Booth notes that this line depicts *Time* piercing the face of youth (see note above and similarity to Hunnis's crest).

25 ***Delves the parallels*** continues the image of ***Time*** disfiguring beauty. ***Parallel*** may also suggest the parallel lives of Neville and Hunnis.

27 As we saw ***labouring*** in Sonnet 59 here we see ***hope***, thus completing the motto ***Spe et labore***.
The couplet refers to ***praise given by the poet that will stand for the future*** (compare with couplet of Sonnet 59 above).

28 *Time's* ***cruel hand*** may evoke the ***hand*** of the clock as an image of piercing; exactly as in Hunnis's crest.

[29] Stopes, *William Hunnis and the Revels of the Chapel Royal*, p. 13.

An adjunct to remember

The coordinates 12-2 would seem to mark the terminus of the *hand of time.* Certainly, one could assign any of the positions 10-4, 11-3 or 13-1. However, 12-2 seems most pleasing as it preserves the proportions of the arrow and sits within the frame of the table as is the point of the arrow.

We have observed that the 154 sonnets are intended as a verse monument or memorial to the love of the poet. Sonnet 122 explores both the impulse and the futility of retaining such a memorial. Moreover, this sonnet seems to illustrate a parallel between the two memorials. In Hunnis's crest the *hand of time* is depicted within his head. In Sonnet 122 Neville's memorial, his tables, are described as being *within his brain.*

	1	2	3	4	5	6	7	8	9	10	11	**12**	13	14	15
1	T	O	T	H	E	O	N	L	I	E	B	E	G	E	T
2	T	E	R	O	F	T	H	E	S	E	I	**N**	S	V	I
3	N	G	S	O	N	N	E	T	S	Mr	**W**	H		A	L
4	L	H	A	P	P	I	N	E	S	**S**	E	A	N	D	T
5	H	A	T	E	T	E	R	N	**I**	T	I	E	P	R	O
6	M	I	S	E	D	B	Y	**O**	V	R	E	V	E	R	-
7	L	I	V	I	**N**	G	**P**	O	E	T	W	I	S	H	E
8	T	H	T	H	**E**	**W**	E	L	L	-	W	I	S	H	I
9	N	G	A	D	**V**	**E**	**N**	T	V	R	E	R	I	N	S
10	E	T	T	**I**	N	G	F	O	R	T	H	T	T		

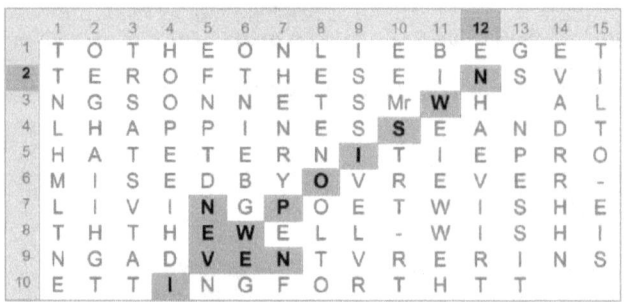

The terminus of the arrow/clock-hand at 12-2

Sonnet 122

TThy guift,, thy tables, are ***within my braine***
Full ***characterd*** *with lasting memory,*
Which shall above that idle rancke remaine,
Beyond all date even to ***eternity.***
Or at the least, so long as braine and heart
Have facultie by nature to subsist,
Til each to raz'd oblivion yeeld his part
Of thee, thy ***record*** *never can be mist:*
That poore ***retention*** *could not so much hold,*
Nor need I tallies thy deare love ***to skore,***
Therefore to give them from me was I bold,
To trust those tables that receave thee more,
To keep an ***adjunct to remember*** *thee,*
Were to import forgetfulnesse ***in mee.***

1 ***Within my brain*** may be read quite literally, in the same way as the *hand of time* in Hunnis's crest is within his head.
2 ***Charactered*** suggests *engraved*, as noted by Booth.[30]
4 ***eternity***
8 ***record***
9 ***retention*** – the holding in memory
10 ***to skore*** means to engrave – as suggested by ***charactered*** in line 2.
13 Sonnet 122 concerns the durability of memory and the need for an ***adjunct to remember*** – a goad, a *GAD*.
14 As in line 1 where the tables are literally within the brain of the poet, so ***in me*** may be taken as ***within me***.

[30] Booth, *Shakespeare's Sonnets*, p. 413.

Like a dial hand

The target of the arrowhead would seem to be the *I* at (y, x) coordinates 10-4, Sonnet 104. The suggestion that the arrow is in fact the hand of a clock becomes stronger in Sonnet 104 in the explicit phrase *a dyall hand,* which Booth takes to refer to the hand of watch or a clock.[31]

We might then ask, what number on the clock would *dial hand* point to? On the grandest clock of the age, the 24-hour clock at Hampton Court Palace this would be the number III (see p. 69 and image on p. 213). Sonnet 104 plays on III (*eye I eyed*) and emphasises the number *three.* Sonnet 104 also refers explicitly to the numeral or "figure" on a clock face.

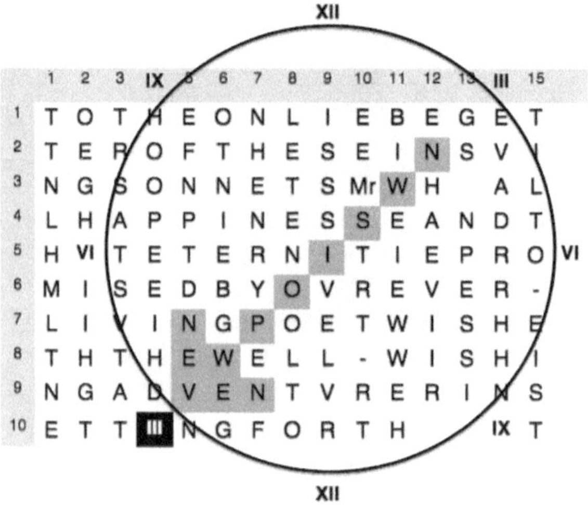

Note. In this table we have squared our usual rectangular cells to approximate the 45 degree diagonal between two points that are the same distance apart horizontally as they are vertically.

[31] Booth, *Shakespeare's Sonnets*, p. 336.

Sonnet 104

To me, faire friend, you never can be olde,
For as you were when first your ***eye I ey'd****,*
Such seemes your beautie still: ***Three*** *Winters colde,*
Have from the forrests shooke ***three*** *Summers pride,*
Three *beautious springs to yellow Autumne* ***turn'd****,*
In processe of the seasons have I seene,
Three *Aprill perfumes in* ***three*** *hot Iunes burn'd,*
Since first I saw you fresh, which yet are greene.
Ah yet doth beauty ***like a Dyall hand****,*
Steale from his figure *and no pace perceived,*
So your sweete hew, which methinks still doth stand,
Hath motion, and mine eye may be deceaved.
For feare of which, heare this thou age unbred,
Ere you were borne was beauties summer dead.

2 ***III*** is the numeral on the 24-hour clock to which the hand points.
3 ***Three***
3 ***Three***
5 ***Three. Turned*** repeats three ideas: the ***revolution*** of Sonnet 59, the ***cruel hand*** of Time in Sonnet 60, and of *TERNIT* in the Dedication.
7 **Three three**
9 ***Like a Dial hand*** – the hand of a clock or watch (as noted by Booth).
10 ***Steal*** is a homophone for ***steel*** meaning to engrave.
The *dial hand* acts in the same way as *Time doth transfix the flourish and delves the parallels* in Sonnet 60. Booth glosses this phrase as: "*The dial's hand (time) takes beauty from the beloved's appearance*".[32]
figure Booth makes the following comment:
figure *(1) number (i.e. character denoting a number on the clock face).*[33]

[32] Booth, *Shakespeare's Sonnets*, p. 336.
[33] Ibid.

Revolution be the same

If one of Neville's central intentions for the Dedication was to acknowledge his theatrical and political predecessor Master William Hunnis, he may also have been acknowledging his own central involvement in the Essex rebellion. At Neville's trial, presumably to protect his family as much as himself, Neville seems to have misrepresented the truth. Unlike the frank and full confession of Hunnis nearly 50 years earlier, Neville sought to minimise his involvement in the Essex uprising. Though he was praised as a patriot, it seems that under King James, Neville maintained this public fiction for the rest of his life. It may be that dishonesty did not sit comfortably with the profoundly ethical Neville, nor in his relations with his family. In citing Hunnis as his role model, it may be that he is also squaring the tally; the confession is there for posterity, but not for disclosure in the near term when it might harm his family.

Indeed, if we take Neville's paralleling of his biography with Hunnis's as, at least in part, a mode of confession, this might explain how his authorship came to be lost to his family forever. That is, if his confession of treason were entwined with his confession of authorship, this might discourage succeeding generations from ever revealing his authorship, even within the family. This scenario might resolve quite simply the valid question as to why the family might, even inadvertently, bury the secret of his authorship for all time.

Timeline

	Mr Richard Farrant	Mr William Hunnis	Sir Henry Neville I	Sir Henry Neville II
1540s		Possible family seat in **Berkshire**. Page to William **1st Earl of Pembroke**. Child of Chapel (?).	Close to Henry VIII. Witness to his will.	**Candidate author of the works of Shakespeare.**
1550s	Gentleman of the Chapel Royal under King Edward and then Queen Mary.	Gentleman of the Chapel Royal under King Edward and Queen Mary. **Plots overthrow of Queen Mary. Not executed. Imprisoned in Tower. Released.**	Close to child King Edward who granted him lands in Berkshire. Active in the Revels. **Opposes Queen Mary** and exiled in Europe.	
1560s	Gentleman of the Chapel Royal. 1564 Master of Children at **Windsor.** Resumes role as Gentleman of the Chapel Royal 1569.	Gentleman of the Chapel Royal under Queen Elizabeth. 1566 Master of the Children of the Chapel Royal. Flourishing of theatre funded by Elizabeth.	Leases the future Blackfriars Theatre. Relocates to **Berkshire** as Forester at **Windsor**.	Born 1562 Early life in the former Office of the Revels in **Blackfriars**.
1570s	1575 Children at Windsor merge with Children of the Chapel. Master of the Children of the Chapel.	Master of Children of the Chapel. Creates many plays at **Blackfriars**. Primary creator of the **Kenilworth** Festivities 1575.	1575 secures lease for the merging of the two Chapel ensembles.	A child in **Berkshire** near Windsor. Possibly, through father's friendships, attends **Kenilworth**. Participates (?). Tour of Europe (1578–1582).
1580s	Dies 1580.	Master of the Children of the Chapel. 1581. Son Robin is page to **Essex**.		Probable diplomatic mission to Scotland with **Essex**.
1590s		Master of the Children of the chapel. Dies 1597.	Dies 1593.	Ambassador to France 1599.
1600 and later				**Plots overthrow of Queen Elizabeth. Not executed. Imprisoned in Tower. Released.** **Kenilworth** festivities in *A Midsummer Night's Dream* and *12th Night.* 1623 First Folio dedicated to **3rd Earl of Pembroke.** Dies July 1615.

Epilogue

The surface meaning of the Dedication seems to have been the perfect camouflage for a remarkable composition. For four centuries commentators have battled, lamented or completely ignored these twelve curious lines. Schoenbaum declared them:

> *... so syntactically ambiguous as to defeat any possibility of consensus among interpreters.*[1]

It is possible that the author under-estimated the difficulty of decrypting the Dedication. But we should be careful not to under-estimate this creative mind. Perhaps the Dedication was not intended to be decrypted. Perhaps it was intended to be unveiled at a time of the author's or his family's choosing. Until that time, if ever it arrived, the Dedication would remain a private work of art.

In Chapter 7 we suggested that the linking of Neville's life with that of William Hunnis might transform the Dedication into a confession of treason. The Dedication as a map of the Sonnets not only reveals the name Sir Henry Neville, but also the living meditations, feelings and vulnerabilities of one of the greatest thinkers of all time.

We may be more confident of the reasons why the Neville would seek anonymity. Our 21st century perspective may struggle with the idea that someone would shun celebrity, but Neville had many reasons for discretion. An early play *Richard II* presents the overthrow of an unjust monarch. To say the least, this was not a work that could assist the advancement of a young statesman in the ascendancy. Indeed, it may well have endangered his life. Being so close to the monarchy, the stakes were always high. In 1601, Neville could have felt the wind from the executioner's axe. Several close friends were beheaded or worse. Imprisoned for two years, he was never free from the same threat. In 1604 the year following his release, the fearful new king briefly imprisoned him again on suspicion of treason. In an instant, fate could turn and destroy Neville, and his family with him.

Neville's greatest fear was civil war; a likely outcome if Elizabeth died without a successor. The threat did not dissolve with the crowning of James in 1603. And as much as they tried, neither Henry Neville nor Robert Cecil was able to temper James' inconsistent, profligate and increasingly absolutist reign. James's son Charles took an even more extreme position which later culminated in the civil war that Neville had so greatly feared. Neville's benign Polybian vision was not realised until 1689, when the English Bill of Rights finally set out limitations on the power of the monarch. His ideas were enthusiastically advanced by his grandson, also Sir Henry Neville, whose writings were influential in the formulation of the American Constitution.

---

[1] Schoenbaum, *Shakespeare's Lives.*

Mark Bradbeer and John Casson have documented a certain bias in the history plays, in which Neville's ancestors are prominent, often cloaked by other names but generally portrayed in a favorable light.[2] Anonymity gave Neville the freedom to write what he wanted.

Beyond Neville's clear need for personal security, his anonymity may also have reflected an artistic and philosophical choice. The works of Shakespeare disdain authoritarianism. They avoid moral judgement and seldom make statements. The author, as Jonson observed of Neville, *seeks the matter to possess.*[3] With a quiet authorial voice, the works reserve a degree of objectivity – the audience must make its own sense of the *matter* – the characters, ideas and events. Perhaps he believed that what was self-evident to him would also be self-evident to readers; that the named author could not be the real author.

At the same time, the author was keenly aware of his place among history's greatest thinkers, and of his works as eternal treasures. In Sonnet 81, which maps to the word *LIE,* he acknowledges this awareness. The identity of the author will remain hidden, and another will enjoy the eternal fame:

Sonnet 81

Or I shall live your Epitaph to make,
Or you survive when I in earth am rotten;
From hence your memory death cannot take,
Although in me each part will be forgotten.
Your name from hence immortal life shall have,
Though I (once gone) to all the world must die:
The earth can yield me but a common grave,
When you entombed in men's eyes shall ***lie****.*
Your ***monument*** *shall be my gentle verse,*
Which eyes not yet created shall o'er-read;
And tongues to be, your being shall rehearse,
When all the breathers of this world are dead;
You still shall live (such virtue hath my Pen)
Where breath most breathes, e'en in the mouths of men.

Shakespeare's Sonnets are famously cryptic; the "Dedication" perhaps even more so. However, one detail is explicit. Repeatedly, the author declares the Sonnets to be a monument. Together, the Dedication and the Sonnets comprise one vivid work of art. This is the hidden monument that the writer promises.

---

[2] Bradbeer and Casson, *Sir Henry Neville, Alias William Shakespeare.*
[3] Jonson's Epigram 109; see Chapter 1 and Appendix 2.

When all the breathers of this world are dead

What then are the conclusions we may make based on the identification of Sir Henry Neville as the author of the works attributed to Shakespeare? The much-maligned Dedication to the Sonnets can be seen to be a work of very precise architecture. Necessarily, the sonnets were published with the author's consent, and the printing was closely supervised. Even ostensible misprints had a clear purpose.

Clearly, not all the Sonnets were written to support the Dedication. In his *Palladis Tamia* (1598) Francis Meres refers to Shakespeare's sugared sonnets circulated *"among his private friends"*. But regardless of when they were written, there is very strong evidence that their sequence was chosen judiciously to align numerically with the Dedication table.

As with all great art, the Sonnets have many layers of meaning, but the function of the Dedication in highlighting less obvious layers of meaning was previously unsuspected. Some sonnets seem to have been written solely to support the encrypted messages, but now we can no longer consider any of the Sonnets without looking to the possibility of a relationship to the Dedication.

While the sonnets serve as confirmation of the encryption, they do much more. In concert with the Dedication, they constitute a unique and undiscovered work of art – a deep insight into the minute workings of the author's mind. It is difficult to think of any other work which so intimately reveals the active mind of an artist, whether immersed in visceral emotion or delighting in logical abstractions. It is almost as if the alignments require the reader to become a poet to follow such a subtle and inventive mind.

While we have come to the view that it is now proven that Sir Henry Neville is the true author, new questions arise. There are many apparent references to biography that have not yet been interpreted. We do not know the identity of the fair youth, although, as noted in Chapter 4, Casson and Rubinstein argue persuasively that this fair youth is Neville's eldest son, who married the heiress Elizabeth Smyth in 1609 shortly before the publication of the Sonnets.[4] The identity of the so-called "dark lady" remains uncertain, though at times it seems to coalesce with that of his jailer, Queen Elizabeth (Sonnets 57, 58, 68, 87). We cannot identify the rival poet, though in some instances transposing William Shakespeare into this role seems to make sense (Sonnets 133–136). The identity of Mr WH still remains conjectural, but Master William Hunnis of the Chapel Royal has numerous attributes which seem to fit (Sonnet 59).[5]

Turning to the plays, we may now revisit the histories with consideration of the many roles of members of the Neville family, and of Neville's own

[4] Casson and Rubinstein, *Sir Henry Neville was Shakespeare*, pp. 200–2.
[5] See Chapter 7.

political vision. It can now be confirmed that the Italianate comedies were inspired and informed by real and intimate knowledge of continental Europe. Many of the settings and characters may have bases in reality. The later tragedies may be seen to be coloured by the personal catastrophe of the Essex rebellion and its aftermath. The late tragic comedies or "problem" plays may reflect Neville's personal efforts to recover his former purpose, while struggling to shape a model of government in which the roles of the monarch and parliament are balanced for stability and the common good, as formulated by Polybius two millennia previously.[6] Remarkably, it was also the coding system of Polybius that was used to encrypt the author's identity.

Our enquiry has abundantly confirmed Brenda James' original discovery that the Dedication reveals the true author to be Sir Henry Neville. We also acknowledge the important pioneering work of John Rollet, who first discovered *HENRY* encrypted in the Dedication, and Rosemary Warner's remarkable discovery that *NEVILLE* is encrypted in Sonnet 134.

Prior to the identification of Neville, questions regarding the life and thoughts of the author seemed forever unanswerable. Luckily, a vast paper trail of Neville's activities and correspondence has survived, of which much remains to be explored.

For hundreds of years audiences have longed for a glimpse of the greatest author. In identifying Sir Henry Neville, Brenda James has set aside both William Shakespeare and the layers of pearl that have accreted around him. Unlike the spontaneous genius who appears fully-formed from nowhere, Neville's life mirrors the works of Shakespeare, and his experience accords with our knowledge of other individuals of genius. There was no great miracle to his learning. Neville's development as a writer was grounded on intensive academic study, enriched with wide reading, extensive travel, brilliant mentors, and the responsibilities of a statesman. Neville is flesh and blood; a man with great conviction, dynamism and a penetrating empathy for humanity.

---

[6] Lesser, *Renaissance Drama and the Politics of Publication*, Chapter 5. This chapter includes an account of Neville's struggles with King James, his promotion of the Polybian model of "mixed government", and the allegorical promotion of this model in Beaumont and Fletcher's *A King and No King*.

Appendices

Appendix 1: Sonnets Supporting the Encrypted Text

In Chapter 5 we presented several examples in which the co-ordinates of individual cells of the encrypted message align with the number and content of individual Sonnets.

For example, the unique letter *Y* in the Dedication is at the intersection of column 7 and row 6. This would correspond to (7, 6) if expressed as (x, y) co-ordinates or (6, 7) as (y, x) co-ordinates. We noted that Sonnets 76 and 67 are the only two which contain three lines beginning with the word *Why.*

In this case, both (x, y) and (y, x) coordinates yield a coherent result, but in general we note a very clear pattern in which text that reads left to right or top to bottom is referenced by (x, y) coordinates. Conversely, when a word reads in a reversed direction cells are referenced by (y, x) coordinates. Such is the case for the reversed fragments *NEV-I-LLE.*

We have also observed many sequential number mappings. The word *GAD,* which we regard as a reinforcement rather than part of the encrypted message, is referenced by its sequential position in the matrix at cell number 122. The number 122 can be associated with Horace's Ode 1.22 which is used as a coded message in *Titus Andronicus.* In this play, Ode 1.22 is inscribed with a *gad of steel.* Moreover, the typography, language and meaning of Sonnet 122 seem very relevant to the context of *GAD* in the dedication.

In Chapter 5 we argued that the precise alignments between numerical properties of the Dedication table and meaning in individual sonnets seem unlikely to be due to chance, and accordingly, that the author of the Dedication is most likely to be the same as the author of the Sonnets. If only a small number of alignments could be demonstrated, doubts should be raised as to whether each may be due to chance or subjective bias; the greater the number of alignments, the stronger the argument that they are intentional.

Many of the sonnets are difficult to understand, and often alignments with the Dedication are illuminating. However, there are instances where a notional alignment can seem to do violence to a sonnet to which we have grown attached based on a fixed or received understanding of its surface meaning. We take some comfort that many other commentators have noted the author's invitation to look for alternative meanings:

... they suggest a multiplicity of additional possible senses if their readers are prepared to try them out, to see how they fit in different narrative settings.[1]

[1] Burrow, C., "Life and Work in Shakespeare's Poems", *Chatterton Lecture on Poetry. Proceedings of the British Academy* 97, 15–50 (1998).

Sonnets Supporting the Encrypted Text

Appendices 1 and 2 constitute the body of evidence which we regard as significant to determine whether the author of the sonnets is the same as the author of the Dedication which encloses the name Sir Henry Neville. This Appendix contains the most compelling mappings that we have found that seem to support the encrypted text.

Sonnet 72 – *HENRY*

***H**ENRY* maps to coordinates 7-2 (x, y), Sonnet 72.

	1	2	3	4	5	6	7	8	9	10	11	12	13	14	15
1	T	O	T	H	E	O	N	L	I	E	B	E	G	E	T
2	T	E	R	O	F	T	H	E	S	E	I	N	S	V	I
3	N	G	S	O	N	N	E	T	S	Mr	W	H		A	L
4	L	H	A	P	P	I	N	E	S	S	E	A	N	D	T
5	H	A	T	E	T	E	R	N	I	T	I	E	P	R	O
6	M	I	S	E	D	B	Y	O	V	R	E	V	E	R	-
7	L	I	V	I	N	G	P	O	E	T	W	I	S	H	E
8	T	H	T	H	E	W	E	L	L	-	W	I	S	H	I
9	N	G	A	D	V	E	N	T	V	R	E	R	I	N	S
10	E	T	T	I	N	G	F	O	R	T	H	T	T		

O Least the world should taske you to recite,
What ***merit*** *liv'd in* ***me*** *that you should love,*
After my death (deare love) for get ***me*** *quite*
For you in ***me*** *can nothing worthy prove.*
Unlesse you would devise ***some vertuous lye,***
To doe more for ***me*** *then mine owne desert,*
And hang more praise upon ***deceased I,***
Then nigard truth would willingly impart.
Oh least your true love may seeme falce in this,
That you for love ***speake well of me untrue,***
My name be buried *where my body is*
And ***live no*** *more to shame nor* ***me*** *nor you*
For I am shamd by ***that which I bring forth***
And so should you to love things nothing worth.

Sonnet 72 repeatedly emphasises a falsehood in relation to the poet's *name.* This falsehood is distilled in line 11, where the poet urges *my name be buried.* In the next line, the name *Nevil* is reversed in the phrase *and live no more.*[2] This abstruse wordplay may extend further. Booth suggests that, given the proximity of *well* to *my name,* the word *well* may pun on Shakespeare's first-name *Will.*[3] In this way, we might then paraphrase lines 10–12 as:

Lest you speak of me as WILL untruthfully,
My name (HENRY) be buried where my body is
And NEVIL no more to shame nor me nor you.

Consistent with this sonnet's mapping to the poet's first name, there are a plethora of first-person pronouns (13 altogether – *me, my, mine, and I*). Indeed, the recurrences of *me* (6 instances) may activate a quiet pun on *merit* as *me-writ* (line 2).[4] In this way, the opening lines may be seen to encapsulate the idea of hidden authorship:

O least the world should taske you to recite what ***me-writ*** *...*

This *me-writ* pun might seem forced were it not for *deceased I* in the same sonnet. Whereas *me-writ* would be a non-grammatical use of the personal pronoun *me* as a subject, *deceased I is* certainly a non-grammatical use of the personal pronoun *I* as an object (line 7). We note too, that the *H* of *HENRY* occurs at sequential letter 22, perhaps reinforcing other lines of evidence that suggest that the initials *TT* may indeed be a "keyword" representing Twenty-Two which directs the reader to *HENRY.*

2 ***me*, *merit*** The archaic use of ***me*** as subject was presumably more available to a 17th century reader, e.g. *methinks* (see lines 7 and 13).

5 The most enduring deceptions are those which are virtuous. We propose that the authorship *lie*, substituting **Will** for **Henry** was a ***virtuous lie.***

7 ***deceased I*** This non-grammatical use of ***I*** as an object is effectively another ***me.*** Occurring at the end of the line it is especially conspicuous. In a sonnet full of the word ***me***, this may activate a pun on "merit" as "me-writ" in line 2

10 ***Speak well of me untrue*** ... *speak of me as Will untruthfully*

11 *My* ***name*** *be buried ...*

12 *And* ***NEVIL*** *no more to shame nor* ***me*** *nor you. NEVIL* is reversed here, as it is in the Dedication table.

13 As noted ***bring forth*** (or "give birth") is a common renaissance metaphor for ***writing***. The concept of ***writing*** would seem to appear unexpectedly, were it not for the pun on ***me-writ*** in line 2.

---

[2] We noted in Chapter 2 that Nevil was a common variant used by Neville himself. "Nevil/Nevel" is the spelling used in early quartos of the Henry VI trilogy.

[3] Booth, *Shakespeare's Sonnets*, p. 259.

[4] Only Sonnet 139 has as many instances of "me", but the number is perhaps less important than the effect of self-centredness that is achieved. The pronoun *me* regularly occurs as a subject in the construct "methinks". *Writ* also occurs frequently, e.g. Sonnet 116 *I never writ nor no man ever loved.*

Sonnet 76 - *YOUR*

YOUR maps to coordinates 7-6 (x, y), Sonnet 76.

	1	2	3	4	5	6	7	8	9	10	11	12	13	14	15
1	T	O	T	H	E	O	N	L	I	E	B	E	G	E	T
2	T	E	R	O	F	T	H	E	S	E	I	N	S	V	I
3	N	G	S	O	N	N	E	T	S	Mr	W	H		A	L
4	L	H	A	P	P	I	N	E	S	S	E	A	N	D	T
5	H	A	T	E	T	E	R	N	I	T	I	E	P	R	O
6	M	I	S	E	D	B	Y	O	V	R	E	V	E	R	-
7	L	I	V	I	N	G	P	O	E	T	W	I	S	H	E
8	T	H	T	H	E	W	E	L	L	-	W	I	S	H	I
9	N	G	A	D	V	E	N	T	V	R	E	R	I	N	S
10	E	T	T	I	N	G	F	O	R	T	H	T	T		

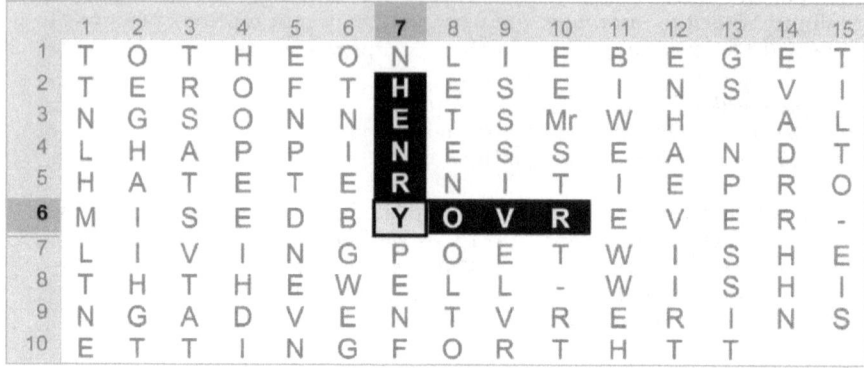

***Why** is my verse so barren of new pride?*
So far from variation or quicke change?
***Why** with the time do I not glance aside*
To new found methods, and to compounds strange?
Why** write I still all one, **ever the same
And keepe invention in a noted weed,
*That **every word doth almost tel my name,***
Shewing their birth, and where they did proceed?
*O know sweet love **I alwaies write of you,***
And you and love are still my argument:
So all my best is dressing old words new,
Spending againe what is already spent:
For as the Sun is daily new and old,
*So is my love still **telling what is told**.*

Sonnet 76 concerns a Poet and a concealed *name*. The three questions that are being asked in Sonnet 76 all begin with *Why*, offering a possible pun on the letter *Y*. The three questions are answered in line 9:

O know sweet love ***I alwaies write of you***.

Alwaies presents a possible summary pun on "all whys". Perhaps more importantly, the one answer to the *Why* questions is that the poet always writes "*of you*". "*Of you*" may be construed, comically, as a *possessive*; the more familiar possessive form is *YOUR*.

In the last line, *telling* and *told* are synonyms for counting and counted respectively (as we use the term Bank Teller). Consistent with the interests of a mathematician (such as Neville), this summary line strongly supports a numerical approach to understanding the *new found methods* of line 4. Moreover, from 1599 to 1601 Neville held the title of Joint Teller of Exchequer.[5]

1 ***Why?*** = Y
3 ***Why?*** = Y
5 ***Why?*** = Y. ***Ever the same*** is the standard translation of Queen Elizabeth's personal motto *Semper eadem.* If YOUR is addressed to Elizabeth, *"ever the same"* may stand for "*Elizabeth*" (see notes on Sonnets 67-68 following).
7 ***every word doth almost tell my name***
9 ***I always write "of you"*** (= YOUR).
14 ***telling what is told*** *Counting what is counted* (see notes above).

[5] *UK History of Parliament*, accessed 7 April 2014. http://www.historyofparliamentonline.org/volume/1558-1603/member/neville-henry-1562-1615.

Sonnet 67 – *YOUR* (continued)

Y*OUR* also maps to coordinates 6-7 (y, x), Sonnet 67.

	1	2	3	4	5	6	**7**	8	9	10	11	12	13	14	15
1	T	O	T	H	E	O	N	L	I	E	B	E	G	E	T
2	T	E	R	O	F	T	**H**	E	S	E	I	N	S	V	I
3	N	G	S	O	N	N	**E**	T	S	Mr	W	H		A	L
4	L	H	A	P	P	I	**N**	E	S	S	E	A	N	D	T
5	H	A	T	E	T	E	**R**	N	I	T	I	E	P	R	O
6	M	I	S	E	D	B	**Y**	**O**	**V**	**R**	E	V	E	R	-
7	**L**	**I**	**V**	**I**	**N**	**G**	P	O	E	T	W	I	S	H	E
8	T	H	T	**H**	**E**	**W**	E	L	L	-	W	I	S	H	I
9	N	G	A	D	V	E	N	T	V	R	E	R	I	N	S
10	E	T	T	I	N	G	F	O	R	T	H	T	T		

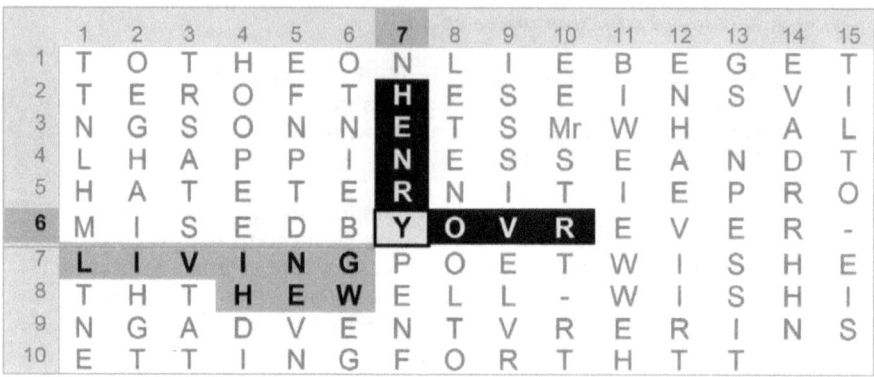

*Ah **wherefore** with infection should he live,*
And with his presence grace impietie,
That sinne by him advantage should atchive,
And lace itselfe with his societie.
***Why** should false painting immitate his cheeke,*
*And steale dead seeing of his **living hew**?*
***Why** should poore beautie indirectly seeke,*
Roses of shaddow, since his Rose is true?
***Why** should he **live, n**ow nature **banckrout** is,*
Beggerd of blood to blush through lively vaines,
*For **she** hath no **exchecker** now but his,*
And proud of many, lives upon his gaines?
  ***O him she stores**, to show what **welth** she had,*
  ***In daies long since**, before these last so bad.*

Sonnet 67 is the other sonnet that has three lines beginning with *Why* and its first line begins with the synonym *Wherefore.* There is only one *Y* in the Dedication and only Sonnets 76 and 67 have multiple lines beginning with *why.*

The term *exchequer* in line 11 would seem to echo the *telling* (counting) of sonnet 76, where we noted that from 1599 to 1601 Neville held the title of Joint *Teller* of the *Exchequer.*

bankrupt (line 9), ***exchequer*** (line 11), ***wealth*** (line 13) – all contribute to a monetary theme. Neville held that the fine Elizabeth imposed on him was disproportionate to his ability to pay. As he was unable to pay he was the last of the rebels to be released. ***Him she stores*** in line 13 would seem to support a context of imprisonment. Indeed, the whole sonnet makes sense if written by a prisoner.

If this sonnet is directed at Elizabeth, this might suggest that Neville is writing about himself in the third person; that is, "*he*" is Neville. An alternative reading may be that "he" is Neville's fellow prisoner Southampton who is known to have suffered from an intermittent form of malaria (quartan ague); hence the concept of "infection" in the opening line.

1 ***Wherefore*** = synonym for **why**
5 ***Why*** = Y
6 ***living hew*** may be significant as it occurs in the Decryption table (shaded on previous page).
7 ***Why*** = Y
9 ***Why*** = Y, ***live now*** (Nevil now?) ***bankrupt***
11 ***She*** is perhaps Queen Elizabeth; ***Exchequer***
13 ***Stores*** may refer to imprisonment, as in line 13 of Sonnet 68 which follows on. ***Wealth***
14 Perhaps *days of yore* (*YOUR*), as in line 14 of Sonnet 68 following.

Sonnet 68 – *YOUR* (continued)

Sonnet 68 seems to follow on from Sonnet 67 to form a larger poem mapping to ***Y****OUR*. Sonnet 68 also maps to ***W****EG*.

	1	2	3	4	5	6	7	8	9	10	11	12	13	14	15
1	T	O	T	H	E	O	N	L	I	E	B	E	G	E	T
2	T	E	R	O	F	T	**H**	E	S	E	I	N	S	V	I
3	N	G	S	O	N	N	**E**	T	S	Mr	W	H		A	L
4	L	H	A	P	P	I	**N**	E	S	S	E	A	N	D	T
5	H	A	T	E	T	E	**R**	N	I	T	I	E	P	R	O
6	M	I	S	E	D	B	**Y**	**O**	**V**	**R**	E	V	E	R	-
7	L	I	V	I	N	G	P	O	E	T	W	I	S	H	E
8	T	H	T	H	E	**W**	E	L	L	-	W	I	S	H	I
9	N	G	A	D	V	**E**	N	T	V	R	E	R	I	N	S
10	E	T	T	I	N	**G**	F	O	R	T	H	T	T		

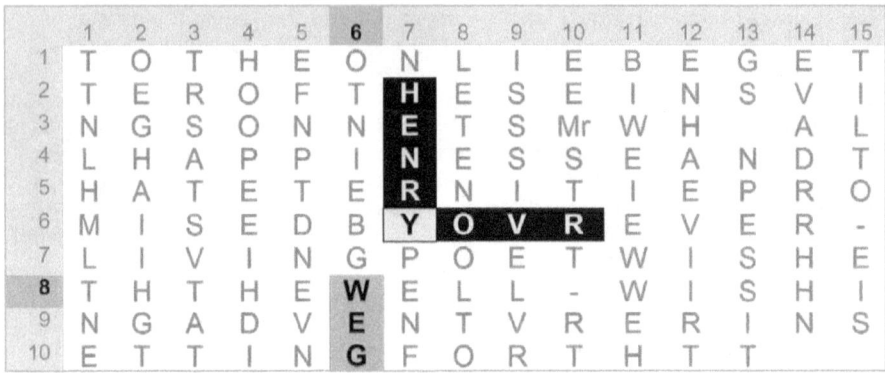

Thus is his cheeke the ***map*** *of daies out-worne,*
When beauty liv'd and dy'ed as flowers do now,
Before these bastard signes of faire were borne,
Or durst inhabit on a living brow:
Before the ***golden tresses*** *of the dead,*
The right of sepulchers, were ***shorne*** *away,*
To live a ***scond*** *life on second head,*
Ere beauties dead ***fleece*** *made another gay:*
In him those holy antique howers are seene,
Without all ***ornament****, it selfe and true,*
Making no summer of an others greene,
Robbing no ould to dresse his beautie new,
And him as for a ***map*** *doth Nature* ***store****,*
To shew faulce Art what beauty was of ***yore****.*

We propose that *"days long since"* in the last line of Sonnet 67 anticipates *"days of yore"* in the last line of Sonnet 68. Indeed, Sonnet 68 can be read as the second half of a larger poem consisting of Sonnets 67 and 68. In this way, the extended poem (67–68) may be seen to map to *YOUR*.

Sonnet 68 also maps to the vertical word WEG (shaded – left). It is an attractive but uncertain possibility that this may be a short form of "periwig", or "periweg" as it was commonly spelt. If *YOUR* is addressed to Elizabeth I, WEG might refer to her famous red woollen wig. Sonnet 68 is the only sonnet that concerns wigs. However, we note that the Oxford English Dictionary gives 1675 as the earliest recorded written use of the word *Wig*, 66 years after the publication of the sonnets.

The word ***map*** in lines 1 and13 may be significant since the most widely reproduced traveller's map of Europe throughout the 16th century was the ***Rom Weg***. It is likely that Neville's father would have used this famous map when in exile, as would Neville on his European Tour and when travelling as Ambassador to France.

1 ***Map*** may be significant in relation to the ***Rom Weg***. See note above.
5 Wig
6 Wig, ***shorne*** – like wool
7 ***Scond,*** ostensibly a misprint for *second*, reinforces the Shakespearean use, meaning roughly *plonked on the head.*[6]
8 Wig, ***fleece*** – like wool
10 ***Ornament*** in Elizabethan slang meant *pubic hair.*
13 ***Map. Store*** is used in the same way in line 13 of Sonnet 67 which we propose refers to Neville's harsh imprisonment.
14 ***YOUR***

[6] Scond: "sconce" is Head. Shakespeare uses *sconce* seven times in four plays.

Sonnet 107 – *FORTH*

***F**ORTH* maps to coordinates 10-7 (y, x), Sonnet 107.

	1	2	3	4	5	6	7	8	9	10	11	12	13	14	15
1	T	O	T	H	E	O	N	L	I	E	B	E	G	E	T
2	T	E	R	O	F	T	H	E	S	E	I	N	S	V	I
3	N	G	S	O	N	N	E	T	S	Mr	W	H		A	L
4	L	H	A	P	P	I	N	E	S	S	E	A	N	D	T
5	H	A	T	E	T	E	R	N	I	T	I	E	P	R	O
6	M	I	S	E	D	B	Y	O	V	R	E	V	E	R	-
7	L	I	V	I	N	G	P	O	E	T	W	I	S	H	E
8	T	H	T	H	E	W	E	L	L	-	W	I	S	H	I
9	N	G	A	D	V	E	N	T	V	R	E	R	I	N	S
10	E	T	T	I	N	G	**F**	**O**	**R**	**T**	**H**	T	T		

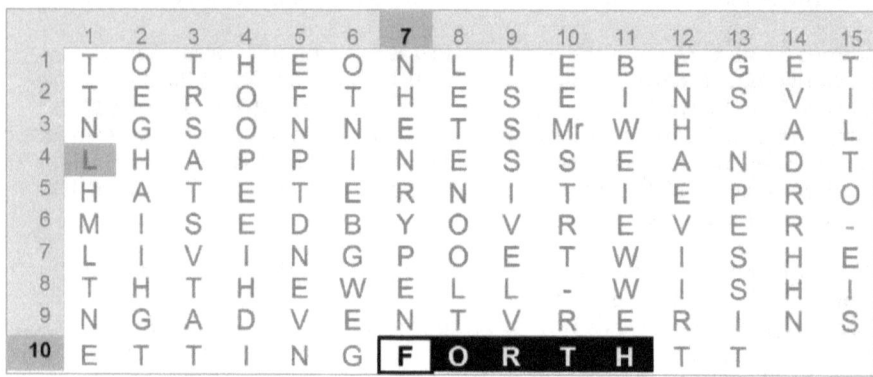

__Not__ mine own feares, nor the __prophetick__ soule,
Of the wide world, __dreaming on things to come__,
Can yet the lease of my true love controule,
Supposde as forfeit to a confin'd __doome__.
The mortall Moone hath her eclipse indur'de,
And the sad __Augurs__ mock their own __presage__,
Incertenties now crowne them-selves assur'de,
And peace proclaimes Olives of __end__lesse age.
Now with the drops of this most balmie time,
My love looks fresh, and death to me subscribes,
Since spight of him Ile live in __this poore rime__,
While he insults ore dull and speachlesse tribes.
And thou __in this__ shalt finde thy monument,
When tyrants crests and tombs of brasse are spent.

FORTH is the last word in Dedication and so may merit closer attention.

Mapping to *FORTH,* Sonnet 107 is a vivid prophecy of *the future.* Many instances of *forth* in Shakespeare carry some sense of *the future,* and often *forth* is synonymous with *the future,* as in *Julius Caesar* IV, iii:

Brutus For, from this day *forth* I'll use you for my mirth ...

Hamlet, IV, iv:

Hamlet Oh, from this time *forth,* my thoughts be bloody ...

We propose that *FORTH* also puns on *fourth,* such that *IN.SETTING.FORTH* would direct the reader to the *fourth (type-) setting* of the grid; specifically the *L* at the start of the *fourth* row which maps to Sonnet 14 (detailed pp. 122–3). Sonnet 107 and 14 are the only sonnets in which the poet compares himself with astrologers and augurs.[7] In fact, Sonnets 14, 107 and Sonnet 55 form a triad: each deals with prediction; each maps to a direction in the grid; and each (and only these three sonnets) begin with *Not* – a familiar abbreviation of the Latin *Nota* meaning "sign", or "direction".[8, 9] Sonnet 107 maps to *FORTH* (10-7), a direction to the fourth line. Sonnet 14 maps to the first letter of the fourth line *L* (1-4), a direction to count 50 letters to assemble *NEVILLE.* Sonnet 55 maps to *TERNIT* (5-5), a direction to reverse *IT* to create *SIR.*

In addition, the imagery of the three sonnets overlaps extensively, as below.

1 ***Not*** The three sonnets that begin with ***Not*** each map to a direction in the grid: Sonnet 107 (10-7 *FORTH*); Sonnet 14 (1-4 *L*), Sonnet 55 (5-5 *TERNIT*).
Prophetic Each of the three ***Not*** sonnets concerns prophecy, but only Sonnets 107 and (its target) 14 have the poet comparing himself to a predictor of the future.
2 ***Dreaming on things to come*** Prophecy
4 ***Doom*** is common to all 3 sonnets 107, 14 and 55.
6 ***Augurs, presage*** Prophecy
8 ***End*** is common to all three sonnets 107, 14 and 55.
13 ***This*** (referring to the text of the sonnet itself) is common to the couplet of all three sonnets 107, 14 and 55.
Sonnet 55 has *You live in* ***this*** *and dwell in lovers' eyes.*
Sonnet 14 has *Or else of thee,* ***this*** *I prognosticate.*

---

[7] Augur: Roman official charged with observing and interpreting omens, for guidance in public affairs.

[8] Dana Sutton, private correspondence.

[9] Given the centrality of the Philomel myth to the dedication code, it may be significant that *notae* was the specific word Ovid used to describe the characters that Philomel weaves in her own "code".

Sonnet 139 – *IN.SETTING.FORTH*

IN.SETTING.FORTH maps to coordinates 13-9 (x, y), Sonnet 139.

	1	2	3	4	5	6	7	8	9	10	11	12	13	14	15
1	T	O	T	H	E	O	N	L	I	E	B	E	G	E	T
2	T	E	R	O	F	T	H	E	S	E	I	N	S	V	I
3	N	G	S	O	N	N	E	T	S	S	Mr	W	H		A	L
4	L	H	A	P	P	I	N	E	S	S	E	A	N	D	T
5	H	A	T	E	T	E	R	N	I	T	I	E	P	R	O
6	M	I	S	E	D	B	Y	O	V	R	E	V	E	R	-
7	L	I	V	I	N	G	P	O	E	T	W	I	S	H	E
8	T	H	T	H	E	W	E	L	L	-	W	I	S	H	I
9	N	G	A	D	V	E	N	T	V	R	E	R	I	N	S
10	E	T	T	I	N	G	F	O	R	T	H	T	T		

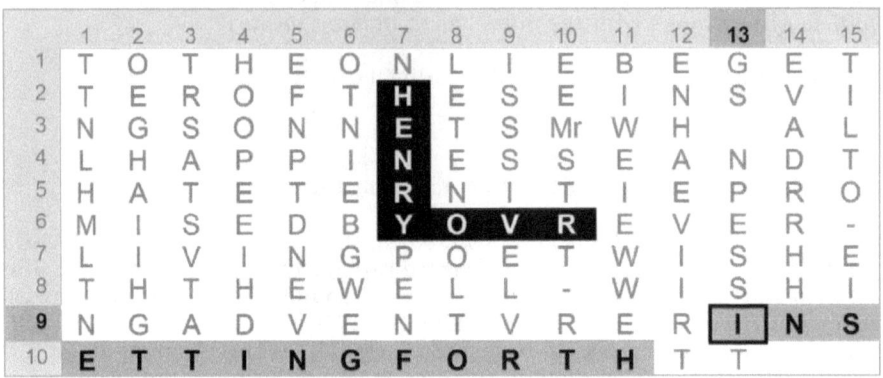

O call not me to justifie the wrong,
That thy unkindnesse layes upon my heart,
Wound me not with thine eye, but with thy toung,
Use power with power, and slay me not by Art,
Tell me thou lov'st ***else-where****; but in my sight,*
Deare heart ***forbeare*** *to glance thine eye aside,*
What needst thou wound with cunning, when thy might
Is more then my ore-prest defence can bide?
Let me excuse thee, ah my love well knowes,
Her prettie lookes have beene mine enemies,
And ***therefore*** *from my face she turnes my foes,*
That they ***else-where*** *might* ***dart*** *their iniuries:*
Yet do not so, but since I am neere slaine,
Kill me *out-right with lookes, and rid my paine.*

The phrase *IN.SETTING.FORTH* encompasses *FORTH* (discussed on pp. 118–119). It is the closing phrase of the Dedication, and as such it is potentially significant. The most obvious meaning is that the *WELL-WISHING. ADVENTURER* is *"setting forth"*. Another possibility is that *IN* indicates a place, as "in bed". Booth notes of Sonnet 139:

Shakespeare may have written the poem for the sake of playing with words and constructions that pertain to place, and can be used for other purposes.[10]

If *IN* does indicate a "place", then that place would be *SETTING.FORTH.* We propose that *SETTING.FORTH* is a specific "place" within the dedication, being the *L* at the start of line 4, the *fourth type-setting.*

In Sonnet 139, the beloved is likened to a warrior or a huntress, whom the poet exhorts to kill him with her ***darts*** (or arrows). In Greek myth this is how the huntress *Artemis* killed *Orion*, whereupon the gods made him into a constellation. The constellation *Orion* (known in folk culture as *The Ell*) is obliquely referred to in Sonnet 14 which maps to the *L* at the start of line 4 (discussed next).

5 ***Else-where*** denotes a place, but here it refers to a person. ***Else-where*** may also pun on ***Ell's where*** – the place where "L" is. *Elsewhere* occurs only 3 times in the sonnets, twice in this sonnet and once in Sonnet 61.

6 In a sonnet that plays on words, ***Forebear*** could indicate "place". When it is read in relation to ***elsewhere*** it might offer a play on 4; i.e. "bear (take the direction – as on a *map*) toward 4". See note on ***therefore*** in line 11.

11 Like ***forebear*** in line 6, in relation to ***elsewhere*** in the next line, **therefore** offers a possible play on "4" being a place, i.e. "there 4".

12 ***else-where*** (see note in line 5). ***Darts*** – see note on line 14.

14 The poet exhorts the beloved to ***kill*** him with looks that are **darts** or arrows, as *Artemis* killed *Orion. Orion* then becomes the constellation *Orion* that is referred to in Sonnet 14 (*L*).

[10] Booth, *Shakespeare's Sonnets*, p. 482.

Sonnet 14 – *The letter L*

L maps to coordinates 1-4 (x, y), Sonnet 14.

	1	2	3	4	5	6	7	8	9	10	11	12	13	14	15
1	T	O	T	H	E	O	N	L	I	E	B	E	G	E	T
2	T	E	R	O	F	T	**H**	E	S	E	I	N	S	V	I
3	N	G	S	O	N	N	**E**	T	S	Mr	W	H		A	L
4	**L**	H	A	P	P	I	**N**	E	S	S	E	A	N	D	T
5	H	A	T	E	T	E	**R**	N	I	T	I	E	P	R	O
6	M	I	S	E	D	B	**Y**	**O**	**V**	**R**	E	V	E	R	-
7	L	I	V	I	N	G	P	O	E	T	W	I	S	H	E
8	T	H	T	H	E	W	E	L	L	-	W	I	S	H	I
9	N	G	A	D	V	E	N	T	V	R	E	R	**I**	**N**	**S**
10	**E**	**T**	**T**	**I**	**N**	**G**	**F**	**O**	**R**	**T**	**H**	T	T		

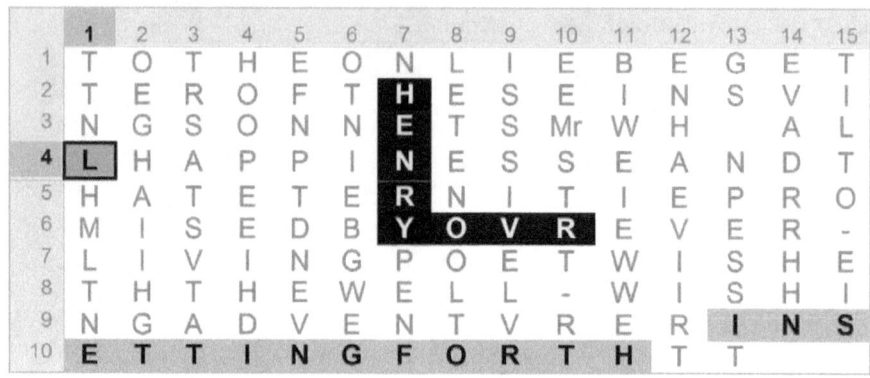

Not from the ***stars*** *do I my judgement plucke,*

And yet me thinkes I have ***Astronomy,***

But not to ***tell*** *of good, or evil lucke,*

Of plagues, of dearths, or ***seasons quallity***

Nor can I fortune to breefe mynuits ***tell;***

Pointing to each his ***thunder, raine and winde,***

Or say with Princes if it shal go ***wel***

By oft predict that I ***in heaven*** *finde,*

But from thine eies my knowledge I derive,

And constant ***stars*** *I read in them such art*

As truth and beautie shal together thrive

If from thyselfe, to store thou wouldst convert:

Or ***else*** *of thee this I prognosticate,*

Thy end is Truthes and Beauties doome and date.

L is the first letter of the fourth row or "setting" as suggested by *FORTH* and *INSETTINGFORTH* (discussed on pp. 118–121). *L* is also the Roman numeral = 50. We propose that this is a direction to count 50 spaces.[11]

The ***Ell*** *or Ell-wand* was the standard measure issued by the crown to towns and villages to measure an "ell" (around 45 inches) and so enable fair commerce. From this measure the most easily recognisable constellation *Orion's Belt* was known as ***the Ell*** in folk astrology.[12]

Sonnet 14 distinguishes the science of astronomy from folk astrology. In folk astrology *Orion* was thought to be the predictor of seasons and especially of bad weather.

Etymologies of Isidore of Seville (7th Century AD):

Orion shines in the south ... If all of its stars are shining, then calm weather is forecast, but if their sharpness is blunted, then a storm is understood to loom.

Taming of a Shrew, 1594 (perhaps quoting Marlowe's *Dr Faustus*, 1592):

... *Longing to view Orion's drizzling looks* ...

1 ***Stars***
2 ***Astronomy*** Sonnet 14 distinguishes *astronomy* – the naming of stars – from folk *Astrology*. Thus, both the names *Orion* and *The Ell* are relevant. Neville studied ***Astronomy*** at Oxford.
4 *Orion's Belt, "The Ell"* was the predictor of the **quality of seasons.**
6 ***thunder, raine and winde*** *Orion* predicted of bad weather.
7 Rhyme on ***well*** and ***tell*** reinforces ***ell***.
8 ***In heaven*** *In the* (starry) *sky*
10 ***Stars***
13 In Sonnet 139, we proposed that ***else-where*** may refer to this sonnet. Here ***else*** (*ells*) may reprise this wordplay.

[11] Sonnet 50 makes reference to the distance to a destination.
[12] Allen, R.H. *Star Names* (Dover, 1963), first published 1889.

Sonnet 57 - *NEV*

***N**EV* maps to coordinates 5-7 (x, y), Sonnet 57.

	1	2	3	4	5	6	7	8	9	10	11	12	13	14	15
1	T	O	T	H	E	O	N	L	I	E	B	E	G	E	T
2	T	E	R	O	F	T	**H**	E	S	E	I	N	S	V	I
3	N	G	S	O	N	N	**E**	T	S	Mr	W	H		A	L
4	**L**	H	A	P	P	I	**N**	E	S	S	E	A	N	D	T
5	H	50		E	T	E	**R**	N	I	T	I	E	P	R	O
6	M	I	S	T	D	B	**Y**	**O**	**V**	**R**	E	V	E	R	-
7	L	I	V	I	**N**	G	P	O	E	T	W	I	S	H	E
8	T	H	T	H	**E**	W	E	L	L	-	W	I	S	H	I
9	N	G	A	D	**V**	**E**	**N**	T	V	R	E	R	I	N	S
10	E	T	T	I	N	G	F	O	R	T	H	T	T		

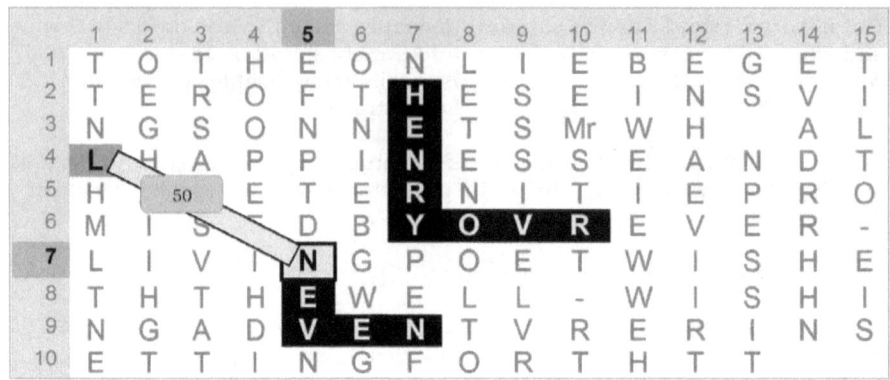

*Being your **slave** what should I doe but **tend**,*
Upon the houres, and times of your desire?
I have no precious time at al to spend;
*Nor **services** to doe, til you require.*
Nor dare I chide the world without end houre,
*Whilst I (my soverain) **watch the clock** for you,*
Nor thinke the bitternesse of absence sowre,
*When you have bid your **servant** once adieue.*
Nor dare I question with my iealious thought
Where you may be, or your affaires suppose,
*But like a sad **slave** stay and think of nought*
***Save** where you are, how happy you make those.*
*So true a **foole** is love, that in your **Will**,*
*(Though you doe anything) **he thinks no ill**.*

In sonnet 57 the ideational word seems to be *knave* which is an excellent homophone for the fragment *NEV.* In Jacobean times *knave* was synonymous with *servant, fool,* and its rhyme *slave,* as in King Lear Act 1, Scene 4:

Lear: Dinner, ho, dinner! Where's my
knave? My **fool**?
....

Lear: My lord's **knave**: you whoreson dog!
You **slave**!

Sonnet 57 is wholly built on the image of a *servant, fool,* and *slave,* possibly evoking the idea "knave" and so *NEV.*

The couplet capitalises *Will* and so raises the possibility that it could be read as the name *Will,* as in Will Shakespeare. The last line both rhymes and equates *Will* with *think no ill. Think no ill* is a fair translation of the Neville motto *Ne vile velis* – effectively Neville's name.

1 ***Slave*** = knave
4 ***services***
6 This idea of *waiting* is made explicit in Sonnets 58 and 97 (following).
8 ***Servant*** = knave
11 ***Slave*** = knave
13 ***Fool*** = knave
14 ***thinks no ill*** = *Ne vile velis,* the Neville motto; effectively his name.

Lines 13–14 might be read:

*So true a fool is love, that in your **Will,***
*(Though you do anything) he thinks **Neville.***

Sonnet 58 – *NEV* (continued)

In the same way as Sonnet 67 extends into Sonnet 68 to form a larger poem evoking *YOUR*, Sonnet 57 seems to extend into 58 and continue to evoke *knave* (*NEV*).

	1	2	3	4	5	6	7	8	9	10	11	12	13	14	15
1	T	O	T	H	E	O	N	L	I	E	B	E	G	E	T
2	T	E	R	O	F	T	H	E	S	E	I	N	S	V	I
3	N	G	S	O	N	N	E	T	S	Mr	W	H		A	L
4	L	H	A	P	P	I	N	E	S	S	E	A	N	D	T
5	H	A	T	E	T	E	R	N	I	T	I	E	P	R	O
6	M	I	S	E	D	B	Y	O	V	R	E	V	E	R	-
7	L	I	V	I	N	G	P	O	E	T	W	I	S	H	E
8	T	H	T	H	E	W	E	L	L	-	W	I	S	H	I
9	N	G	A	D	V	E	N	T	V	R	E	R	I	N	S
10	E	T	T	I	N	G	F	O	R	T	H	T	T		

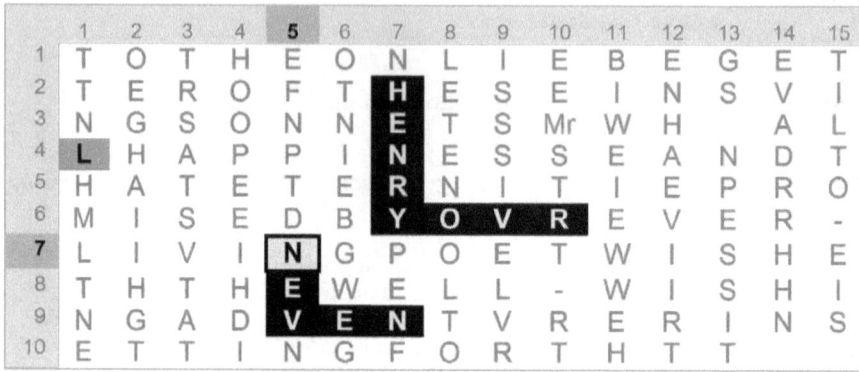

*That God forbid, that made me first your **slave**,*
*I should in thought controule your times of **pleasure**,*
*Or at your hand th'account of houres to **crave**,*
*Being your **vassail**, bound to staie your leisure.*
Oh let me suffer (being at your beck)
*Th'**imprison'd** absence of your libertie,*
And patience tame, to sufferance, bide each check,
Without accusing you of iniury.
*Be where you list, your **charter** is so strong,*
That you your selfe may priviledge your time
To what you will, to you it doth belong,
*Your selfe to pardon of selfe-doing **crime**.*
*I am to **waite**, though **waiting** so be hell,*
*Not blame **your pleasure** be it **ill or well**.*

As well as the synonyms *slave* and *vassal,* Sonnet 58 also introduces the notion of *imprisonment* (line 6) which is central to Neville's biography. Looking back, line 6 of Sonnet 57 could also be read as evoking an image of imprisonment. One might then conjecture the identity of the jailer to be Queen Elizabeth herself. We see at least three possible references to the Queen in these two sonnets. In addition to the servility of the relationship, Sonnet 57 has *my sovereign,* and Sonnet 58 has *your vassal* (a menial to a lord or king), and *your charter* (a royal right). While great inequalities of status are standard in traditional Petrarchan sonnets, throughout *Shakespeares Sonnets* the author was burlesquing these conventions.

1 ***slave*** = knave. Rhyme with *crave* in line 3 echoes *knave.*
2 Imprisonment "at the Tower" was referred to as "at her majesty's **pleasure**" Only this sonnet and Sonnet 97 (following) both introduce and reprise the word ***pleasure*** (see line 14).
3 ***Crave***
4 ***vassal*** = knave
6 ***imprisoned***
9 ***charter*** = a royal right
13 ***wait, waiting*** = serving
14 ***Your pleasure*** may refer to the Tower as in line 2.
ill or well seems to echo the rhyming of *Will* and *no ill* in the couplet of Sonnet 57.

Sonnet 97 – *NEV (reversed)*

***NE**V* maps to coordinates 9-7 (y, x) because the word is reversed; Sonnet 97.

	1	2	3	4	5	6	**7**	8	9	10	11	12	13	14	15
1	T	O	T	H	E	O	N	L	I	E	B	E	G	E	T
2	T	E	R	O	F	T	**H**	E	S	E	I	N	S	V	I
3	N	G	S	O	N	N	**E**	T	S	Mr	W	H		A	L
4	L	H	A	P	P	I	**N**	E	S	S	E	A	N	D	T
5	H	A	T	E	T	E	**R**	N	I	T	I	E	P	R	O
6	M	I	S	E	D	B	**Y**	**O**	**V**	**R**	E	V	E	R	-
7	L	I	V	I	**N**	G	P	O	E	T	W	I	S	H	E
8	T	H	T	H	**E**	W	E	L	L	-	W	I	S	H	I
9	N	G	A	D	**V**	**E**	**N**	T	V	R	E	R	I	N	S
10	E	T	T	I	N	G	F	O	R	T	H	T	T		

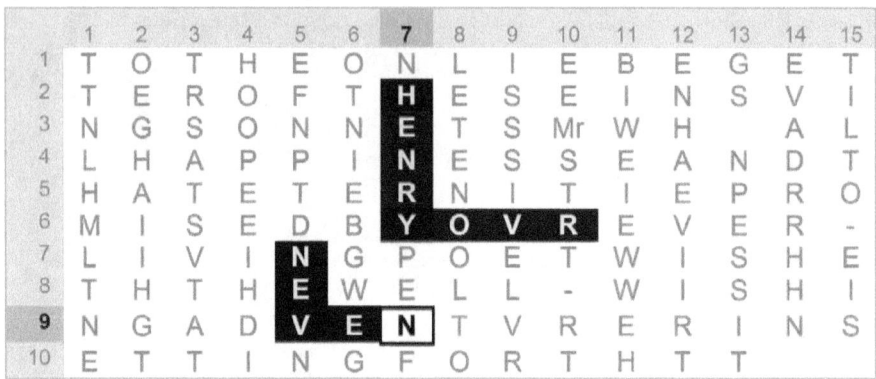

*How like a **winter** hath my **absence** beene*
*From thee, the **pleasure** of the fleeting year?*
What freezings have I felt, what darke daies seen?
What old Decembers barenesse everywhere?
*And yet this **time removd** was **sommers** time,*
*The **teeming** Autumne, **big** with ritch **increase**,*
***Bearing** the wanton **burthen** of the prime,*
*Like widdowed **wombes** after their Lords decease:*
*Yet this aboundant **issue** seem'd to me,*
*But **hope of Orphans**, and **unfather'd fruite**,*
*For **Sommer** and his **pleasures waite** on thee,*
And thou away, the very birds are mute.
Or, if they sing, tis with so dull a cheere,
*That leaves looke pale, dreading the **Winters** neere.*

Sonnet 97 extends the standard Renaissance conceit that equates writing poetry with childbirth (e.g. Sonnets 59.4, 76.8, 77.11). We propose that this poem expresses the pain of the anonymous poet (the father of the poems) separated from his poetry/children. Moreover, the noted (and inexplicable) switch from children already born to children not yet born suggests the possibility of the children being fathered after they are born. This would make sense if the children were poems, and the author is, or might be, named post publication.

Images of the pregnant belly evoke the ideational pun on *nave* – the navel/belly = *NEV*, and *ne* = born – phonetically reinforcing *NEV*. This evocation of *navel* is extended in Sonnet 98 (following).

Nave meaning *navel* is perhaps most easily recalled from *Macbeth* I, ii

> *...unseam'd him from the* ***nave*** *to the chops*

Like Sonnet 58 (which maps to the vertical *NEV*), this sonnet contains muted references to imprisonment via ***pleasure*** to evoke "Her Majesty's Pleasure" (lines 2 and 11), and ***time removed*** (line 5).

We propose that in this sonnet (and others) *Summer* may be a pseudonym for Neville. A summer is one who sums. Neville was both a mathematician and Joint Teller of the Exchequer. Line 1 might introduce a mock logic that it is like *Winter* because of *my absence* (i.e. he is the *Summer*).

1 We propose that ***Summer*** may be a pseudonym for Neville (see note above).
2 ***pleasure*** Only this sonnet and Sonnet 58 (*NEV*) both introduce and reprise the word ***pleasure*** (see note on line 11).
5 Confinement – for childbirth/poetic creation, possibly imprisonment.
6 Pregnant.
7 Pregnant.
8 Pregnant.
9 ***issue*** conflates "printed poetry" with "children".
10 Though the children (the poems) are already born, as yet they have no named father (author).
11 ***Summer*** may signify **Neville**. ***Pleasures*** (and in line 2) repeats the reference to the Tower in Sonnet 58 (lines 2 and 14).
12 ***wait*** = *serve* as in Sonnet 58. In fact, ***wait*** only occurs in Sonnets 58 and 97; each instance refers to *serving*. The extended Sonnets 57–58 and 97–98 map to the two instances of ***NEV*** in the Dedication.
14 ***Winter*** – the opposite of ***Summer*** in lines 5 and 11.

Sonnet 98 – *NEV (reversed)*

In the same way as Sonnet 57 extends into Sonnet 58 to form a larger poem evoking *KNAVE*, Sonnet 97 extends into Sonnet 98 to evoke *NAVE*.

	1	2	3	4	5	6	**7**	8	9	10	11	12	13	14	15
1	T	O	T	H	E	O	N	L	I	E	B	E	G	E	T
2	T	E	R	O	F	T	H	E	S	E	I	N	S	V	I
3	N	G	S	O	N	N	E	T	S	Mr	W	H		A	L
4	L	H	A	P	P	I	N	E	S	S	E	A	N	D	T
5	H	A	T	E	T	E	R	N	I	T	I	E	P	R	O
6	M	I	S	E	D	B	Y	O	V	R	E	V	E	R	-
7	L	I	V	I	N	G	P	O	E	T	W	I	S	H	E
8	T	H	T	H	E	W	E	L	L	-	W	I	S	H	I
9	N	G	A	D	V	E	N	T	V	R	E	R	I	N	S
10	E	T	T	I	N	G	F	O	R	T	H	T	T		

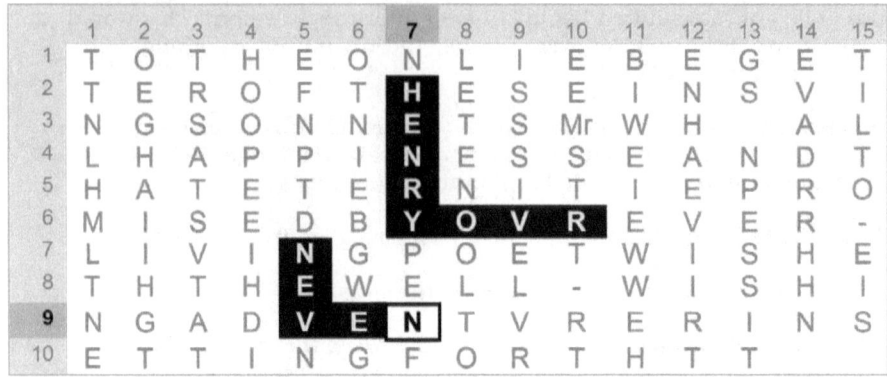

From you have I beene absent in the spring,
When ***proud*** *pide Aprill (drest in all his trim)*
Hath put a spirit of youth in every thing:
That ***heavie*** *Saturne laught and leapt with him.*
Yet nor the laies of birds, nor the sweet smell
Of different flowers in odor and in hew,
Could make me any ***summers story*** *tell:*
Or from their proud lap pluck them where they grew:
Nor did I wonder at the Lillies white,
Nor praise the deepe vermillion in the Rose,
They weare but sweet, but figures of delight:
Drawne after you, you patterne of all those.
Yet seem'd it ***Winter*** *still, and you away,*
As with your ***shaddow*** *I with these did play.*

Following on from Sonnet 97, Sonnet 98 develops the theme of the poet separated from his writing via the metaphor of childbirth, and expands on the homophone of *NEV,* being *NAVE.*

Indeed, Sonnet 98 offers a precise reference to the *navel* or *nave*, but rather than a human *nave* that is evoked, it is the *nave* of a flower. Lines 6-8:

> *Of different* ***flowers*** *in odour and in hue*
> ...
> *Or from their* ***proud lap pluck*** *them where they grew:*

Booth notes the "dormant" sexual (reproductive) suggestiveness of this line:

> *Proud* ... (2) swelling, luxuriant, pregnant ...
>
> *"laps" in Othello IV, iii ("[husbands] pour our treasures into foreign laps"; "pluck"* and *"pluck a sweet"* meaning "deflower" in *Loves Labours Lost* IV, iii
>
> ... since flowers cannot be plucked from their own laps, a reader must come to understand *"their ... lap"* as the place where they grow, the ground ("the lap of mother earth" is the traditional and obvious conceit ...) [13]

In this way, the flower's stem may be imagined as the umbilical cord from "mother earth" (compare with *wombs* in Sonnet 97). And, the precise location at which the flower is detached (plucked) from the stem would be its *nave.*

2 ***Proud*** As noted above, Booth suggests *swelling, luxuriant, pregnant*
4 ***Heavy*** continues the large-bellied imagery from Sonnet 97
7 ***summer's story*** As in Sonnet 97, we propose *Summer* is a pseudonym for the anonymous author.
8 We propose that the stem of the flower is associated with an umbilical cord to "mother earth", thus activating an obscure but precise allusion to ***Nave.*** See notes above.
13 ***Winter*** confirms that Sonnet 98 looks back to and extends Sonnet 97.
14 ***shadow*** It might make sense that the horizontal *NEV* in the grid resembles the *shadow* of the vertical *NEV.*

[13] Booth, *Shakespeare's Sonnets*, pp. 217–18.

Sonnet 122 - *GAD*

***G**AD* maps to sequential letter 122; Sonnet 122.[14]

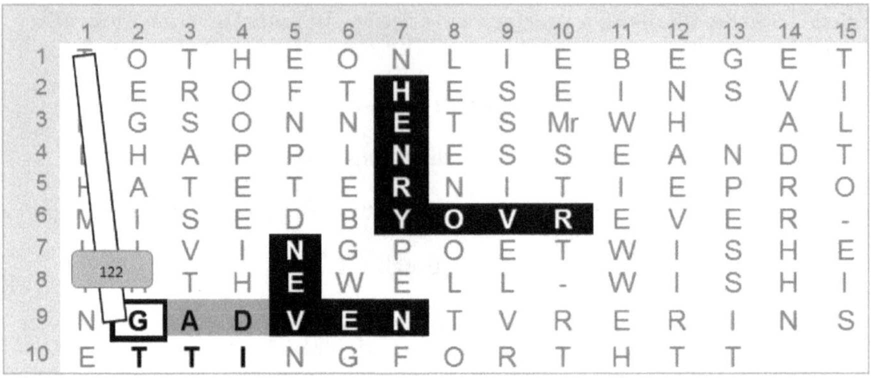

TThy guift,,thy tables, are within my braine
*Full **characterd** with lasting **memory,***
*Which shall above that idle **rancke** remaine,*
*Beyond all date even **to** eternity.*
Or at the least, so long as braine and heart
*Have facultie by nature **to** subsist,*
*Til each **to** raz'd oblivion yeeld his part*
Of thee, thy record never can be mist:
That poore retention could not so much hold,
Nor need I tallies** thy deare love to **skore,
*Therefore **to** give them from me was I bold,*
***To** trust those **tables** that receave thee more,*
***To** keep an **adjunct to remember** thee,*
*Were **to** import forgetfulnesse in mee.*

[14] As Ambassador to France, Neville used the code word b.122 to refer to his eponymous adversary the French Secretary – Villeroy, Nicholas de **Neufville** (see list of Neville's code words on p. 44).

A GAD is a sharp point, a spear-head or arrow-head. In the dedication table, *GAD* is adjacent to the "arrow-head" created by the two *NEV*s, and sits above the *TT* that we propose signifies "count *22* letters" (to complete NEVI-LLE). *GAD* is a variant of *goad*, a pointed stick for driving cattle and a metaphor for a prompt or reminder. The central concern of Sonnet 122 is an *adjunct to remember*, a *GAD*. The *adjunct* is a *table book* inscribed with characters.

In *Titus Andronicus* IV, i a *GAD* inscribes Horace's Ode 1.22 (cf. 122):

I will go get a leaf of brass,
And with a ***gad*** *of steel will write these words*[15]

Echoing the **coded** message in the *Myth of Philomel* upon which the play is based, Titus uses Ode 1.22 as a **code**:

The man of pure and upright life
Has no need of Moorish spears, or bow,
Or a quiver full of poison arrows ...[16]

Philomel is also evoked in Sonnet 102 which maps to *TT* below *GAD*. This sonnet highlights her silencing; by excision of her tongue (pp. 142–3).

Together with the *TT* at the start of Sonnet 122, the points above lead us to conclude that *TT* may signify "count 22". However, in Chapter 6 we proposed that *TT* might also signify 15, since *TT* occurs at the 15th character in the dedication (in *BEGETTER*). In this way, the acrostic *TTMAP* might signify *15MAP*, a *table* of 15 columns. In Sonnet 122 a second "error" follows *TT;* the two commas after "guift" (see below and image on page 60). These may be seen to resemble the number 99. Sonnet 99 is the only sonnet with 15 lines.

1 The "erroneous" ***TT*** and **,,** seem deliberate. See page 138. ***Tables*** may refer to the *table* setting of the Dedication. *Table books* consisted of waxed pages that were marked with a stylus (a *GAD*), rather than an ink pen.
2 ***Charactered*** suggests *engraved*, as noted by Booth,[17] and accords with the use of a stylus, or a **gad,** on waxed pages in a ***table*** book.
3 ***Rank*** Booth: "*rank* also suggests lines of letters (characters) written in rows"
4 ***to*** (=2) occurs more often in Sonnet 122 than any other sonnet (9 instances). Booth notes the *welter of infinitives* in lines 10–14.
10 ***Tallies*** – In Ode 1.22 Horace has no need of spears or arrows (sticks); in Sonnet 122, the author has no need of tallies (sticks).
11 ***Score*** means either to account for, or to inscribe – as suggested by ***charactered*** in line 2 (and as with a *GAD* in *Titus Andronicus*).
12 We note the acrostic ***To To*** *(22)* across lines 12 and 13. ***Tables***.
13 Sonnet 122 concerns the durability of memory and the need for an ***adjunct to remember*** – a goad, a *GAD*.

---

[15] This may be referred to in Jonson's lines to Shakespeare's engraving in the *First Folio*. Jonson wishes that the engraving would *surpass/ All, that was ever* ***writ in brass***.
[16] See photograph of Neville's annotated copy of Horace's Ode 1.22 on p. 162.
[17] Booth, *Shakespeare's Sonnets*, pp. 413–15 for *Charactered*, *Rank*, and the "Welter of infinitives".

Sonnet 104 – *I*

I maps to coordinates 10-4 (y, x) because *NEVILLE* is reversed; Sonnet 104.

	1	2	3	4	5	6	7	8	9	10	11	12	13	14	15
1	T	O	T	H	E	O	N	L	I	E	B	E	G	E	T
2	T	E	R	O	F	T	H	E	S	E	I	N	S	V	I
3	N	G	S	O	N	N	E	T	S	Mr	W	H		A	L
4	L	H	A	P	P	I	N	E	S	S	E	A	N	D	T
5	H	A	T	E	T	E	R	N	I	T	I	E	P	R	O
6	M	I	S	E	D	B	Y	O	V	R	E	V	E	R	-
7	L	I	V	I	N	G	P	O	E	T	W	I	S	H	E
8	T	H	T	H	E	W	E	L	L	-	W	I	S	H	I
9	N	G	A	D	V	E	N	T	V	R	E	R	I	N	S
10	E	T	T	I	N	G	F	O	R	T	H	T	T		

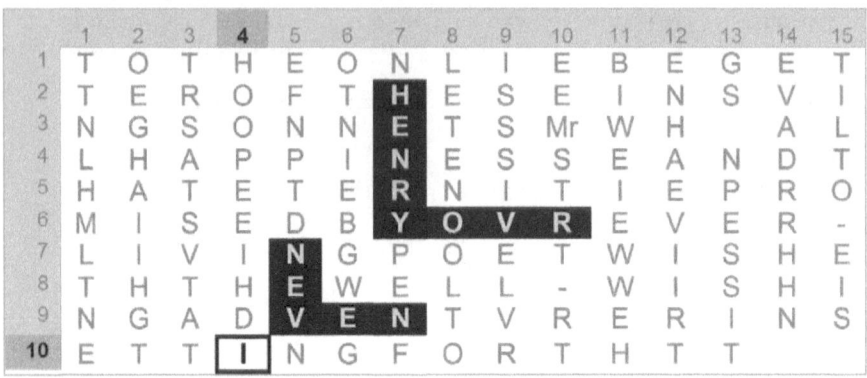

To me, faire friend, you never can be olde,

For as you were when first your ***eye I ey'd****,*

Such seemes your beautie still: ***Three*** *Winters colde,*

Have from the forrests shooke ***three*** *Summer's pride,*

Three *beautious springs to yellow Autumne* ***turn'd****,*

In processe of the seasons have I seene,

Three *Aprill perfumes in* ***three*** *hot Iunes burn'd,*

Since first I saw you fresh, which yet are greene.

Ah yet doth beauty like a ***Dyall hand****,*

Steale *from his* ***figure*** *and no pace perceived,*

So your sweete hew, which methinks still doth stand,

Hath motion, and ***mine eye may be deceaved****.*

For feare of which, heare this thou age unbred,

Ere you were borne was beauties ***summer*** *dead.*

Sonnet 104 plays on the sound *I* in *eye I ey'd* (line 2). There are also five instances of the number *three*. In Roman numerals, the number *three* is written iii (*eye I ey'd*). This *I* is both the letter *I* in NEVILLE as well as the number "1" of ITT (as in Horace's Ode 1.22).

The suggestion that the arrow is in fact the hand of a clock becomes stronger in Sonnet 104 in the explicit phrase *a dyall hand* (line 9) which Booth takes to refer to the hand of watch or a clock.[18]

We might then ask what number on the clock the dial hand would point to?[19] On the grandest clock of the age, the 24-hour clock at Hampton Court Palace (see image on page 213), this would be the number III. Sonnet 104 plays on III (*eye I eyed*) and emphasises the number *three.* Sonnet 104 also refers explicitly to the numeral or "figure" on a clock face.

As far as we know, in the 400+ years since this sonnet was published no commentator has previously associated *eye I ey'd* to the Roman numeral iii via the word *three.*

2 ***III*** is the numeral on the 24-hour clock to which the hand points.

3 ***Three***

4 ***Three***

5 ***Three.***
Turned repeats the idea of the ***revolution*** as seen in Sonnet 59, in the ***cruel hand*** of Time in Sonnet 60, and *TERNIT* in the Dedication.

7 ***Three. Three.***

9 ***Dial hand*** – the hand of a clock or watch, noted by Booth.

10 ***Steal*** is a homophone for ***steel***, meaning *to engrave*. The ***dial hand*** acts in the same way in Sonnet 60, where *Time doth transfix the flourish* and *delves the parallels*, which Booth glosses as "*The dial's hand (time) takes beauty from the beloved's appearance*".[20]
Booth continues: ***figure*** (1) number (i.e. character denoting a number on the clock face).[21]

14 See Sonnet 97; ***summer*** may refer to Neville as *one who "sums"*.

---

[18] Booth, *Shakespeare's Sonnets*, p. 336.

[19] We are grateful to Lewis Leyland for posing this question and suggesting that it may be significant.

[20] Booth, *Shakespeare's Sonnets*, p. 336.

[21] Ibid.

***Sonnet 105 – I* (continued)**

Sonnet 105 seems to follow on from Sonnet 104.

	1	2	3	4	5	6	7	8	9	10	11	12	13	14	15
1	T	O	T	H	E	O	N	L	I	E	B	E	G	E	T
2	T	E	R	O	F	T	H	E	S	E	I	N	S	V	I
3	N	G	S	O	N	N	E	T	S	Mr	W	H		A	L
4	L	H	A	P	P	I	N	E	S	S	E	A	N	D	T
5	H	A	T	E	T	E	R	N	I	T	I	E	P	R	O
6	M	I	S	E	D	B	Y	O	V	R	E	V	E	R	-
7	L	I	V	I	N	G	P	O	E	T	W	I	S	H	E
8	T	H	T	H	E	W	E	L	L	-	W	I	S	H	I
9	N	G	A	D	V	E	N	T	V	R	E	R	I	N	S
10	E	T	T	I	N	G	F	O	R	T	H	T	T		

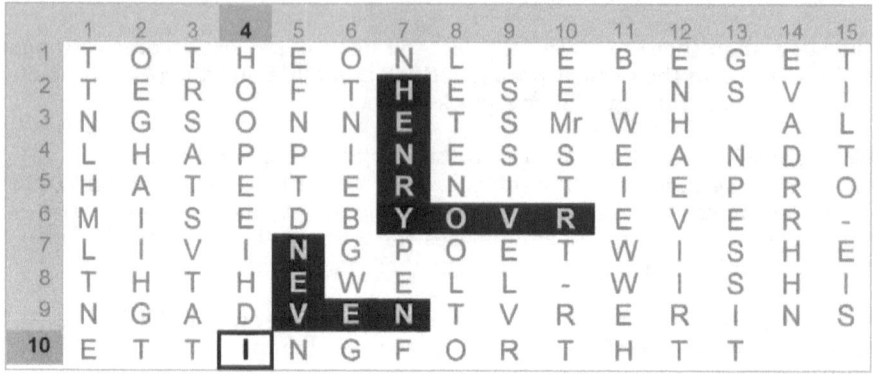

*Let not **my** love be cal'd **Idolatrie**,*
*Nor **my** beloved as an **Idoll** show,*
*Since all **alike my** songs and praises be*
*To **one**, of **one**, still such, and ever so.*
***Kinde** is my love to day, to morrow **kinde**,*
*Still constant in a **wondrous** excellence,*
*Therefore my verse to constancie **confin'de**,*
***One** thing expressing, leaves out difference.*
*Faire, **kinde**, and true, is all **my** argument,*
*Faire, **kinde**, and true, varrying to other words,*
*And in this change is **my** invention spent,*
***Three** theams in **one**, which **wondrous** scope affords.*
*Faire, **kinde**, and true, have often liv'd **alone**,*
*Which **three** till now, never kept seate in **one**.*

Sonnet 104 merges with Sonnet 105 to form one poem which ends on the word "one" to support I – the numeral one (1).

Sonnet 104 expresses the impermanence of beauty, but Sonnet 105 answers this with the miracle of art to hold beauty eternally.

The last line of Sonnet 105 *Which three till now, never kept seat in one* perfectly describes the "*III*" wordplay in Sonnet 104, where III may be the numeral on the 24-hour clock face.

Sonnet 105 is also significant because, following the transformation *TERNIT,* it maps to the *I* of the new word *SIR at* coordinates 10-5 (x, y).

1 ***i, Idolatry*** Capitalisation of *I* in lines 1 and 2. Long ***i*** sounds abound.
2 ***i, i***
3 ***i, i***
4 ***one, one***
5 ***i, i***
6 ***wondrous*** one
7 ***i***
8 ***one***
9 ***i, i***
10 ***i***
11 ***i***
12 ***Three, one, wondrous*** one
13 ***i, alone*** one
14 ***Three*** in ***one*** is an explicit distillation of the wordplay of Sonnets 104 and 105.

Sonnet 151 – TT

TT maps to coordinates 15-1 (x, y); Sonnet 151 and its complement Sonnet 152. *TT* is also discussed in detail in Chapter 6.

	1	2	3	4	5	6	7	8	9	10	11	12	13	14	**15**
1	T	O	T	H	E	O	N	L	I	E	B	E	G	E	**T**
2	**T**	E	R	O	F	T	H	E	S	E	I	N	S	V	I
3	N	G	S	O	N	N	E	T	S	Mr	W	H		A	L
4	L	H	A	P	P	I	N	E	S	S	E	A	N	D	T
5	H	A	T	E	T	E	R	N	I	T	I	E	P	R	O
6	M	I	S	E	D	B	Y	O	V	R	E	V	E	R	-
7	L	I	V	I	N	G	P	O	E	T	W	I	S	H	E
8	T	H	T	H	E	W	E	L	L	-	W	I	S	H	I
9	N	**G**	**A**	**D**	V	E	N	T	V	R	E	R	I	N	S
10	E	**T**	**T**	I	N	G	F	O	R	T	H	T	T		

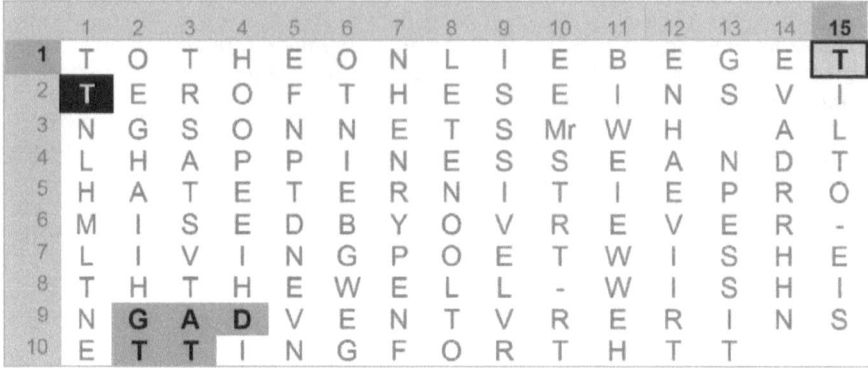

__Love is too young__ to know what __conscience__ is,
Yet who knowes not __conscience__ is born of love;
Then gentle cheater urge not my amisse,
Least guilty of my faults thy sweet selfe prove.
For thou betraying me, I doe betray
__My nobler part__ to my __grose bodies treason__,
My soule doth tell my body that he may
Triumph in love, __flesh__ staies no farther reason,
But __rysing__ at thy name doth point out thee,
As his triumphant prize, proud of this pride,
He is contented thy poore drudge to be
***To stand in thy affaires, fall by thy side**.*
No want of conscience hold it that I call,
Her love, for whose deare love __I rise and fall__.

The very first *TT* of the Dedication is the *TT* of *BEGETTER*. This *TT* occurs at the 15th space and activates the sense of the acrostic *TTMAP* as *15MAP*; a *MAP* of *15* columns.

There are many instances where two sonnets are placed together to form a longer poem of 28 lines – Sonnets 57–58, 59–60, 67–68, 77–78, 97–98, 104–105, 113–114 and 133–134. The mapping of these longer poems refers to the number of the first sonnet in the pair.

In this case, Sonnet 151 clearly forms a pair with Sonnet 152 (over page). Both are concerned with a double falsehood in love, and refer very explicitly to the sexual act. Indeed, it is the unusual and graphic reference to sex that links the two most directly and confirms that they are two halves of a longer poem. Most importantly, the second half of this poem (Sonnet 152) presents the only reference in *Shakespeare's Sonnets* to the number *twenty-two.*

Booth's comments below and on page 141 are in quotes and italics;[22] ours are in non-italics.

1 ***Conscience*** in lines 1 and 2 of this most important sonnet may be the *conscience* that Ben Jonson refers to in the dedication of his *Epigrams* (1616) which also refers to a *cipher* (see p. 52).

3 Lines 3-4 refer to the double-false-hood that is reprised in line 2 of Sonnet 152 below.

6 *"... playing on* ***part*** meaning *"bodily part" and specifically the male member,"*

9 ***rising*** *"...The overt reference is to sexual erection ..."*

12 *"... the overt reference is sexual;"*

14 *"'rising and falling' is singularly appropriate to [the poem's] theme of involuntary lust; the point is that* ***it is not a metaphor****."* (Our bold.)

[22] Booth, *Shakespeare's Sonnets*, pp. 524–9.

Sonnet 151–152 – TT

TT maps to coordinates 15-1 (x, y); Sonnet 151 and its complement Sonnet 152. *TT* is also discussed in detail in Chapter 6.

	1	2	3	4	5	6	7	8	9	10	11	12	13	14	**15**
1	**T**	**O**	**T**	**H**	**E**	O	N	L	I	E	B	E	G	E	**T**
2	**T**	E	R	O	F	T	H	E	S	E	I	N	S	V	I
3	N	G	S	O	N	N	E	T	S	Mr	W	H		A	L
4	L	H	A	P	P	I	N	E	S	S	E	A	N	D	T
5	H	A	T	E	T	E	R	N	I	T	I	E	P	R	O
6	M	I	S	E	D	B	Y	O	V	R	E	V	E	R	-
7	L	I	V	I	N	G	P	O	E	T	W	I	S	H	E
8	T	H	T	H	E	W	E	L	L	-	W	I	S	H	I
9	N	G	A	D	V	E	N	T	V	R	E	R	I	N	S
10	E	T	T	I	N	G	F	O	R	T	H	T	T		

Two and twenty *OTHES* are broken

In loving thee thou know'st I am forsworne,
But thou art twice forsworne to me love swearing,
***In act thy bed-vow broake** and new faith torne,*
In vowing new hate after new love bearing:
*But why of **two othes** breach doe I accuse thee,*
*When **I breake twenty**: I am perjur'd most,*
*For all my vowes are **othes** but to misuse thee:*
And all my honest faith in thee is lost.
*For I have sworne deepe **othes** of thy deepe kindnesse,*
***Othes** of thy love, thy truth, thy constancie,*
*And to inlighten thee **gave eyes to blindnesse**,*
Or made them swere against the thing they see.
For I have sworne thee faire: more perjurde eye,
To swere against the truth so foule a lie.

As noted, Sonnet 152 follows on from, and forms a pair with Sonnet 151. This longer poem is concerned with falsehoods in love, and refers very explicitly to the sexual act. Indeed, it is the unusual and graphic reference to sex that links the two and directs us to read them as two halves of a longer poem. Most importantly, the second half of this poem (Sonnet 152) presents the only reference in *Shakespeare's Sonnets* to the number *twenty-two.*

Two and twenty oaths are broken.[23]

2 ***Twice forsworn*** reprises the *double falsehood* referred to in line 3–4 above.

3 ***In act thy bed-vow broke*** *"performing the sexual act".*

5 ***Two***

6 ***Twenty*** Two and Twenty oaths are broken by the poet and the addressee.

7 Lines 7–14 detail the broken ***othes*** (see OTHE in grid on previous page).

11 ***Eyes to blindness*** This reference to Cupid returns to the image of baby Cupid right back at line 1 of the paired Sonnet 151, *Love is too Young ...*

[23] *OTHE* occurs in the first row at co-ordinates 2-1. Sonnet 21 illustrates false poetic oaths and is discussed in Appendix 2.

Sonnet 102 - *TT*

The ***TT*** that joins *NEVI* and *LLE* maps to coordinates 10-2; Sonnet 102.[24]

	1	2	3	4	5	6	7	8	9	10	11	12	13	14	15
1	T	O	T	H	E	O	N	L	I	E	B	E	G	E	T
2	T	E	R	O	F	T	H	E	S	E	I	N	S	V	I
3	N	G	S	O	N	N	E	T	S	Mr	W	H		A	L
4	L	H	A	P	P	I	N	E	S	S	E	A	N	D	T
5	H	A	T	E	T	E	R	N	I	T	I	E	P	R	O
6	M	I	S	E	D	B	Y	O	V	R	E	V	E	R	-
7	L	I	V	I	N	G	P	O	E	T	W	I	S	H	E
8	T	H	T	H	E	W	E	L	L	-	W	I	S	H	I
9	N	G	A	D	V	E	N	T	V	R	E	R	I	N	S
10	E	T	T	I	N	G	F	O	R	T	H	T	T		

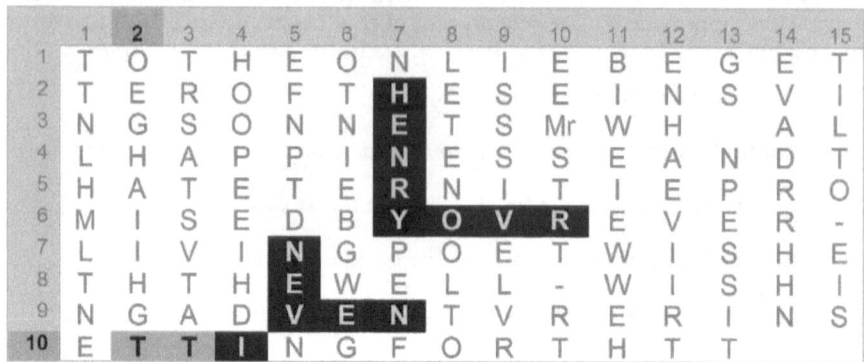

My love is strengthned though more weake in seeming
I love not lesse, thogh lesse the show appeare,
That love is marchandiz'd, whose ritch esteeming,
The owners ***tongue*** *doth* ***publish*** *every where.*
Our love was new, and then but in the spring,
When I was wont to greet it with my laies,
As ***Philomell*** *in summers front doth sing,*
And stops ***his*** *pipe in growth of riper daies:*
Not that the ***summer*** *is lesse pleasant now*
Than when her ***mournefull himns*** *did* ***hush the night,***
But that wild musick burthens every bow,
And sweets growne common loose their deare delight.
Therefore like her, ***I some-time hold my tongue****:*
Because I would not ***dull*** *you with my songe.*

---

[24] Arguably the mapping should be to 103 to allow *TT* to be read right-to-left as in *ITT*. However, 103 is reserved for *Mr.* discussed later.

This sonnet invokes the myth of Philomel, the story at the heart of *Titus Andronicus.* Philomel (the nightingale) is raped by a King who cuts out her tongue to silence her. Imprisoned, she alerts her sister via a **code** (see *GAD* pp. 132–3).

In Ovid's retelling of the Philomel myth, Philomel's tongue writhes on the ground as if trying to speak. The seemingly callous reference to Philomel's tongue being cut out (lines 4 and 13) may be clearer in the context of a writer who is silenced. We propose that, like Philomel, Neville is imprisoned and silenced and, like Philomel, he communicates via a **code**.

We propose *TT* means *count twenty-two letters.*[25] This theory arose when we saw that there are twenty-two characters between the two fragments *NEVI* and *LLE*. There is a certain symmetry in that the conspicuous initials *TT* in the dedication may also have been intended to direct the reader to the 22nd letter in the dedication – the *H* of *HENRY.* This is the most rewarding starting point for decryption as *HENRY* is apparent as soon as the Dedication is set in 15 columns.

(Notes on *TT* at coordinates 15-1 are presented in Chapter 6 and above, pp. 138–41.)

4 This may be the ***tongue*** of the writer that ***publishes***.
7 ***Philomel*** is raped by a monarch who cuts out her tongue. Imprisoned, she alerts her sister via a coded message.
8 ***His*** allows the female *Philomel* to be a man also.
9 ***summer*** may be a pseudonym for Neville.
10 ***mournful hymns*** = perhaps *mournful hims* – "thugs", perhaps "prison guards".
hush the night = perhaps *silence the* ***knight***
13 The image of the poet *"holding"* his severed ***tongue*** is a vivid declaration that he has been silenced.
14 To ***dull*** a knife is to blunt it.

[25] The story of Philomel the mythical ***coder*** is re-told in *Titus Andronicus.* In this play the ***code*** is reconceived as Horace's Ode ***1.22***, and it is inscribed using a ***gad***. In the dedication grid the ***code*** is ***TT*** meaning ***22*** and may also be seen to have been written with a ***gad,*** being the arrow head of ***NEVs*** adjacent to the word ***GAD*** (see pp. 132–3).

Sonnet 108 - *Hyphen*

The *hyphen* which links *NEVI* to *LLE* maps to coordinates 10-8; Sonnet 108.

	1	2	3	4	5	6	7	8	9	10	11	12	13	14	15
1	T	O	T	H	E	O	N	L	I	E	B	E	G	E	T
2	T	E	R	O	F	T	H	E	S	E	I	N	S	V	I
3	N	G	S	O	N	N	E	T	S	Mr	W	H		A	L
4	L	H	A	P	P	I	N	E	S	S	E	A	N	D	T
5	H	A	T	E	T	E	R	N	I	T	I	E	P	R	O
6	M	I	S	E	D	B	Y	O	V	R	E	V	E	R	-
7	L	I	V	I	N	G	P	O	E	T	W	I	S	H	E
8	T	H	T	H	E	W	E	L	L	-	W	I	S	H	I
9	N	G	A	D	V	E	N	T	V	R	E	R	I	N	S
10	E	T	T	I	N	G	F	O	R	T	H	T	T		

***What's in the brain**, that **ink** may **character**,*
*Which hath not **figur'd** to thee my true spirit?*
***What's new to speak,** what now to register,*
That may express my love, or thy dear merit?
***Nothing, sweet boy**; but yet, like prayers divine,*
I must each day say o'er the very same;
Counting no old thing old, thou mine, I thine,
*Even as when first I hallow'd **thy fair name**.*
So that eternal love in love's fresh case,
Weighs not the dust and injury of age,
Nor gives to necessary wrinkles place,
But makes antiquity for aye his page;
Finding the first conceit of love there bred,
Where time and outward form would show it dead.

Unlike all the other mappings, a hyphen is not a letter of the alphabet, nevertheless Sonnet 108 seems to acknowledge this in its opening lines:

What's in the brain that ink may character,
Which hath not figured to thee my true spirit?

Booth notes that "The coincidence of *figured* and *charactered* can activate a gentle and incidental play on their common denominator in nouns meaning "a letter of the alphabet".[26] We note that sonnet 115 which maps sequentially to this hyphen begins *Those lines that I before have writ do lie.* Hyphens could be described playfully as *lines* that are horizontal and so *lie.*

1 ***character*** Both *ink* and *character* refer explicitly to writing.

2 ***figured*** referring to an alphabetical character. See Booth's note above.

3 ***What's in the brain*** and ***what's new to speak*** may both suggest the absurdity of a mapping to a non-alphabetic character.

5 The answer to the two opening questions is ***Nothing***. A **hyphen** was frequently used to representing a null value, a zero, i.e. ***nothing***. ***sweet boy*** If, as in sonnet 1–17, the fair youth is Neville's eldest son,[27] who also became Sir Henry Neville, the following lines become clearer.

8 In this case, ***thy fair name*** would also be *Sir Henry Neville,* and the remaining lines describe the renewing nature of succession.

---

[26] Booth, *Shakespeare's Sonnets*, p. 348.
[27] See p. 48.

Sonnet 89 – *LLE*

***L**LE* maps to coordinates 8-9 (y, x) because *NEVILLE* is reversed; Sonnet 89.

	1	2	3	4	5	6	7	8	9	10	11	12	13	14	15
1	T	O	T	H	E	O	N	L	I	E	B	E	G	E	T
2	T	E	R	O	F	T	H	E	S	E	I	N	S	V	I
3	N	G	S	O	N	N	E	T	S	Mr	W	H		A	L
4	L	H	A	P	P	I	N	E	S	S	E	A	N	D	T
5	H	A	T	E	T	E	R	N	I	T	I	E	P	R	O
6	M	I	S	E	D	B	Y	O	V	R	E	V	E	R	-
7	L	I	V	I	N	G	P	O	E	T	W	I	S	H	E
8	T	H	T	H	E	W	E	L	L	-	W	I	S	H	I
9	N	G	A	D	V	E	N	T	V	R	E	R	I	N	S
10	E	T	T	I	N	G	F	O	R	T	H	T	T		

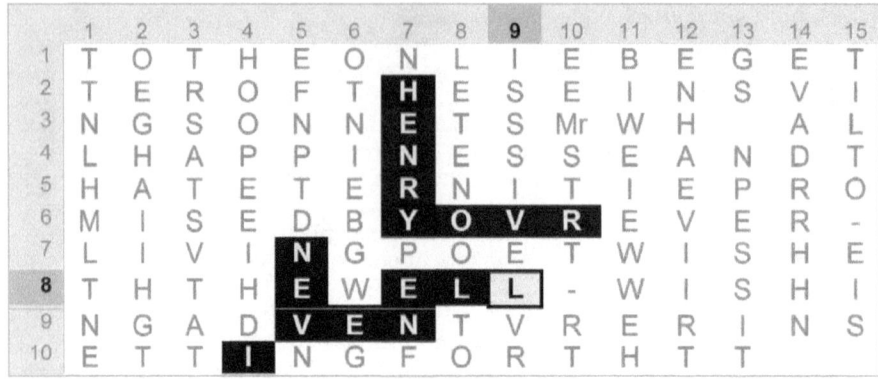

*Say that thou didst forsake me for some **falt**,*
And I will comment upon that offence,
Speake of my lamenesse, and I straight will halt:
Against thy reasons making no defence.
*Thou canst not (love) **disgrace me halfe so ill**,*
To set a forme upon desired change,
*As **ile my selfe disgrace**, knowing thy wil,*
*I will **acquaintance strangle**, and **look strange**:*
Be absent from thy walkes and in my tongue,
***Thy sweet beloved name** no more shall dwell,*
*Least I (too much prophane) should do it **wronge:***
*And haplie of our old acquaintance **tell**.*
*For thee, **against my self** ile vow **debate**,*
For I must nere love him whom thou dost hate.

LLE is a fragment that is broken from the stem, *NEVI*. At this point, we might reflect on the challenge facing a poet who seeks to evoke the meaningless fragment *LLE* in a sonnet.

In this sonnet, the author offers to disfigure himself – as indicated by ***disgrace***,[28] so that he will ***look strange***. Possibly he (Nevi-lle) will be broken in half – as suggested by ***half so ill***.

The poet will not say ***thy name*** (line 10), but seems to play on the many spellings of the last syllable of Neville, via *will* (4 instances), *I'll* (2 instances), *ill,* and *ell*. There were several variations on the ending of *Neville* used by the Neville family and by Neville himself, e.g. Nevell, Newell, Newil, Nevile, Nevill, Nevil, and of course Neville.

This faultiness of the spellings may be reinforced by ***falt*** in line 1 and the inverted acrostic *FALT,* lines 10–13.

1 ***fault*** See acrostic ***falt*** in lines 10–13 below.

5 ***Disgrace*** means *disfigure.*
Possibly, "*disfigure me so that I am in two halves*"; one *half* is "*ill*".

7 *I'll disfigure myself* – perhaps disfigure his *name* – so that the poet is in two pieces.

8 ***Acquaintance strangle*** continues the violent dis-figuration image.
look strange "be estranged", but also "appear strange", as does *NEVI-LLE.*

10 We propose that ***thy name*** means *the name in question, NEVILLE,* rather than the name of the addressee.

13 ***Against my self*** extends the image of a poet in two halves.
Debate means *battle* as in the preceding violence.

[28] Booth, *Shakespeare's Sonnets*, p. 293. "***disgrace*** (1) disfigure, deprive of beauty.

Sonnet 55 – *TERN.IT.OVRE*

***T**ERN.IT.OVRE* maps to coordinates 5-5, Sonnet 55.

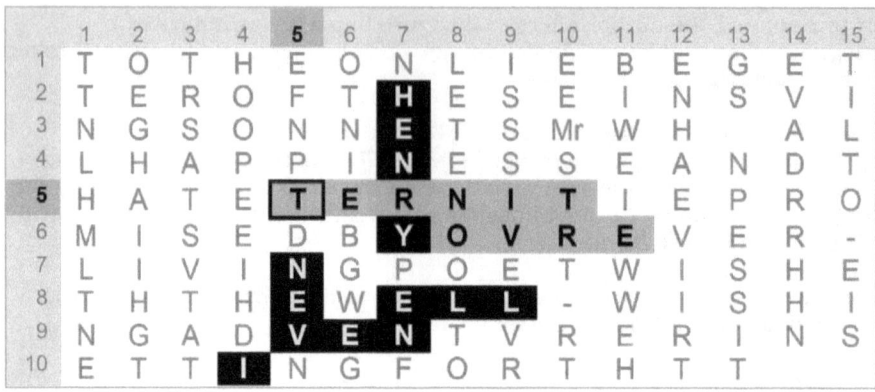

	1	2	3	4	5	6	7	8	9	10	11	12	13	14	15
1	T	O	T	H	E	O	N	L	I	E	B	E	G	E	T
2	T	E	R	O	F	T	H	E	S	E	I	N	S	V	I
3	N	G	S	O	N	N	E	T	S	Mr	W	H		A	L
4	L	H	A	P	P	I	N	E	S	S	E	A	N	D	T
5	H	A	T	E	T	E	R	N	I	T	I	E	P	R	O
6	M	I	S	E	D	B	Y	O	V	R	E	V	E	R	-
7	L	I	V	I	N	G	P	O	E	T	W	I	S	H	E
8	T	H	T	H	E	W	E	L	L	-	W	I	S	H	I
9	N	G	A	D	V	E	N	T	V	R	E	R	I	N	S
10	E	T	T	I	N	G	F	O	R	T	H	T	T		

Not marble, nor the guilded monument,
Of Princes shall out-live ***this powrefull rime****,*
But you shall shine more bright in these contents,
Then unswept stone, besmeered with sluttish time.
When wastefull warre shall statues ***over-turne****,*
And broiles roote out the workes of masonry,
Nor Mars his sword, nor warres quick fire shall burne:
The living record of your memory.
Gainst death, and all oblivious emnity
Shall you pace forth, your praise shall still finde room,
Even in the eyes of all posterity
That weare this world out to the ending doome.
So til the judgement that ***your selfe arise****,*
You live in this, and dwell in lovers eies.

We propose that *TERN IT OVRE* is a direction to reverse the letters ***IT*** to generate the nonce word *MRSIR.*

While there are 10 occurrences of the word *turn* in the sonnets, Sonnet 55 has the only instance of a rhyme on ***turn***, and the only instance of a pairing of ***turn*** with ***over*** (line 5).

In this sonnet the poet seeks to make the addressee *shine more brightly.* We propose that this is consistent with the intention of *TERN (IT) OVRE* – a transposition that creates the knight's title *SIR.*

The couplet also seems to invoke the knighting ceremony.

2 ***This powerful rhyme*** This sonnet literally ***rhymes*** on ***turn*** (line 5).
5 ***over-turn*** This is the only pairing of *turn* and *over.*
13 ***Arise*** occurs in the ceremony at which a knight is created:
Arise Sir ...

Sonnet 95 – *IT*

IT maps to coordinates 9-5 (x, y), Sonnet 95.

	1	2	3	4	5	6	7	8	**9**	10	11	12	13	14	15
1	T	O	T	H	E	O	N	L	I	E	B	E	G	E	T
2	T	E	R	O	F	T	**H**	E	S	E	I	N	S	V	I
3	N	G	S	O	N	N	**E**	T	S	Mr	W	H		A	L
4	L	H	A	P	P	I	**N**	E	S	S	E	A	N	D	T
5	H	A	T	E	**T**	**E**	**R**	**N**	**I**	**T**	I	E	P	R	O
6	M	I	S	E	D	B	**Y**	**O**	**V**	**R**	**E**	V	E	R	-
7	L	I	V	I	**N**	G	P	O	E	T	W	I	S	H	E
8	T	H	T	H	**E**	W	**E**	**L**	**L**	-	W	I	S	H	I
9	N	G	A	D	**V**	**E**	**N**	T	V	R	E	R	I	N	S
10	E	T	T	**I**	N	G	F	O	R	T	H	T	T		

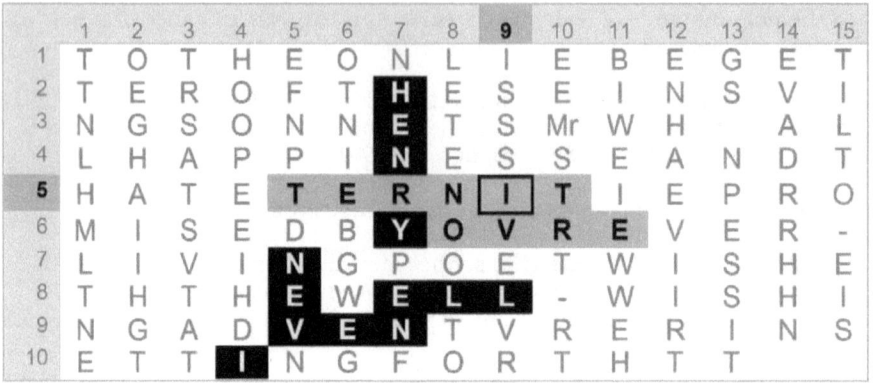

How sweet and lovely dost thou make the shame,
Which like a canker in the fragrant Rose,
  Dot*h* ***spot*** *the beautie of thy budding name?*
  O*h in what sweets doest thou thy sins inclose!*
  T*hat tongue that tells the story of thy daies,*
(Making lascivious comments on thy sport)
Cannot dispraise, but in a kinde of praise,
Naming thy name*, blesses an ill report.*
Oh what a mansion have those vices got,
Which for their habitation chose out thee,
Where beauties vaile ***dot****h cover every* ***blot****,*
And all ***things turnes*** *to faire, that* ***eies*** *can see****!***
  Take heed (deare heart) of this large priviledge,
  The hardest knife ill vs'd ***dot****h lose his edge.*

Line 12 of this sonnet seems to encapsulate the process whereby reversing the letters *IT* of *TERN(IT)OVER,* creates the title *SIR*, and ***all things turns to fair that eyes*** (i's) ***can see!***

Since, "i" is the only dotted letter in the Elizabethan alphabet, ***spot*** and ***blot*** may suggest the "i" of *TERN (IT) OVER.*

The word ***dot*** occurs four times and may also buttress the dotted ***i***. However, *dot* is not found elsewhere in Shakespeare. At the time the Sonnets were published, *dot* referred to the head of a pimple or boil.

3 ***dot***, ***spot, dot*** (acrostic) may all relate to the letter ***i***.
8 ***Naming thy name***
11 ***dot, blot***
12 Both ***thing*** and ***it*** are neutral pronouns. The ***thing*** that is being ***turned*** is ***IT***, and particularly the letter ***I,*** as in ***eyes can see!*** The exclamation mark is in the original. Indeed, given its placement, this exclamation mark may be intended as an inverted "i".
14 ***dot***

Sonnet 103 – *MrSIR*

***Mr**SIR* maps to coordinates 10-3 (x, y), Sonnet 103.

	1	2	3	4	5	6	7	8	9	**10**	11	12	13	14	15
1	T	O	T	H	E	O	N	L	I	E	B	E	G	E	T
2	T	E	R	O	F	T	**H**	E	S	E	I	N	S	V	I
3	N	G	S	O	N	N	**E**	T	S	**Mr**	W	H		A	L
4	L	H	A	P	P	I	**N**	E	S	**S**	E	A	N	D	T
5	H	A	T	E	**T**	**E**	**R**	**N**	**T**	**I**	I	E	P	R	O
6	M	I	S	E	D	B	**Y**	**O**	**V**	**R**	**E**	V	E	R	-
7	L	I	V	I	**N**	G	P	O	E	T	W	I	S	H	E
8	T	H	T	H	**E**	W	**E**	**L**	**L**	-	W	I	S	H	I
9	N	G	A	D	**V**	**E**	**N**	T	V	R	E	R	I	N	S
10	E	T	T	**I**	N	G	F	O	R	T	H	T	T		

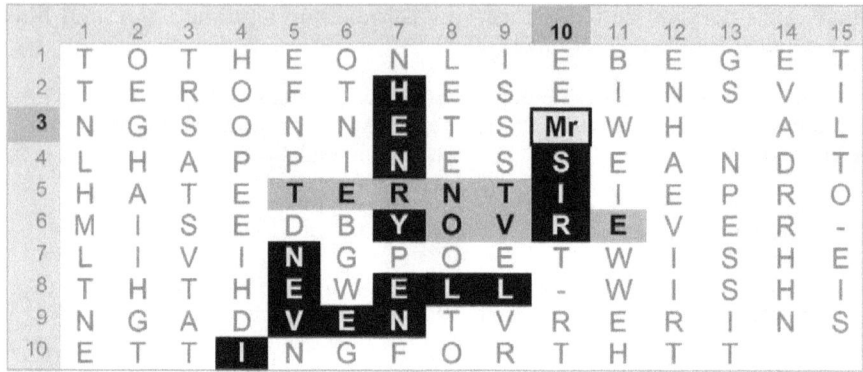

***Alack** what **pouerty** my Muse brings forth,*
That having such a skope to show her pride,
*The argument all bare is of **more** worth*
Then when it had my added praise beside.
*Oh blame me not if I no **more** can write!*
*Look in your **glasse** and there appears a face,*
*That over-goes **my blunt invention** quite,*
***Dulling my lines**, and doing me **disgrace**.*
*Were **it** not sinfull then striving **to mend**,*
***To marre the subject** that before was well,*
For to no other passe my verses tend,
*Then of your graces and **your gifts** to tell.*
*And **more**, much **more** then i**n my verse** can sit,*
Your own glasse** shows you **when you look in it.

Sonnet 103 deals with impoverishment. We propose that it may be read to refer to the stripping of a title (*SIR*) and the comic invention *MrSIR*. *Poverty* occurs only in this sonnet and Sonnet 40 which maps sequentially to *MrSIR*.

This sonnet emphasises ***more*** (four instances).[29] *More* may have some phonetic similarity to the spelling of *Mr*, and it draws attention to ***mar*** in line 10, which provides a closer comic echo of *Mr* or ***M.R.*** The cryptic reinforcement of *MrSIR* is not revealed until the last line, which directs the reader to reverse *I* and *T:*

> *Your own glass* (mirror)*shows you when you look in it* (IT).

A mirror reverses *IT*.

We propose that Queen Elizabeth is central to the sonnets. Elizabeth sentenced Neville to life imprisonment, stripped him of his offices and knighthood and fined him 10,000 pounds.

1 ***Alack*** Booth notes – *The context of the words that follow generates a delayed pun on "a lack".*[30] The pun is accentuated by the typography (as below). We propose this refers to the "lack" of Neville's title (Sir).

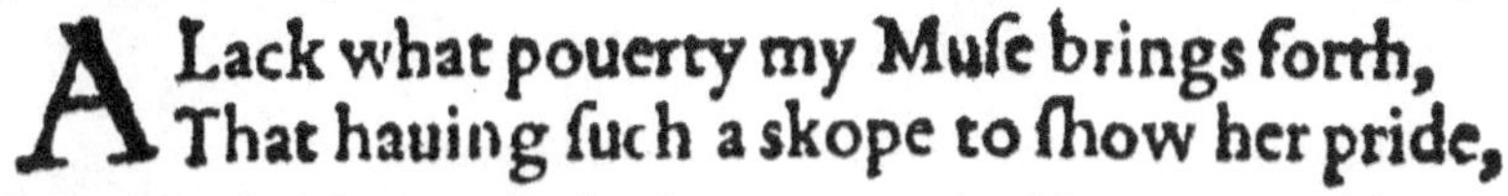

A Lack what pouerty my Mufe brings forth,
That hauing fuch a skope to fhow her pride,

Poverty only occurs twice in the sonnets – in this sonnet and in Sonnet 40, which also maps sequentially to this cell.

3 ***More*** (see above).

5 ***More***

6 ***glass*** a mirror (see line 14).

7 ***My blunt invention*** may refer to the invented word ***MrSIR***.

8 ***My lines*** may be *my lineage*; dulled. He and his heirs are ***dis-graced*** as he is stripped of his title (see line 12 also).

9 ***it*** See line 14. **To mend** is to correct morally (e.g. by imprisonment and changing Neville's title from Sir to Mr).

10 ***To mar*** Perhaps *To M.R. the subject* – To make a ***Mr.*** out of Queen Elizabeth's ***subject*** who was formerly SIR.

12 The most conspicuous **gift** that Neville received from Queen Elizabeth was his knighthood – the title *SIR*.

13 ***More***, ***More***

14 ***your own glass shows you when you look in it***
IT is a very weak word on which to end a Sonnet. However, a *glass* (a mirror) will reverse ***IT*** (see also line 6).

---

[29] Noted by Vendler. See Vendler, H, *The Art of Shakespeare's Sonnets, Volume 1* (Harvard University Press, Cambridge, Mass, 1997), p. 437.
[30] Booth, p. 331.

Sonnet 77 - *POET/PEN*

The Intersection of ***POET*** and ***PEN*** maps to coordinates 7-7, Sonnet 77.

	1	2	3	4	5	6	**7**	8	9	10	11	12	13	14	15
1	T	O	T	H	E	O	N	L	I	E	B	E	G	E	T
2	T	E	R	O	F	T	H	E	S	E	I	N	S	V	I
3	N	G	S	O	N	N	E	T	S	Mr	W	H		A	L
4	L	H	A	P	P	I	N	E	S	S	E	A	N	D	T
5	H	A	T	E	T	E	R	N	T	I	I	E	P	R	O
6	M	I	S	E	D	B	Y	O	V	R	E	V	E	R	-
7	L	I	V	I	N	G	P	O	E	T	W	I	S	H	E
8	T	H	T	H	E	W	E	L	L	-	W	I	S	H	I
9	N	G	A	D	V	E	N	T	V	R	E	R	I	N	S
10	E	T	T	I	N	G	F	O	R	T	H	T	T		

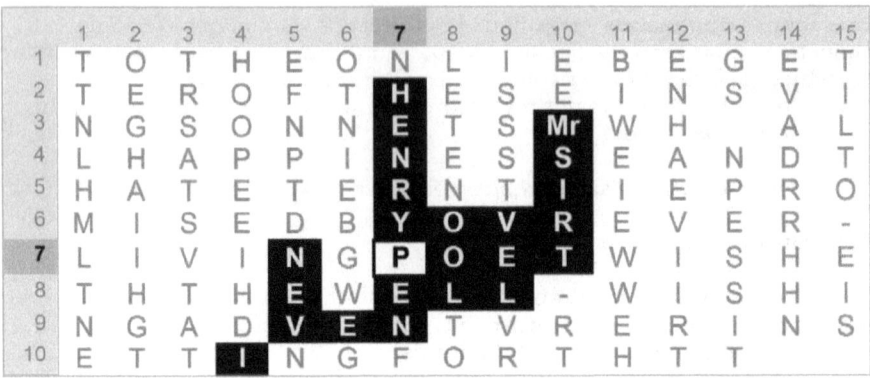

Thy glasse will shew thee how thy beauties were,
Thy dyall how thy pretious mynuits waste,
The vacant leaves thy mindes imprint will ***beare,***
And of ***this booke****, this* ***learning*** *maist* ***thou taste.***
The wrinckles which thy glasse will truly show,
Of ***mouthed graves*** *will give thee memorie,*
Thou by thy dyals shady stealth maist know,
Times theevish progresse to eternitie.
Looke what thy memorie cannot containe,
Commit to these waste blacks, and thou shalt finde
Those ***children*** *nursed,* ***deliverd from thy braine,***
To take a new acquaintance of thy minde.
These ***offices****, so* ***oft*** *as thou wilt looke,*
Shall ***profit*** *thee and much inrich* ***thy booke****.*

At the centre of the series of 154 sonnets, Sonnet 77 seems to urge the reader either to write poetry, or to read poetry closely. POET/PEN may also be read as an imperative urging the reader to write. No other sonnet is so concerned with the poet's process.

Note. In addition to this mapping of *POET*, a very explicit mapping to the phrase *LIVING.POET* is discussed on pages 184–5.

Ben Jonson's Epigram 77 conceals the identity of the addressee and seems to echo Sonnet 77.

> *To one that desired me* ***not to name him***
>
> *Be* ***safe****, nor fear thy self so good a* ***fame****,*
> *That,* ***any way, my book*** *should* ***speak thy name***
> *For, if thou shame, rank'd with my friends, to go,*
> *I am more ashamed to have thee thought my foe.*

We propose that in Epigram 77 Jonson is referring to Sonnet 77, and that Neville did choose safety and shunned ***fame.*** Ben Jonson knew and admired Sir Henry Neville (see also Jonson's epigram *To Sir Henry Nevil*, Epigram 109 in Chapter 1).

John Casson suggests that "anyway" in line 2 of Jonson's *Epigram 77* may hint at N-E-V.[31] If it does indeed hint at Neville this reversal would add a fillip of wit to Jonson's brief verse which professes discretion. Indeed this disclosure is not unlike Jonson's *Epigram 13 To Dr Empiric* with the acrostic WOLF that we cited in Chapter 3.

3 See notes on poems as children, below and in Sonnet 97.

4 ***this book*** (see Jonson's *Epigram 77* above and line 14). The poet emphasises the learning in ***this book***.
The learning that one ***tastes*** is common to both *Titus Andronicus* and to the Philomel myth, where dead children are eaten as a lesson.

6 ***Mouthed graves*** intensifies the idea of eating/tasting in line 4 (indeed of eating death). It may also refer to *whispered* or *coded engravings* as found in *Titus Andronicus.*

11 Poems as ***children*** *of the* ***brain*** is a common early-modern conceit which revives the idea of ***children*** eaten.

13 ***offices***, ***oft***, ***profit*** This emphasis on the sound ***off*** links Sonnet 77 to 78, which begins ***So oft have I***... (discussed pp. 184–5)

14 ***thy book*** Jonson refers to ***my book***.

[31] Casson, J., "A new interpretation of Epigram 77 by Ben Jonson", *Journal of Neville Studies* Vol. 1, No. 1, p. 31 (2008).

Sonnet 78 – *POET/PEN (continued)*

Sonnet 78 follows on from Sonnet 77 to form a longer poem.

	1	2	3	4	5	6	7	8	9	10	11	12	13	14	15
1	T	O	T	H	E	O	N	L	I	E	B	E	G	E	T
2	T	E	R	O	F	T	H	E	S	E	I	N	S	V	I
3	N	G	S	O	N	N	E	T	S	Mr	W	H		A	L
4	L	H	A	P	P	I	N	E	S	S	E	A	N	D	T
5	H	A	T	E	T	E	R	N	T	I	I	E	P	R	O
6	M	I	S	E	D	B	Y	O	V	R	E	V	E	R	-
7	L	I	V	I	N	G	P	O	E	T	W	I	S	H	E
8	T	H	T	H	E	W	E	L	L	-	W	I	S	H	I
9	N	G	A	D	V	E	N	T	V	R	E	R	I	N	S
10	E	T	T	I	N	G	F	O	R	T	H	T	T		

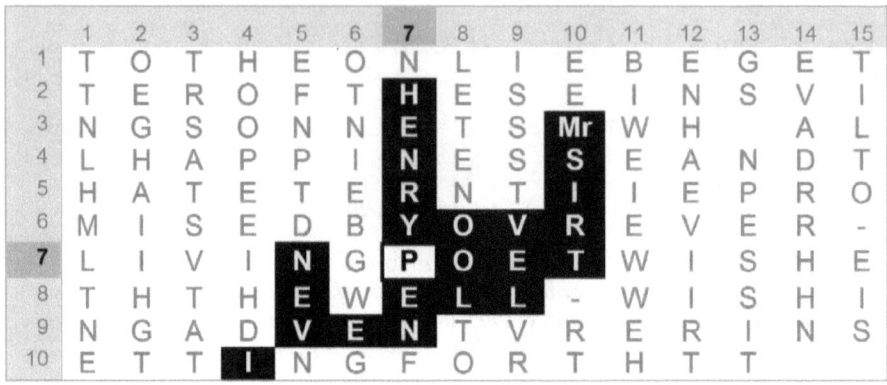

So ***oft*** *have I invok'd thee for my muse*
And found such faire assistance in my verse,
As every Alien ***pen*** *hath got my use,*
And under thee their ***poesie*** *disperse.*
Thine eyes, that taught the dumbe on high to sing,
And heavie ignorance ***aloft to flie,***
Have ***added fethers to the learneds wing,***
And given grace a double majestie.
Yet be most proud of that which I compile,
Whose influence is thine, and borne of thee,
In others workes thou doost but ***mend the stile,***
And Art with thy sweete graces graced be.
But thou art all my art, and doost advance
As ***high as learning****, my rude ignorance.*

Sonnet 78 contains complex wordplay on *PEN* which means both ***feather*** and ***stylus*** (for writing). This wordplay has long been regarded as inexplicable or subconscious. However, the imagery relates directly to the decrypted word *PEN.*

At a loss to account for the clarity of the imagery and its apparent irrelevance to the surface meaning of the sonnet, Booth suggests that while the wordplay is real, it may be unconscious on the part of the author.[32]

We propose that this wordplay is intentional.

1 ***Oft*** links the couplet of Sonnet 77 to Sonnet 78.
3 The old word ***PEN*** was still in use, meaning *feather.*
4 ***Poesy*** echoes *POET.*
6 ***Aloft to fly*** is the central image of Sonnet 78 and repeats the "oft" that links Sonnets 77 and 78.
7 ***Adding feathers*** to lengthen the wings of a captive bird of prey is a specialist practice in falconry to enable the bird to fly higher. This technique was known as *Imping.*
11 ***Stile*** means both ***style*** and ***stylus*** or ***writing instrument*** such as a *Feather, i.e.* a *PEN.* So that, ***mend the stile*** means all of: improve the writing; sharpen the pen; and "fix the feather", which re-states the obscure *imping* image above.

[32] Booth writes in detail on this baffling ideational wordplay. Booth, *Shakespeare's Sonnets*, p. 269.

Sonnet 33 – *SONNETS*

***S**ONNETS* maps to coordinates 3-3, and sequentially to the 33rd letter of the Dedication, Sonnet 33.

	1	2	3	4	5	6	7	8	9	10	11	12	13	14	15
1	T	O	T	H	E	O	N	L	I	E	B	E	G	E	T
2	T	E	R	O	F	T	H	E	S	E	I	N	S	V	I
3	N	G	S	O	N	N	E	T	S	Mr	W	H		A	L
4	L	H	A	P	P	I	N	E	S	S	E	A	N	D	T
5	H	A	T	E	T	E	R	N	T	I	I	E	P	R	O
6	M	I	S	E	D	B	Y	O	V	R	E	V	E	R	-
7	L	I	V	I	N	G	P	O	E	T	W	I	S	H	E
8	T	H	T	H	E	W	E	L	L	-	W	I	S	H	I
9	N	G	A	D	V	E	N	T	V	R	E	R	I	N	S
10	E	T	T	I	N	G	F	O	R	T	H	T	T		

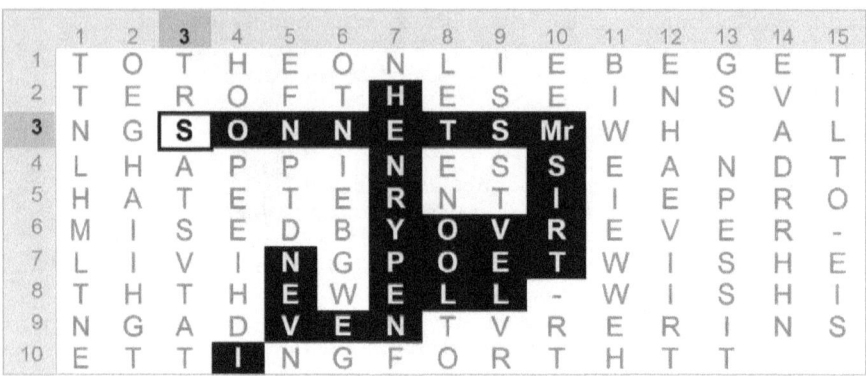

Full many a glorious morning have I seene,
Flatter the mountaine tops with ***soveraine eie****,*
Kissing with ***golden face*** *the meddowes greene;*
Guilding *pale streams with heavenly alcumy:*
Anon permit the basest cloudes to ride,
With ougly rack on his ***celestiall face****,*
And from the for-lorne world ***his visage*** *hide*
Stealing unseene to west with this disgrace:
Even so ***my Sunne*** *one early morne did shine,*
With all triumphant splendour on my brow,
But out alack, he was but one hour mine,
The region cloude hath mask'd him from me now.
Yet him for this, my love no whit disdaineth,
Suns *of the world may staine, when heavens* ***sun*** *staineth.*

Sonnet 33 deals with the idea of a "son", but the word "son" or "sonne" is never used.[33] This sonnet invokes the loss of the warmth and beauty of the sun as a metaphor for the loss of a living son. The word "son" is evoked by its homophone *sun.*

***S**ONNETS* is the only word that maps via both (x, y) and (y, x) coordinates as well as sequentially since it sits at the 33rd letter of the dedication.

Note. In 1599, Neville apologised for the brevity of his diplomatic dispatch:

*...by reason of some domestical misfortune in the loss of my **son** lately born.*

2 ***(sun)***
3 ***(sun)***
4 ***(sun)***
6 ***(sun)***
7 ***(sun)***
9 ***Sun***
14 ***Sun, sun***

[33] In Sonnets 7 and 41 *son* is spelt "sonne". In Sonnet 13 it is spelt "son".

Appendix 2: Sonnets supporting additional text

In Chapter 5 and in Appendix 1 we examined possible alignments between sonnets and encrypted words in the Dedication grid. However, we have noted that there are many other words in the Dedication that are generated vertically, horizontally and diagonally.

The generation of new words is not remarkable in itself, but numerical and thematic alignments may be. As isolated instances, each association of a word with a sonnet does not prove intent on the part of the author, since each Sonnet contains myriad images and poetic devices within its 140 syllables. However, if the associations are strong and there are many of them we propose that a case should be examined for intentionality.
To evaluate each alignment of a word to a sonnet, we have adapted the rules of thumb we applied to the primary encrypted text. In a few instances no particular relationship is discernible, for example *HATE* in row 5, and *HOOP* in column 4. However, we have observed that in the great majority of instances one or more of the following phenomena can be observed:

- the word itself is emphasised in the sonnet

- the meaning of the word is central to the meaning of the sonnet

- there is wordplay on the word

Altogether, we have observed alignments that we find persuasive in more than 45 sonnets. Of these, we believe we can point to several cases where the sonnet not only evokes the letter or word, but is unique among the 154 sonnets because its content most closely aligns with the letter or word. Ultimately, readers will decide for themselves how strong or pleasing any particular alignment may be. Perhaps the most important point is that the alignments, if they were designed by the author of the sonnets, are more likely to reflect artistic rather than mechanistic choices.

In the first part of this Appendix we have detailed those sonnets that seem to be referenced by *Polybian coordinates* in the Dedication Table. In the second part we have detailed those sonnets that seem to be referenced by *sequential position* (i.e. in the 15-column table, where the top left cell is position 1, and the bottom right hand cell is position 150).

Sonnets supporting additional text

Polybian coordinates

Sequential mapping

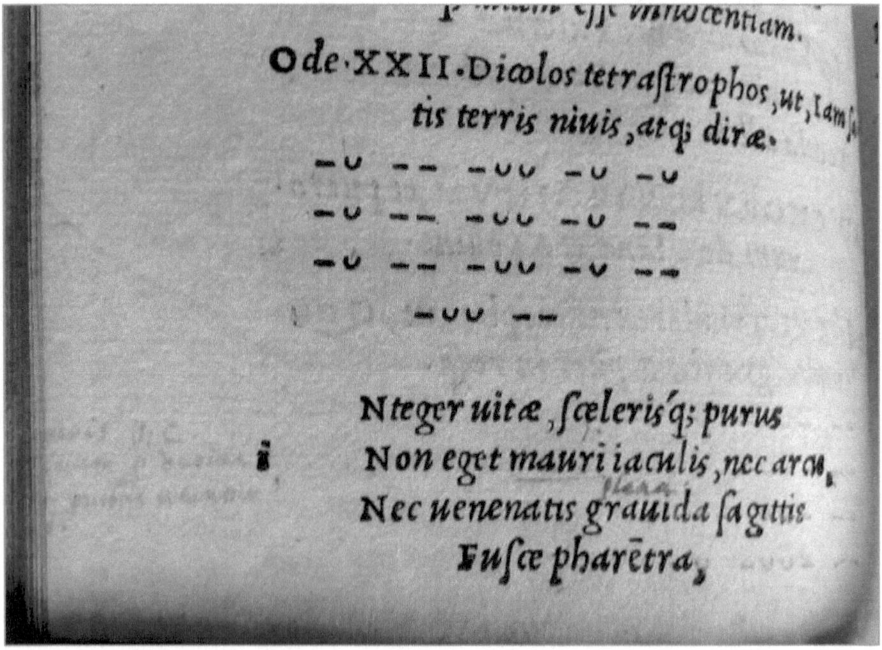

innocentiam.

Ode.XXII.Dicolos tetraſtrophos,ut,Iam
tis terris niuis,atq; diræ.

– ∪ – – – ∪ ∪ – ∪ – ∪
– ∪ – – – ∪ ∪ – ∪ – –
– ∪ – – – ∪ ∪ – ∪ – –
– ∪ ∪ – –

Nteger uitæ,ſceleris'q; purus
Non eget mauri iaculis,nec arcu,
Nec uenenatis grauida ſagittis
Fuſce pharētra,

Neville's annotated copy of Horace's *Carmina* (Odes) Book 1.
Private collection. Photograph courtesy of John Casson[1]

This is the first stanza of Ode 22. Remarkably, this edition also sets out the Sapphic metre of 38 beats which we propose inspired the numbering of Sonnet 38 (a sonnet evoking the poet Sappho and numbers) as discussed below.

[1] Casson and Rubinstein, *Sir Henry Neville was Shakespeare*, p. 73.

Coordinate Mappings

In the following pages we detail those sonnets that seem to be referenced by *Polybian coordinates*[2] in the Dedication Table.

[2] This system of (x, y) co-ordinates is commonly known as Cartesian co-ordinates, in honour of Rene Descartes who formalised it in 1637, but as described in Chapter 3, it was known to Polybius some 1700 years previously.

Sonnet 38 – *TEN/TEN*

TEN maps to (y, x) coordinates 3-8 since the word is reversed, and sequentially to 38, being the 38th character; Sonnet 38.

	1	2	3	4	5	6	7	**8**	9	10	11	12	13	14	15
1	T	O	T	H	E	O	N	L	I	E	B	E	G	E	T
2	T	E	R	O	F	T	H	E	S	E	I	N	S	V	I
3	N	G	S	O	N	**N**	**E**	**T**	S	Mr	W	H		A	L
4	L	H	A	P	P	I	N	**E**	S	S	E	A	N	D	T
5	H	A	T	E	T	E	R	**N**	I	T	I	E	P	R	O
6	M	I	S	E	D	B	Y	O	V	R	E	V	E	R	-
7	L	I	V	I	N	G	P	O	E	T	W	I	S	H	E
8	T	H	T	H	E	W	E	L	L	-	W	I	S	H	I
9	N	G	A	D	V	E	N	T	V	R	E	R	I	N	S
10	E	T	T	I	N	G	F	O	R	T	H	T	T		

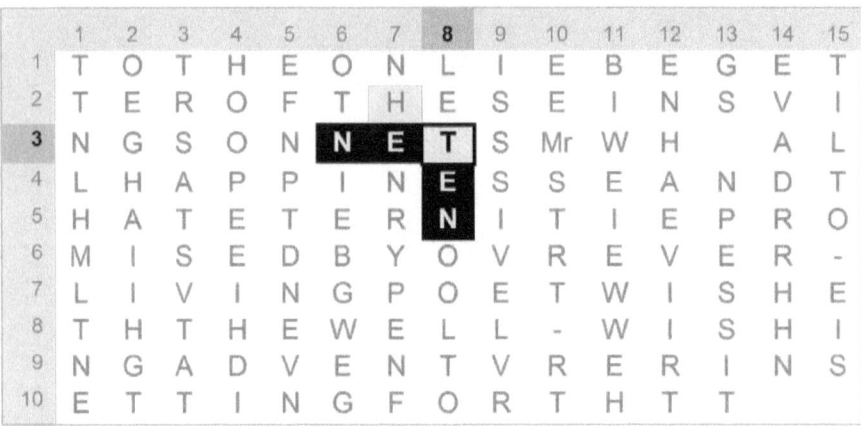

*How can my **Muse** want subject **to** invent,*
*While thou dost breath that poor'st in**to** my verse,*
*Thine owne sweet argument, **to** excellent,*
*For every vulgar paper **to** rehearse:*
*Oh give thy selfe the thanks if **ought** in me,*
Worthy perusal stand against thy sight,
*For who's so dumbe that cannot write **to** thee,*
When thou thyselfe doth give invention light?
*Be thou the **tenth Muse, ten times** more in worth*
*Then those old **nine** which **rimers invocate**,*
*And he that **calls on thee**, let him bring **forth***
Eternal numbers to out-live long date.
*If my **slight Muse** doe please these curious daies,*
The paine be mine, but thine shal be the praise.

Sonnet 38 concerns the ***tenth muse*** and maps to the intersection of two *TEN*s. Sappho of Lesbos was named "*the tenth muse*" by Plato, and was an enormously influential poet famous for her *Sapphic stanza*, consisting of 38 beats which we propose is reflected in the numbering of this sonnet.

Probably the most famous instance of this form is Horace's Ode 1.22 which we propose is central to the dedication code (image on page 162).

Supporting this attention to ***eternal numbers*** (line 12), we note that Sonnet 38 contains a ***nine*** and two ***tens*** among several possible numerical puns: *to* (=2), *forth* (=4); *ought* (=0); and possibly *invocate* (=8).

Sappho of Lesbos is famous for her erotic poetry which is addressed to both men and women, hence the 19th century coinage of the word *lesbian*. The two *TEN*s may also direct the reader to Sonnet 20 which concerns uncertain gender identity.

1 ***Muse.*** Sappho was the ***tenth muse*** (see note above and line 9).
2 ***To*** (=2) is emphasised via repetition and placement in lines 1-4, 7, 12.
5 ***ought*** = a cipher, zero.
9 ***tenth Muse*** Sappho was the 10th Muse.
ten times Sonnet 38 is at the intersection of two TENs.
10 **rimers:** see Sonnet 134 (Appendix 3, page 206).
11 ***forth***. *"Who now **calls on thee**, NEVIL, is a **Muse**..."* See Ben Jonson's Jonson's epigram *To Sir Henry Nevil*, in Chapter 1.
12 ***Eternal numbers to out-live long date*** perfectly encapsulates the immortality of an ancient verse form, such as the Sapphic stanza. **Numbers** in the context of poetry refers directly to the syllables within the lines. In the Sapphic stanza, the number of syllables is 38.
13 George Carleton also refers to the *slight muse*, albeit in Latin, when writing of Sir Henry Neville. See Chapter 1.

Sonnet 77 - *PEN*

The P of ***PEN*** maps to coordinates 7-7, Sonnet 77.

	1	2	3	4	5	6	**7**	8	9	10	11	12	13	14	15
1	T	O	T	H	E	O	N	L	I	E	B	E	G	E	T
2	T	E	R	O	F	T	H	E	S	E	I	N	S	V	I
3	N	G	S	O	N	N	E	T	S	Mr	W	H		A	L
4	L	H	A	P	P	I	N	E	S	S	E	A	N	D	T
5	H	A	T	E	T	E	R	N	I	T	I	E	P	R	O
6	M	I	S	E	D	B	Y	O	V	R	E	V	E	R	-
7	L	I	V	I	N	G	**P**	O	E	T	W	I	S	H	E
8	T	H	T	H	E	W	**E**	L	L	-	W	I	S	H	I
9	N	G	A	D	V	E	**N**	T	V	R	E	R	I	N	S
10	E	T	T	I	N	G	F	O	R	T	H	T	T		

Thy glasse will shew thee how thy beauties were,
Thy dyall how thy pretious mynuits waste,
***The vacant leaves thy mindes imprint will beare**,*
And of this booke, this learning maist thou taste.
The wrinckles which thy glasse will truly show,
*Of **mouthed graves** will give thee memorie,*
Thou by thy dyals shady stealth maist know,
Times theevish progresse to eternitie.
Looke what thy memorie cannot containe,
***Commit to these waste blacks**, and thou shalt finde*
*Those children nursed, **deliverd from thy braine**,*
To take a new acquaintance of thy minde.
*These **offices**, so **oft** as thou wilt looke,*
*Shall **profit** thee and much **inrich thy booke**.*

Sonnets supporting additional text

In Appendix 1 we examined Sonnet 77 in support of the intersection of *POET* and *PEN.* Sonnet 77 seems to urge the reader to write poetry. Similarly, *POET/PEN* may be read as an imperative to the reader to write.

No other sonnet is so concerned with the writing process of a *poet.*

PEN is comprised of three letters that are each within other decrypted fragments ***P***_OET, LL_***E***_, and_ ***N***_EV._

PEN may be seen to map to coordinates 7-7, 7-8, and 7-9, and so to Sonnets 77, 78 and 79 (detailed below).

3 (write)
6 Possibly, *whispered writing.*
10 *(write)*
11 *(writing)*
13 ***offices, oft, profit*** This emphasis on the sound ***off*** links Sonnet 77 to 78, which begins ***So oft have I...***
14 *(write)*

Sonnet 78 - *PEN/WELL*

The E of *P**E**N* maps to coordinates 7-8, Sonnet 78.

	1	2	3	4	5	6	7	8	9	10	11	12	13	14	15
1	T	O	T	H	E	O	N	L	I	E	B	E	G	E	T
2	T	E	R	O	F	T	H	E	S	E	I	N	S	V	I
3	N	G	S	O	N	N	E	T	S	Mr	W	H		A	L
4	L	H	A	P	P	I	N	E	S	S	E	A	N	D	T
5	H	A	T	E	T	E	R	N	I	T	I	E	P	R	O
6	M	I	S	E	D	B	Y	O	V	R	E	V	E	R	-
7	L	I	V	I	N	G	**P**	O	E	T	W	I	S	H	E
8	T	H	T	H	E	**W**	**E**	**L**	**L**	-	W	I	S	H	I
9	N	G	A	D	V	E	**N**	T	V	R	E	R	I	N	S
10	E	T	T	I	N	G	F	O	R	T	H	T	T		

So oft have I invok'd thee for my muse,
And found such faire assistance in my verse,
As every Alien ***pen*** *hath got my use,*
And under thee their poesie disperse.
Thine eyes, that taught the dumbe on high to sing,
And heavie ignorance ***aloft to flie****,*
Have ***added fethers to the learneds wing****,*
And given grace a double majestie.
Yet be most proud of that which I compile,
Whose influence is thine, and borne of thee,
In others workes thou doost but ***mend the stile****,*
And Art with thy sweete graces graced be.
But thou art all my art, and doost advance
As ***high as learning****, my rude ignorance.*

Sonnet 78 contains complex wordplay on *mending a pen* in which *PEN* means both ***feather*** and ***stylus*** (for writing). This wordplay has long been regarded as inexplicable or subconscious. However, the imagery does relate directly to the decrypted word PEN and the intersecting word WELL, so that ***mend the stile*** (stylus) can be taken to mean *make the pen well.*

At a loss to account for the clarity of the imagery and its apparent irrelevance to the surface meaning of the sonnet, Booth suggests that while the wordplay is real, it may be unconscious on the part of the author.[3] However, the intersection of *PEN* and *WELL* in the decryption seems to provide a logical reference.

3 The old word ***PEN*** was still in use, meaning *feather.*

7 ***Adding feathers*** to lengthen the wings of a captive bird of prey was a specialist practice in falconry to enable the bird to fly higher. This technique was known as "imping".

11 ***Stile*** means both ***style*** and ***stylus*** or ***writing instrument*** such as a feather, i.e. a *PEN.* So that, ***mend the stile*** (fix the pen) re-states the obscure "imping" image above.

[3] Booth writes in detail on this baffling ideational wordplay. Booth, *Shakespeare's Sonnets,* p. 269.

Sonnet 79 – *PEN*

The N of ***PEN*** maps to coordinates 7-9, Sonnet 79.

	1	2	3	4	5	6	7	8	9	10	11	12	13	14	15
1	T	O	T	H	E	O	N	L	I	E	B	E	G	E	T
2	T	E	R	O	F	T	H	E	S	E	I	N	S	V	I
3	N	G	S	O	N	N	E	T	S	Mr	W	H		A	L
4	L	H	A	P	P	I	N	E	S	S	E	A	N	D	T
5	H	A	T	E	T	E	R	N	I	T	I	E	P	R	O
6	M	I	S	E	D	B	Y	O	V	R	E	V	E	R	-
7	L	I	V	I	N	G	**P**	O	E	T	W	I	S	H	E
8	T	H	T	H	E	W	**E**	L	L	-	W	I	S	H	I
9	N	G	A	D	V	E	**N**	T	V	R	E	R	I	N	S
10	E	T	T	I	N	G	F	O	R	T	H	T	T		

Whilst I alone did call upon thy ayde,
My verse alone had all thy gentle grace,
But now my gracious numbers are decayed,
And my sick Muse doth give another place.
I grant (sweet love) ***thy lovely argument***
Deserves the travaile of a worthier ***pen****,*
Yet what of thee ***thy Poet*** *doth invent*
He robs thee of, and payes it thee againe
He lends thee vertue, and he stole that word,
From thy behaviour, beautie doth he give
And found it in thy cheeke: he can afford
No praise to thee, but what in thee doth live.
Then thanke him not, for that which he doth say,
Since what he owes thee, thou thy selfe doth pay.

Sonnet 79 continues the association of *PEN* and *POET*. *PEN* is conspicuous since, together with *argument*, it is the subject of a double entendre.

There are eight other sonnets that use the word ***pen***, and all in the context of writing poetry, but only Sonnet 78 and 79 explicitly refer to *poetry*. [4] Sonnet 78 refers ***poesy*** and Sonnet 79 to ***poet***.

5 ***argument*** = vagina (cf. French *l'argument*)[5]

6 ***pen*** The close association of *Argument* and *Pen* (penis) suggests a bawdy reading.[6]

7 ***Poet***

---

[4] The other sonnets using the word ***pen*** are 16, 19, 32, 81, 84, 85, 100 and 106.

[5] Booth, *Shakespeare's Sonnets*, pp. 196, 273.

[6] Booth suggests a similar potentially bawdy reading of *sweet argument* in Sonnet 38 where it would be the topic of a *vulgar paper* (see p. 164 lines 3–4).

Sonnet 81 – *LIE*

LIE maps to coordinates 8-1, Sonnet 81.

	1	2	3	4	5	6	7	**8**	9	10	11	12	13	14	15
1	T	O	T	H	E	O	N	**L**	**I**	**E**	B	E	G	E	T
2	T	E	R	O	F	T	H	E	S	E	I	N	S	V	I
3	N	G	S	O	N	N	E	T	S	Mr	W	H		A	L
4	L	H	A	P	P	I	N	E	S	S	E	A	N	D	T
5	H	A	T	E	T	E	R	N	I	T	I	E	P	R	O
6	M	I	S	E	D	B	Y	O	V	R	E	V	E	R	-
7	L	I	V	I	N	G	P	O	E	T	W	I	S	H	E
8	T	H	T	H	E	W	E	L	L	-	W	I	S	H	I
9	N	G	A	D	V	E	N	T	V	R	E	R	I	N	S
10	E	T	T	I	N	G	F	O	R	T	H	T	T		

Or I shall live your Epitaph to make,

Or you survive when I in earth am rotten,

From hence your memory death cannot take,

Although in me each part will be forgotten.

***Your name** from hence immortall life shall have,*

Though I (once gone) to all the world must dye,

The earth can yeeld me but a common grave,

***When you intombed in mens eyes shall lye**,*

***Your monument shall be my gentle verse**,*

Which eyes not yet created shall ore-read,

And toungs to be, your beeing shall rehearse,

When all the breathers of this world are dead,

You still shall live (such virtue hath my pen)

Where breath most breaths, even in the mouths of men.

Sonnets supporting additional text

No Sonnet can be taken as directly autobiographical, but they all seem to make some sort of personal statement based on real or imagined experience. Sonnet 81 seems to contradict the biography of Shakespeare of Stratford and no conjecture on its central meaning makes sense in the context of what little we know about his life. However, the essence – *you will be remembered, and I will be forgotten* – is unambiguous. We propose that the attribution of the works to Shakespeare is the *LIE*, and that the writer is addressing this sonnet to the front-man.

The illustrious Sir Henry Neville was buried in the family tomb at Waltham St Lawrence with no epitaph at all.

There are 25 instances of the word *lie* in the sonnets, but we would argue that none relates so closely to a misrepresentation of authorship as Sonnet 81.[7]

5 ***Your name*** We propose this is the *name* of the front-man.

8 ***lie*** We propose that the double meaning of ***lie*** encapsulates the need for the encrypted message in the dedication. ***intomb`ed*** The meter demands *IN-TOMB-BED* which amplifies the word *bed*. *Bed* offers much greater wit and weight to the mapped word *LIE*.

12 See notes on Sonnet 18 (reversing 81) following.

[7] The spelling *ONLIE* as it appears in the dedication is extremely rare, though this was the preferred spelling in the letters of King James.

Sonnet 18 – *L'ETE*

L'ETE is the French word for ***summer***.

	1	2	3	4	5	6	7	**8**	9	10	11	12	13	14	15
1	T	O	T	H	E	O	N	**L**	I	E	B	E	G	E	T
2	T	E	R	O	F	T	H	**E**	S	E	I	N	S	V	I
3	N	G	S	O	N	N	E	**T**	S	Mr	W	H		A	L
4	L	H	A	P	P	I	N	**E**	S	S	E	A	N	D	T
5	H	A	T	E	T	E	R	N	I	T	I	E	P	R	O
6	M	I	S	E	D	B	Y	O	V	R	E	V	E	R	-
7	L	I	V	I	N	G	P	O	E	T	W	I	S	H	E
8	T	H	T	H	E	W	E	L	L	-	W	I	S	H	I
9	N	G	A	D	V	E	N	T	V	R	E	R	I	N	S
10	E	T	T	I	N	G	F	O	R	T	H	T	T		

Shall I compare thee to a ***Summers*** *day?*
Thou art more lovely and more temperate:
Rough windes do shake the darling buds of Maie,
And ***Sommers lease*** *hath all too short a date:*
Sometime too hot the eye of heaven shines,
And often is his gold complexion dimm'd,
And every faire from faire some-time declines,
By chance, or natures changing course untrim'd:
But thy ***ete****rnall* ***Sommer*** *shall not fade,*
Nor loose possession of that faire thou ow'st,
Nor shall death brag thou wandr'st in his shade,
When in eternall lines to time thou grow'st,
So long as men can breath or eyes can see,
So long lives this, and this gives life to thee,

L'ETE is the French word for ***summer.***

This Sonnet has the most instances of ***Summer*** – all of which are capitalised. *L'ETE* may also be ***Summer's lease*** (line 4), since if *Summer* is *Leased*, so it is *let* (L'ETE). A similar pun on *lease* and *let* can be found in Sonnet 13 (lines 5, 9).

In 1599, Sir Henry Neville was Ambassador to France which required him to speak fluent French. As a mathematician and Joint Teller (counter) of the Exchequer, he may also be termed a "summer".

L'ETE is an exception to the pattern of (x, y) coordinates for words that are in natural reading order (not reversed). It seems logical that (y, x) might be used in this instance, if the author intended to give precedence to *LIE* which aligns to Sonnet 81 using the expected (x, y) coordinates. In addition, there are a number of parallels between Sonnet 18 and 81. Sonnet 18, begins *Shall I ...*; Sonnet 81 begins *Or I shall ...* Sonnet 18 has *death brag thou wandr'st in his shade* (line 11); Sonnet 81 has *your memory death cannot take* (line 3). The similarities around the couplet are shown below.

1 ***Summer***

4 We propose that L'ETE is a pun on ***Summer's lease***, since *L'ETE* is both ***summer*** (in French) and ***let*** (*leased*).

9 ***Summer***

12 Compare with lines 12-14 of Sonnet 81:
When all the breathers of this world are dead,
*You still shall **live** (such virtue hath my pen)*
*Where **breath** most **breathes**, even in the mouths of **men**.*

14 ***Comma*** It is not clear whether the comma at the end of the sonnet is intentional. However, it is in the precise location that one might expect an apostrophe to follow *L* and so complete *L'ETE.*

Sonnet 151 – *TILT*

***T**ILT* maps to coordinates 15-1, Sonnet 151.

	1	2	3	4	5	6	7	8	9	10	11	12	13	14	**15**
1	T	O	T	H	E	O	N	L	I	E	B	E	G	E	**T**
2	T	E	R	O	F	T	H	E	S	E	I	N	S	V	**I**
3	N	G	S	O	N	N	E	T	S	Mr	W	H		A	**L**
4	L	H	A	P	P	I	N	E	S	S	E	A	N	D	**T**
5	H	A	T	E	T	E	R	N	I	T	I	E	P	R	O
6	M	I	S	E	D	B	Y	O	V	R	E	V	E	R	-
7	L	I	V	I	N	G	P	O	E	T	W	I	S	H	E
8	T	H	T	H	E	W	E	L	L	-	W	I	S	H	I
9	N	G	A	D	V	E	N	T	V	R	E	R	I	N	S
10	E	T	T	I	N	G	F	O	R	T	H	T	T		

Love is too young to know what conscience is,
Yet who knowes not conscience is born of love;
Then gentle cheater urge not my amisse,
Least guilty of my faults thy sweet selfe prove.
For thou betraying me, I doe betray
***My nobler part** to my **grose bodies treason**,*
My soule doth tell my body that he may
***Triumph** in love, flesh staies no farther reason,*
*But **rysing** at thy name doth point out thee,*
*As his **triumphant prize**, proud of this pride,*
He is contented thy poore drudge to be
***To stand in thy affaires, fall by thy side**.*
No want of conscience hold it that I call,
*Her love, for whose deare love **I rise and fall**.*

Jousting at the *TILT* is the most familiar image of knighthood. Sir Henry Neville was stripped of his knighthood for his part in the Essex rebellion.

Sonnet 151 is the most sexually explicit of all the sonnets and appears to be inexplicably gratuitous.[8] However, we propose that the word *TILT* in the Dedication completes a traditional metaphor in which the services of a knight represent the sexual services of the lover. The image of the raising and lowering of a lance is particularly suggestive. Sonnet 151 reverses this metaphor; the sexual services of the lover – described so graphically – represent the services of a knight (Neville). See Booth's comments below.

Neville mentions the *tilt* twice in letters to Winwood.[9] Shakespeare mentions *tilt* three times:

> *Henry VI Part 1*, III.ii.51:
> *... will you...run a-tilt at death within a chair?*
>
> *Henry VI Part 2*, I.iii.49:
> *... in the city Tours*
> *Thou rannest a tilt in honour of my love...*
>
> *Two Gentlemen of Verona*, I.iii.30:
> *There shall he practise tilts and tournaments.*

References to both the tilt and male erection may also be invoked in Sonnet 15 which maps sequentially to *TILT*, and is described on p. 178.

Booth's comments below are in quotes and italics;[10] ours are in non-italics.

6 *"... playing on* ***part*** meaning *"bodily part" and specifically the male member"*
gross body's treason may conflate lust with the *treason* that cost Neville his knighthood.

8 Schmidt notes ***triumph*** as – "a public festivity ... Particularly a tournament, e.g. hold those jousts and triumphs. R2 5.ii.52".[11]
A joust was, of course, a **tilt.**

9 ***rising*** *"... The overt reference is to sexual erection ..."*

10 ***triumphant prize*** see note on *triumph* above

12 *"... the overt reference is sexual; here the metaphor is of the soldier's loyalty ... or of a* ***knight's*** *loyalty to his king"* (our bold).

14 *"'rising and falling' is singularly appropriate to [the poem's] theme of involuntary lust; the point is that* ***it is not a metaphor.****"* [our bold]

---

[8] Sonnets 151–152 are considered in detail in Chapter 6: TT.
[9] Winwood, Ralph, *Memorials of Affairs of State,* ed. Edmund Sawyer, i, 271, 274.
[10] Booth, *Shakespeare's Sonnets,* pp. 524–9.
[11] Schmidt, A., *Shakespeare Lexicon and Quotation Dictionary* (Dover, New York, 1971).

Sonnet 15 - *TILT*

***T**ILT* maps sequentially to 15, Sonnet 15 (see Sonnet 151 also).

	1	2	3	4	5	6	7	8	9	10	11	12	13	14	15
1	T	O	T	H	E	O	N	L	I	E	B	E	G	E	**T**
2	T	E	R	O	F	T	H	E	S	E	I	N	S	V	**I**
3	N	G	S	O	N	N	E	T	S	Mr	W	H		A	**L**
4	L	H	A	P	P	I	N	E	S	S	E	A	N	D	**T**
5	H	A	T	E	T	E	R	N	I	T	I	E	P	R	O
6	M	I	S	E	D	B	Y	O	V	R	E	V	E	R	-
7	L	I	V	I	N	G	P	O	E	T	W	I	S	H	E
8	T	H	T	H	E	W	E	L	L	-	W	I	S	H	I
9	N	G	A	D	V	E	N	T	V	R	E	R	I	N	S
10	E	T	T	I	N	G	F	O	R	T	H	T	T		

When I consider ***every thing that growes***
Holds in perfection but a little moment.
That ***this huge stage*** *presenteth nought but showes*
Whereon the Stars *in secret influence comment.*
When I perceive that men as plants increase,
Cheared and checkt even by the selfe-same skie:
Vaunt in their youthful sap, at height decrease,
And were their ***brave state*** *out of memory.*
Then the conceit of this inconstant stay,
Sets you most rich in youth before my sight,
Where wastfull Time ***debateth*** *with decay*
To change your day of youth to ***sullied night,***
And ***all in war*** *with Time for love of you*
As he takes from you, I ***ingraft*** *you new.*

Jousting at the *TILT* is the most familiar emblem of knighthood. Sir Henry Neville was stripped of his knighthood for his part in the Essex rebellion.

In line with the biography of William Shakespeare, Sonnet 15 is generally taken to evoke imagery of a theatrical stage. However, it may relate more closely to the outdoor spectacle of the *Tilt.*

Given the explicit references to male erection and detumescence in Sonnet 151, we note that lines 1, 2 and 7 offer similar if more decorous potential.

1 ***Every thing that grows*** may refer to male erection (see lines 2, 7).

2 ***Holds in perfection but a little moment***

3 ***huge stage*** A huge performance space (cf. a tilt-yard).

4 ***Whereon the stars*** Perhaps suggesting open air performance.

7 Possible reference to tumescence and detumescence.

8 ***state*** is generally taken to refer to fine clothes. However, *state* is synonymous with titles. Only titled men (knights) were eligible for the *Tilt.*

11 ***debate*** Strive or fight (with)

12 Possibly *diminished* ***knight*** due to the removal of his title.
The ***tilt*** is simulated ***war***, very often beginning with a *melee* – a mock battle.
Booth notes that the couplet conflates multiple images of penetration, around ***Ingraft.*** Grafting involves the insertion of a pointed graft into another tree.[12] We propose that this image intensifies the association of ***tilt*** with male erection.

[12] Booth, *Shakespeare's Sonnets,* pp. 157–8.

Sonnet 43 - *OPE/OPE*

The intersection of ***O**PE* with ***O**PE* maps to coordinates 4-3, Sonnet 43.

	1	2	3	**4**	5	6	7	8	9	10	11	12	13	14	15
1	T	O	T	H	E	O	N	L	I	E	B	E	G	E	T
2	T	E	R	O	F	T	H	E	S	E	I	N	S	V	I
3	N	G	S	**O**	N	N	E	T	S	Mr	W	H		A	L
4	L	H	A	**P**	**P**	I	N	E	S	S	E	A	N	D	T
5	H	A	T	**E**	T	**E**	R	N	I	T	I	E	P	R	O
6	M	I	S	E	D	B	Y	O	V	R	E	V	E	R	-
7	L	I	V	I	N	G	P	O	E	T	W	I	S	H	E
8	T	H	T	H	E	W	E	L	L	-	W	I	S	H	I
9	N	G	A	D	V	E	N	T	V	R	E	R	I	N	S
10	E	T	T	I	N	G	F	O	R	T	H	T	T		

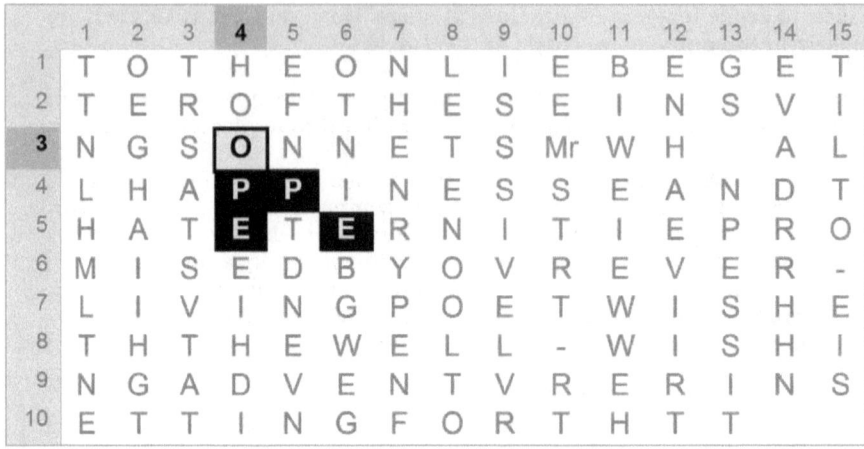

When most I winke, then doe mine eyes best see,
For all the day they ***view*** *things unrespected,*
But when I sleepe, in dreames they ***look*** *on thee,*
And darkely bright, are bright in dark directed.
Then thou, whose shaddow shaddowes doth make bright,
How would thy shadowes form, form happy show,
To the cleere day with thy much cleerer light,
When to ***un-seeing eyes*** *thy shade shines so?*
How would (I say) ***mine eyes*** *be blessed made,*
By ***looking*** *on thee in the living day?*
When in dead night thy faire imperfect shade
Through heavy sleepe on ***sightlesse eyes*** *doth stay?*
All dayes are nights ***to see till I see thee,***
And nights bright daies when dreams do shew thee me.

Ope is a common variant of *open.* There are around 150 instances of the word *open* in Shakespeare, and around 30 of *ope.*

Sonnet 43 deals explicitly with seeing when eyes are not *open.* The word *ope* is ideational in Sonnet 43. The word is never used but the sonnet evokes its meaning.

We propose that this sonnet, like Sonnet 33 (discussed on pp. 158–9), is a poignant reflection on the death of Neville's infant son. We note the interplay of *shade, shadows, dead night* and *living day.*

1 ***wink*** means to close the eyes. ***see***
2 ***view***
3 ***look***
8 ***unseeing eyes***
9 ***eyes***
10 ***looking***
12 ***sightless eyes***
13 ***see***, ***see***

Sonnet 116 – *EVER*

***E**VER* maps to coordinates 11-6, Sonnet 116.

	1	2	3	4	5	6	7	8	9	10	**11**	12	13	14	15
1	T	O	T	H	E	O	N	L	I	E	B	E	G	E	T
2	T	E	R	O	F	T	H	E	S	E	I	N	S	V	I
3	N	G	S	O	N	N	E	T	S	Mr	W	H		A	L
4	L	H	A	P	P	I	N	E	S	S	E	A	N	D	T
5	H	A	T	E	T	E	R	N	I	T	I	E	P	R	O
6	M	I	S	E	D	B	Y	O	V	R	**E**	**V**	**E**	**R**	-
7	L	I	V	I	N	G	P	O	E	T	W	I	S	H	E
8	T	H	T	H	E	W	E	L	L	-	W	I	S	H	I
9	N	G	A	D	V	E	N	T	V	R	E	R	I	N	S
10	E	T	T	I	N	G	F	O	R	T	H	T	T		

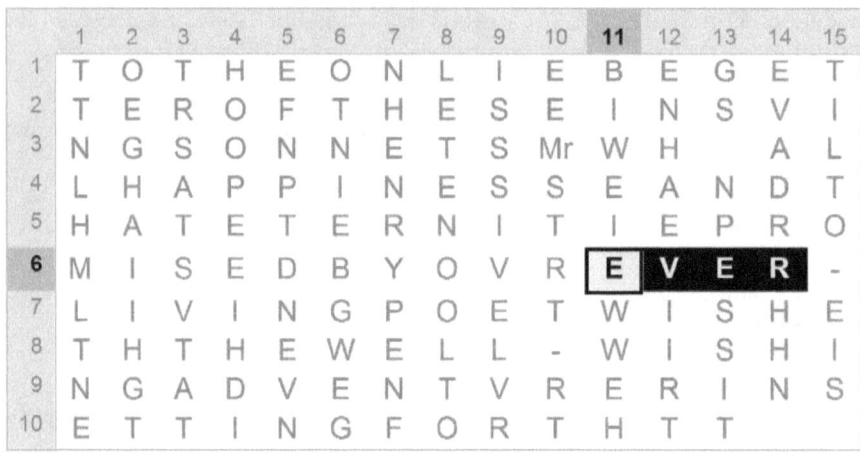

Let me not to the marriage of true mindes
Admit impediments, love is not love
Which alters when it alteration findes,
Or bends with the remover to remove.
*O no, it is an **ever**-fixed marke*
*That lookes on tempests and is **never** shaken;*
*It is the star to **every** wandring barke,*
Whose worths unknowne, although his higth be taken.
Lov's not Times foole, though rosie lips and cheeks
Within his bending sickles compass come,
Love alters not with his breef houres and weekes,
But beares it out even to the edge of doome:
If this be error and upon me proved,
*I **never** writ, nor no man **ever** loved.*

Sonnet 116 includes the greatest number of instances of ***ever*** of any sonnet.

This sonnet declares that love will endure forever – love is *ever-living.* Similarly, *LIVING* in Sonnet 17 is built upon the assumption that poetry is eternal.[13]

Given that both Sonnets 116 and 17 address the idea of immortality, it seems possible that *EVER-LIVING* was also intended to be included in the primary decrypted phrase:

MrSIR HENRY NEVILLE YOUR EVER-LIVING SONNETS POET.

There are five instances of ***ever*** in Sonnet 116, including two in the final line.

5 ***ever***
6 ***never***
7 ***every***
14 ***never, ever***

[13] See *LIVING,* p. 184.

Sonnet 17 – *LIVING.POET*

***L**IVING* maps to coordinates 1-7, Sonnet 17.

	1	2	3	4	5	6	7	8	9	10	11	12	13	14	15
1	T	O	T	H	E	O	N	L	I	E	B	E	G	E	T
2	T	E	R	O	F	T	H	E	S	E	I	N	S	V	I
3	N	G	S	O	N	N	E	T	S	Mr	W	H		A	L
4	L	H	A	P	P	I	N	E	S	S	E	A	N	D	T
5	H	A	T	E	T	E	R	N	I	T	I	E	P	R	O
6	M	I	S	E	D	B	Y	O	V	R	E	V	E	R	-
7	**L**	**I**	**V**	**I**	**N**	**G**	**P**	**O**	**E**	**T**	W	I	S	H	E
8	T	H	T	H	E	W	E	L	L	-	W	I	S	H	I
9	N	G	A	D	V	E	N	T	V	R	E	R	I	N	S
10	E	**T**	**T**	I	N	G	F	O	R	T	H	T	T		

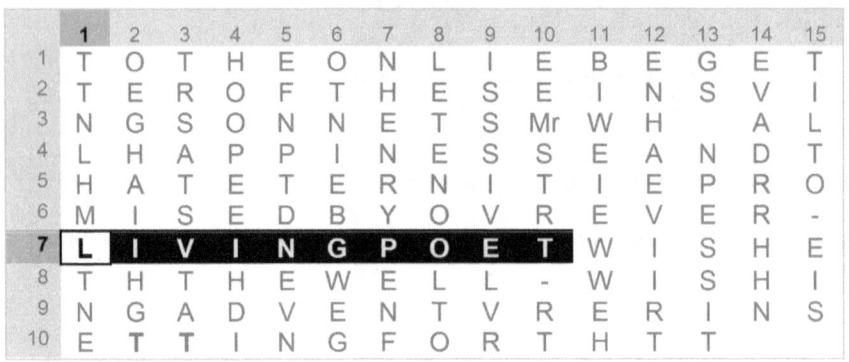

*Who will **beleeve** my verse in time to come,*
If it were fild with your most high deserts?
Though yet heaven knowes it is but a tombe
*Which **hides your life**, and shewes not halfe your parts:*
If I could write the beauty of your eyes,
*And in fresh **numbers number** all your graces,*
*The age to come would say **this Poet lies**,*
Such heavenly touches nere toucht earthly faces.
So should my papers (yellowed with their age)
*Be scorn'd like **old men** of **lesse truth** then tongue,*
*And your true rights be termed a **Poets** rage,*
And stretched miter of an Antique song.
*But were some childe of yours **alive** that time,*
*You should **live** twise in it, and in my rime.*

Sonnet 17 compares the poet living on through his poems with the addressee living on through his children. ***Life, alive, live*** and ***poet***, ***poet's*** all underscore the mapped phrase *LIVING.POET.*

Similarly, *EVER* in Sonnet 116 declares that love is eternal.[14] Given that both sonnets deal with immortality, it seems likely that *EVER-LIVING.POET* was intended to be included in the decryption:

> *MrSIR HENRY NEVILLE YOUR EVER-LIVING POET.*

Sonnet 17 also acknowledges a *life* hidden by a *Poet,* and refers to verses as *numbers* in the which *this poet lies.*

Note. Also mapping to *LIVING.POET,* Sonnet 71 graphically imagines the dead poet – whose poetry nevertheless lives on. We may also hear a comic echo of the Neville motto *Ne vile velis* in lines 4 and 5:

> *From this* ***vile*** *world with* ***vildest*** *worms to dwell:*
> ***Nay*** *if you read this line...*

1 ***believe*** approximates the sound of *live* and may call attention to the variants below.
4 ***life***
7 ***this poet lies***
10 ***old men*** *Compare with "ever-living"*?
11 ***poet's***
13 ***alive***
14 ***live***

[14] See *EVER,* p. 182.

Sonnet 21 - *OTHE*

***O**THE* maps to coordinates 2-1, Sonnet 21.

	1	2	3	4	5	6	7	8	9	10	11	12	13	14	15
1	**T**	**O**	**T**	**H**	**E**	O	N	**L**	**I**	**E**	B	E	G	E	**T**
2	**T**	E	R	O	F	T	H	E	S	E	I	N	S	V	I
3	N	G	S	O	N	N	E	T	S	Mr	W	H		A	L
4	L	H	A	P	P	I	N	E	S	S	E	A	N	D	T
5	H	A	T	E	T	E	R	N	I	T	I	E	P	R	O
6	M	I	S	E	D	B	Y	O	V	R	E	V	E	R	-
7	L	I	V	I	N	G	P	O	E	T	W	I	S	H	E
8	T	H	T	H	E	W	E	L	L	-	W	I	S	H	I
9	N	G	A	D	V	E	N	T	V	R	E	R	I	N	S
10	E	T	T	I	N	G	F	O	R	T	H	T	T		

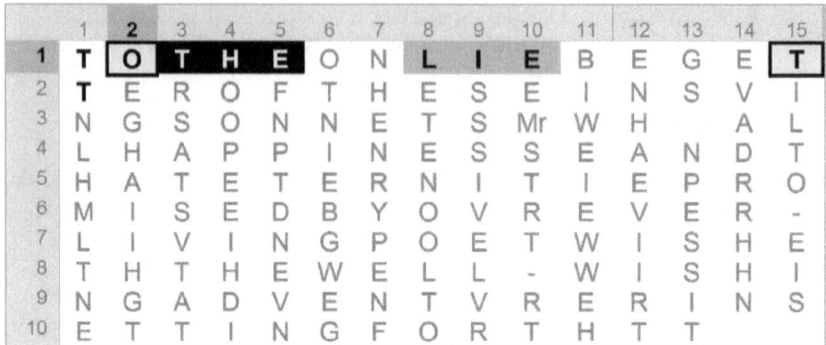

So is it not with me as with that Muse,
Stird by a painted beauty to his verse,
*Who heaven it selfe for ornament **doth** use*
*And every faire with his faire **doth reherse**,*
Making a coopelment of proud compare
With Sunne and Moone, with earth and seas rich gems:
With Aprills first borne flowers and all things rare,
That heavens ayre in this huge rondure hems,
*O let me true in love but **truly write**,*
And then beleeve me, my love is as faire,
*As any **mothers** childe, though not so bright*
As those gould candells fixt in heavens ayer:
*Let them **say more** that like of **heare-say** well,*
I will not prayse that purpose not to sell.

Sonnet 21, which maps to *OTHE,* satirises the shallow techniques of would-be poets. Written and spoken poetic oaths of love are presented and shown to be ridiculous.

OTHE is the most common Early Modern spelling of *oath.* In the Dedication grid, *OTHE* sits adjacent to the vertical *TT* in column 1. In Chapter 6 we note that the twenty-two broken ***othes*** of Sonnet 152 supply the mapping that confirms that *TT* = 22.

Sonnet 81, as we have observed, maps to the antonym of *OTHE,* that is *LIE.* Sonnet 81 concerns the one falsehood in the author's own eternal poetry – its authorship.

3 Incidental echoes of ***oath*** occur in ***doth*** and ***mother*** in lines 3, 4 and 10.

4 ***Doth rehearse*** suggests a practised and artificial spoken oath as in line 13.

9 ***truly write***. Booth remarks on the casual wit in the sound of *truly "right"*. This wordplay would seem to encapsulate the concept of ***oath.***[15]

[15] Booth, *Shakespeare's Sonnets,* p. 169.

Sonnet 56 – *TIDE/EDGE*

The intersection of *TI**D**E* and *E**D**GE* maps to coordinates 5-6, Sonnet 56.

	1	2	3	4	5	6	7	8	9	10	11	12	13	14	15
1	T	O	T	H	E	O	N	L	I	E	B	E	G	E	T
2	T	E	R	O	F	T	H	E	S	E	I	N	S	V	I
3	N	G	S	O	N	N	E	T	S	Mr	W	H		A	L
4	L	H	A	P	P	I	N	E	S	**S**	**E**	**A**	N	D	T
5	H	A	T	**E**	T	**E**	R	N	I	T	**I**	E	P	R	O
6	M	I	S	E	**D**	B	Y	O	V	R	**E**	V	E	R	-
7	L	I	V	**I**	N	**G**	P	O	E	T	W	I	S	H	E
8	T	H	**T**	H	E	W	**E**	L	L	-	W	I	S	H	I
9	N	G	A	D	V	E	N	T	V	R	E	R	I	N	S
10	E	T	T	I	N	G	F	O	R	T	H	T	T		

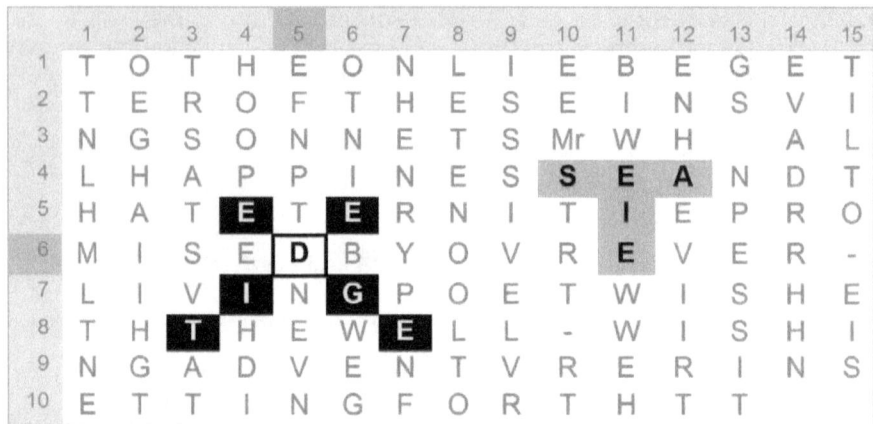

Sweet love renew thy force, be it not said
*Thy **edge** should **blunter** be than apetite,*
Which but to daie by feeding is alaied,
*To morrow **sharpned** in his former might.*
So love be thou, although to daie thou fill
Thy hungrie eies, even till they winck with fulnesse,
*Too morrow **see** again, and do not kill*
*The spirit of love, with a perpetual **dulnesse**:*
*Let this sad Intrim like the **Ocean be***
*Which parts **the shore**, where two contracted new,*
*Come daily to **the banckes**, that when they **see***
*Returne of love, more blest may be the **view.***
As cal it Winter, which being ful of care,
Makes Somers welcome, thrice more wish'd, more rare.

The images of *tide* and *edge* recur throughout Sonnet 56.

In Chapter 5 we noted Sonnet 56 as an example of obscure ideational punning. Booth writes of lines 9 and 11:

> "The word *see* rhymes phonetically with *be* and, through the intermediary of "sea", rhymes ideationally with *ocean*".[16]

The idea that is invoked is *sea,* but the word *sea* is missing from the sonnet. However at coordinates 5-6 in the dedication, *TIDE* intersects with *EDGE.* The first and second quatrains discuss the *sharp* and *blunt* ***edge*** of appetite. The third quatrain uses the ***sea*** as a metaphor for separation. There are two other mappings to Sonnet 56. At (y, x) coordinates 5-6, *TID**E*** intersects with *T**E**RN,* and at sequential position 56, *S**E**A* intersects with ***E**IE.* First, we will examine *TIDE/EDGE.*

2 ***edge***, ***blunter***
4 ***sharpened*** (as of an edge)
7 ***see*** = sea
8 ***dullness*** = *bluntness* (as of an edge)
9 ***ocean***
10 ***the shore***
11 ***the banks, see*** = sea

[16] Booth, *Shakespeare's Sonnets,* p. 231.

Sonnet 56 – *TIDE/TERN*

The intersection of *TID**E*** and *T**E**RN* maps to (y, x) coordinates 5-6, Sonnet 56.

	1	2	3	4	5	6	7	8	9	10	11	12	13	14	15
1	T	O	T	H	E	O	N	L	I	E	B	E	G	E	T
2	T	E	R	O	F	T	H	E	S	E	I	N	S	V	I
3	N	G	S	O	N	N	E	T	S	Mr	W	H		A	L
4	L	H	A	P	P	I	N	E	S	**S**	**E**	**A**	N	D	T
5	H	A	T	E	**T**	**E**	**R**	**N**	I	T	**I**	E	P	R	O
6	M	I	S	E	**D**	B	Y	O	V	R	**E**	V	E	R	-
7	L	I	V	**I**	N	G	P	O	E	T	W	I	S	H	E
8	T	H	**T**	H	E	W	E	L	L	-	W	I	S	H	I
9	N	G	A	D	V	E	N	T	V	R	E	R	I	N	S
10	E	T	T	I	N	G	F	O	R	T	H	T	T		

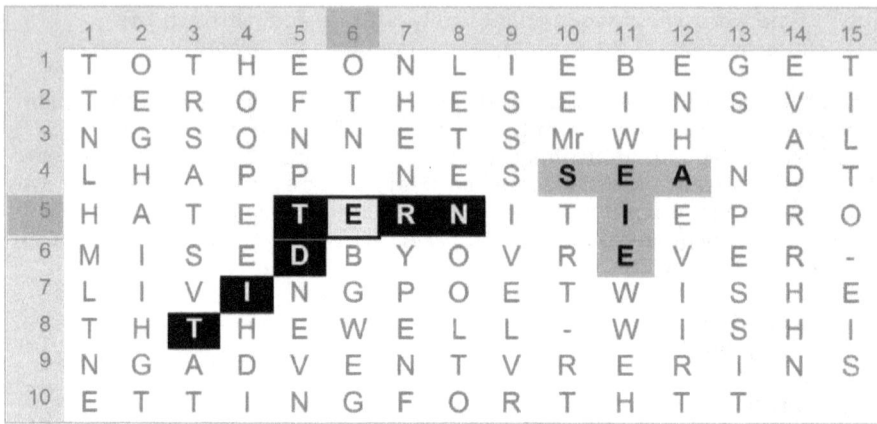

Sweet love renew thy force, be it not said
Thy edge should blunter be than apetite,
Which but to daie by feeding is alaied,
To morrow sharpned in his former might.
So love be thou, although to daie thou fill
Thy hungrie eies, even till they winck with fulnesse,
Too morrow ***see*** *again, and do not kill*
The spirit of love, with a perpetual dulnesse:
Let this sad Intrim like the ***Ocean be***
Which ***parts the shore****, where two contracted new,*
Come daily to the banckes, that when they ***see***
Returne *of love, more blest may be the view.*
As cal it Winter, which being ful of care,
Makes Somers welcome, thrice more wish'd, more rare.

Sonnets supporting additional text

In Chapter 5 and directly above, we have noted Sonnet 56 as an example of obscure ideational punning. The idea that is invoked is *sea,* but the word *sea* is missing from the sonnet.

At coordinates 5-6, *TIDE* intersects with *TERN.* The *turning of the tide* is the central metaphor in this sonnet.

Note. This mapping *TERN* would seem to support our earlier observation of *TERNIT.*

7 ***see*** = sea
9 ***Ocean*** Lines 9-12 exploit the simile of the *turning tide.*
10 ***parts the shore***
11 ***see*** = sea
12 ***Return*** (as of the tide)

56

Sweet loue renew thy force, be it not ſaid
Thy edge ſhould blunter be then apetite,
Which but too daie by feeding is alaied,
To morrow ſharpned in his former might.
So loue be thou, although too daie thou fill
Thy hungrie eies, euen till they winck with fulneſſe,
Too morrow ſee againe, and doe not kill
The ſpirit of Loue, with a perpetual dulneſſe:
Let this ſad *Intrim* like the Ocean be
Which parts the ſhore, where two contracted new,
Come daily to the banckes, that when they ſee:
Returne of loue, more bleſt may be the view.
  As cal it Winter, which being ful of care,
  Makes Somers welcome, thrice more wiſh'd, more rare:

Sequential Mappings

In the following pages, we detail those sonnets that seem to be referenced by the cell number, where the top left hand cell in the Dedication is number 1, and reading like a book, the bottom right hand cell is number 150.

Sonnet 56 – *SEA/EIE*

The intersection of *S**E**A* and ***E**IE* maps *sequentially* to cell 56, Sonnet 56.

	1	2	3	4	5	6	7	8	9	10	11	12	13	14	15
1	T	O	T	H	E	O	N	L	I	E	B	E	G	E	T
2	T	E	R	O	F	T	H	E	S	E	I	N	S	V	I
3	N	G	S	O	N	N	E	T	S	Mr	W	H		A	L
4	L	H	A	P	P	I	N	E	S	**S**	**E**	**A**	N	D	T
5	H	A	T	**E**	**T**	**E**	**R**	**N**	I	T	**I**	E	P	R	O
6	M	I	S	E	**D**	B	Y	O	V	R	**E**	V	E	R	-
7	L	I	V	**I**	N	**G**	P	O	E	T	W	I	S	H	E
8	T	H	**T**	H	E	W	**E**	L	L	-	W	I	S	H	I
9	N	G	A	D	V	E	N	T	V	R	E	R	I	N	S
10	E	T	T	I	N	G	F	O	R	T	H	T	T		

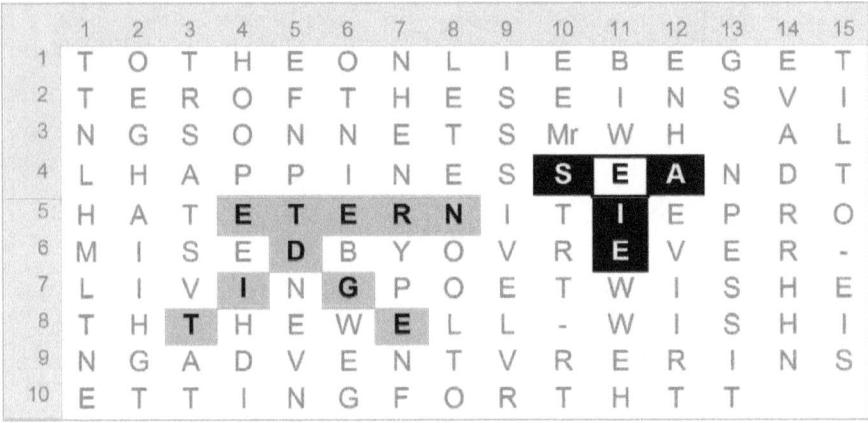

Sweet love renew thy force, be it not said
Thy edge should blunter be than apetite,
Which but to daie by feeding is alaied,
To morrow sharpned in his former might.
So love be thou, although to daie thou fill
*Thy hungrie **eies**, even till they **winck** with fulnesse,*
*Too morrow **see** again, and do not kill*
The spirit of love, with a perpetual dulnesse:
*Let this sad Intrim like the **Ocean be***
Which parts the shore, where two contracted new,
*Come daily to the banckes, that when they **see***
*Returne of love, more blest may be the **view**.*
As cal it Winter, which being ful of care,
Makes Somers welcome, thrice more wish'd, more rare.

We have noted in the two mappings above Sonnet 56 as an example of obscure ideational punning. The idea that is invoked is *sea,* but the word itself is missing from the sonnet.

However, at sequential position 56 in the dedication, *SEA* intersects with *EIE* in a complementary ideational association. In this case the linking word is *see.*

6 ***eyes, wink***
7 ***see*** = sea
9 ***Ocean be***
11 ***see*** = sea
12 ***view***

Sonnet 111 - *WELL*

***W**ELL* maps *sequentially* to cell 111, Sonnet 111.

	1	2	3	4	5	6	7	8	9	10	11	12	13	14	15
1	T	O	T	H	E	O	N	L	I	E	B	E	G	E	T
2	T	E	R	O	F	T	H	E	S	E	I	N	S	V	I
3	N	G	S	O	N	N	E	T	S	Mr	W	H		A	L
4	L	H	A	P	P	I	N	E	S	S	E	A	N	D	T
5	H	A	T	E	T	E	R	N	I	T	I	E	P	R	O
6	M	I	S	E	D	B	Y	O	V	R	E	V	E	R	-
7	L	I	V	I	N	G	P	O	E	T	W	I	S	H	E
8	T	H	T	H	E	**W**	E	L	L	-	W	I	S	H	I
9	N	G	A	D	V	E	N	T	V	R	E	R	I	N	S
10	E	T	T	I	N	G	F	O	R	T	H	T	T		

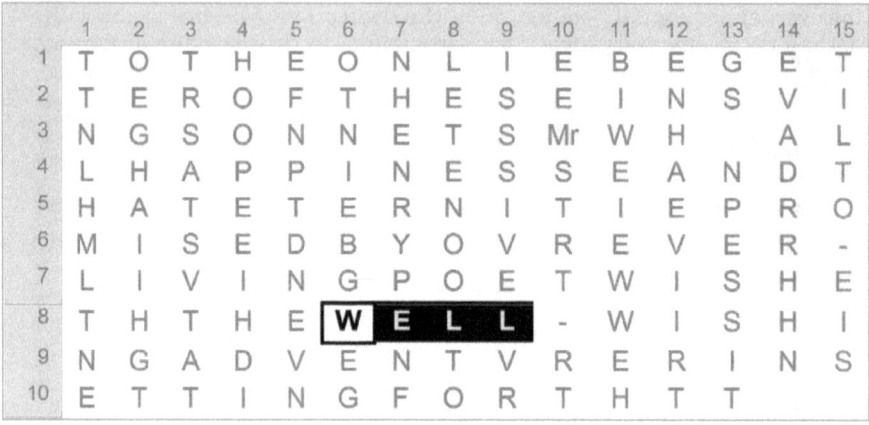

O for my sake do you wish fortune chide,
The guiltie goddesse of my harmfull deeds,
That did not ***better*** *for my life provide*
Then publick meanes which publick manners breeds.
Thence comes it that my name receives ***a brand,***
And almost thence my nature is subdu'd
To what it works in, like the dyer's hand,
Pitty me then, and wish I were ***renu'de,***
Whilst like a ***willing pacient*** *I* ***will*** *drinke,*
Potions of Eysell gainst my strong infection,
No ***bitternesse*** *that I* ***will bitter*** *thinke,*
Nor double pennance to ***correct*** *correction.*
Pitty me then deare friend, and I assure yee,
Even that your pittie is enough to ***cure mee.***

Sonnet 111 invokes the image of a patient "getting better" – becoming ***well.***

The similarity of the sounds of *Will* and *Well* are played on frequently in the sonnets and in the plays. Rhyming on *Jill, ill,* and *well* occurs in *A Midsummer Night's Dream* III ii; punning on *well* and *will* occurs in *Merry Wives of Windsor* I iii.

3 When someone is ***better*** – they are ***well*** (see note on *bitter/ bitterness* below).
4 ***Better*** is the comparative form of the adverb ***well.***
5 Neville was convicted for treason in 1601. Traitors were commonly branded with the letter *T* on the forehead, though it is not known if Neville suffered this fate.
8 ***renewed*** = well
9 ***willing patient*** = welling patient. ***will***
11 Of line 11 Booth writes, "*Note the echo of* better *in line 3; in pronunciation bitter and better were like enough to invite punning.*"[17]
better = well/recovered from illness.
12 ***correct*** = to make ***well***
14 ***cure me*** = to make me ***well***

[17] Booth, *Shakespeare's Sonnets*, p. 362.

Sonnet 50 – *PINES*

***P**INES* maps *sequentially* to cell 50, Sonnet 50.

	1	2	3	4	5	6	7	8	9	10	11	12	13	14	15
1	T	O	T	H	E	O	N	L	I	E	B	E	G	E	T
2	T	E	R	O	F	T	H	E	S	E	I	N	S	V	I
3	N	G	S	O	N	N	E	T	S	Mr	W	H		A	L
4	L	H	A	P	**P**	**I**	**N**	**E**	**S**	S	E	A	N	D	T
5	H	A	T	E	T	E	R	N	I	T	I	E	P	R	O
6	M	I	S	E	D	B	Y	O	V	R	E	V	E	R	-
7	L	I	V	I	N	G	P	O	E	T	W	I	S	H	E
8	T	H	T	H	E	W	E	L	L	-	W	I	S	H	I
9	N	G	A	D	V	E	N	T	V	R	E	R	I	N	S
10	E	T	T	I	N	G	F	O	R	T	H	T	T		

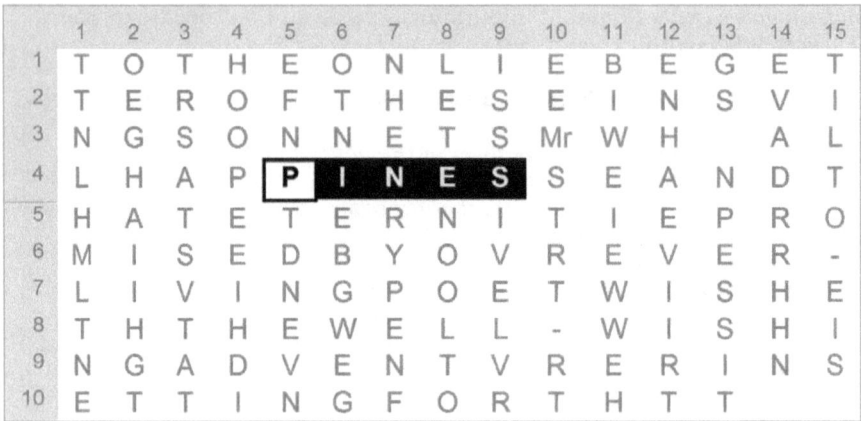

How heavie doe I journey on the way,

When what I seeke (my wearie travels end)

Doth teach that ease and that repose to say

Thus farre the miles are measurde from thy friend.

*The beast that **beares** me, tired with my woe,*

*Plods duly on, to **beare** that waight in me,*

As if by some instinct the wretch did know

His rider lov'd not speed, being made from thee:

The bloody spurre cannot provoke him on,

That some-times anger thrusts into his hide,

*Which heavily he answers with a **grone**,*

More sharpe to me than spurring to his side,

For that same grone doth put this in my mind,

My greefe lies onward and my joy behind.

The word *pains* and *pines* were almost interchangeable in meaning and very closely related phonetically (for *pine,* see also Sonnets 75 and 146, and *pain* see Sonnets 38, 132, 139, 140, 141).

Sonnet 50 compares two *pains*, physical and emotional. The physical pain of spurring is compared to the emotional pain of longing, or *pining.*

5 ***Bears*** = *carries* but also *suffers pain*
6 ***Bear*** as above.
11 ***groan***
12 Two *pains.* Physical pain is compared with emotional pain.
13 ***groan***

Sonnet 123 – *ADVENT*

***A**DVENT* maps *sequentially* to cell 123, Sonnet 123.

	1	2	3	4	5	6	7	8	9	10	11	12	13	14	15
1	T	O	T	H	E	O	N	L	I	E	B	E	G	E	T
2	T	E	R	O	F	T	H	E	S	E	I	N	S	V	I
3	N	G	S	O	N	N	E	T	S	Mr	W	H		A	L
4	L	H	A	P	P	I	N	E	S	S	E	A	N	D	T
5	H	A	T	E	T	E	R	N	I	T	I	E	P	R	O
6	M	I	S	E	D	B	Y	O	V	R	E	V	E	R	-
7	L	I	V	I	N	G	P	O	E	T	W	I	S	H	E
8	T	H	T	H	E	W	E	L	L	-	W	I	S	H	I
9	N	G	**A**	**D**	**V**	**E**	**N**	**T**	V	R	E	R	I	N	S
10	E	T	T	I	N	G	F	O	R	T	H	T	T		

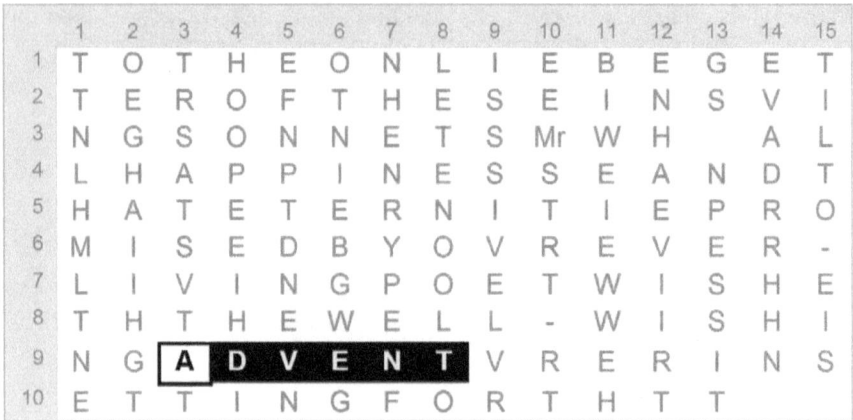

No! Time, thou shalt not boast that I doe change,
Thy ***pyramyds*** *buylt up with newer might*
To me are nothing ***nouell****, nothing strange,*
They are but dressings of a former sight:
Our dates are breefe, and therefor we admire,
What thou dost foyst upon us that is ould,
And rather make them ***borne*** *to our desire*
Then thinke ***that we before have heard them tould****:*
Thy registers and thee I both defie,
Not wondring at the present, nor the past,
For thy records, and what we see doth lye,
Made more or les by thy continuall hast:
This I doe vow and this shall ever be,
I will be true dispight thy syeth and thee.

Advent is both the arrival of a person or thing, as well as the season celebrating the birth of Christ.

This Sonnet concerns innovation and plays on the word *novel.*

If Sonnet 122 refers to Horace's Ode I.22, we may see a numerical reference in Sonnet 123 to Matteo Bandello's famous ***Novelle*** 1, 23: *Marvellous subtlety used by a thief in robbing and cozening the King of Egypt* (cf. *pyramid* and *nouell*). We can be certain that the author greatly admired Bandello, because he used his *novelle* in the plots of 5 plays: *Cymbeline* (Part 1, Story 19); *Romeo & Juliet* (2, 6); *Twelfth Night* (2, 28); *Much Ado About Nothing* – Claudio sub-plot (1, 20); *Edward III* (2, 29).

2 ***Pyramid*** – the emblem of Egypt (see comment on Bandello 1, 23 above).

3 ***Nouell*** is a homophone for ***Nowell***, or Advent, the season celebrating the birth of Christ; ***Novelle*** the 16th Century literary innovation of Matteo Bandello (see above), and possibly ***Neville*** himself.

7 ***Born*** (Advent, the birth of Christ)

8 Shakespeare ***re-told*** several stories of Bandello, who was in turn *re-telling* older stories (see above).

Sonnet 59 – *D*

D maps *sequentially* to cell 59, Sonnet 59.

	1	2	3	4	5	6	7	8	9	10	11	12	13	14	15
1	T	O	T	H	E	O	N	L	I	E	B	E	G	E	T
2	T	E	R	O	F	T	H	E	S	E	I	N	S	V	I
3	N	G	S	O	N	N	E	T	S	Mr	W	H		A	L
4	L	H	A	P	P	I	N	E	S	S	E	A	N	**D**	T
5	H	A	T	E	T	E	R	N	I	T	I	E	P	R	O
6	M	I	S	E	D	B	Y	O	V	R	E	V	E	R	-
7	L	I	V	I	N	G	P	O	E	T	W	I	S	H	E
8	T	H	T	H	E	W	E	L	L	-	W	I	S	H	I
9	N	G	A	D	V	E	N	T	V	R	E	R	I	N	S
10	E	T	T	I	N	G	F	O	R	T	H	T	T		

If their bee nothing new, but that which is,
Hath beene before, how are our braines beguild,
Which labouring for invention beare amisse
The second burthen of a former child
Oh that record could with back-ward looke
Even of ***five hundreth*** *courses of the sunne,*
Show me your image in some antique book,
Since minde at first in carrecter was done
That I might see what the old world could say,
To this composed wonder of your frame,
Whether we are mended, or where better they,
Or whether revolution be the same.
Oh sure I am the wits of ***former daies***
To subjects worse have given admiring praise.

Sonnet 59 recalls the writing of ancient times, and includes the number ***five hundred***, being the Roman numeral *D*.

In Chapter 7 we examined Sonnet 59 in relation to the biography of Mr. William Hunnis which seems to parallel that of Sir Henry Neville.

There are 2 other instances of the letter *D* in the dedication but neither maps to a sonnet that is associated with the number five hundred.

6 **Five hundred** is represented in Roman numerals as *D*.
8 The Roman numeral *D* may be regarded as an ***antique character***.
13 Perhaps phonetically ***former dees***

Sonnet 18 – *ROPE*

R*OPE* maps *sequentially* to cell 18, Sonnet 18.

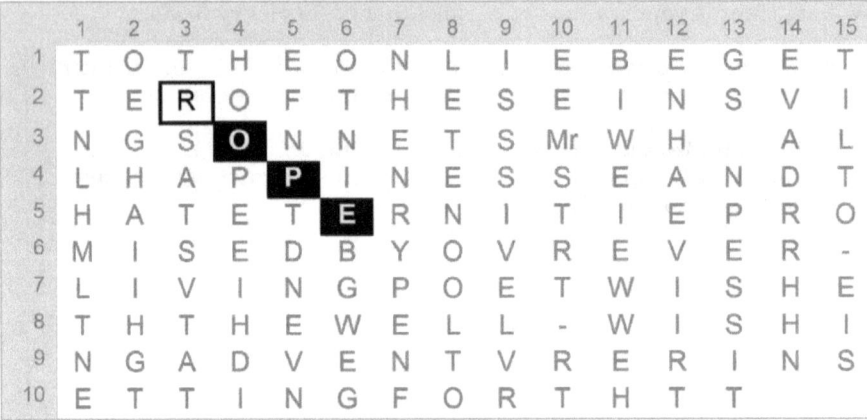

	1	2	3	4	5	6	7	8	9	10	11	12	13	14	15
1	T	O	T	H	E	O	N	L	I	E	B	E	G	E	T
2	T	E	**R**	O	F	T	H	E	S	E	I	N	S	V	I
3	N	G	S	**O**	N	N	E	T	S	Mr	W	H		A	L
4	L	H	A	P	**P**	I	N	E	S	S	E	A	N	D	T
5	H	A	T	E	T	**E**	R	N	I	T	I	E	P	R	O
6	M	I	S	E	D	B	Y	O	V	R	E	V	E	R	-
7	L	I	V	I	N	G	P	O	E	T	W	I	S	H	E
8	T	H	T	H	E	W	E	L	L	-	W	I	S	H	I
9	N	G	A	D	V	E	N	T	V	R	E	R	I	N	S
10	E	T	T	I	N	G	F	O	R	T	H	T	T		

Shall I compare thee to a Summers day?
Thou art more lovely and more temperate:
Rough windes do shake the darling buds of Maie,
And Sommers ***lease*** *hath all too short a date:*
Sometime too hot the eye of heaven shines,
And often is his gold complexion dimm'd,
And every faire from faire some-time declines,
By chance, or natures changing course untrim'd:
But thy eternall Sommer shall not fade,
Nor loose possession of that faire thou ow'st,
Nor shall death brag thou wandr'st in his shade,
When in eternall lines to time thou grow'st,
So long as men can breath or eyes can see,
So long lives this, and this gives life to thee,

On the surface Sonnet 18 seems far removed from any consideration of *rope*, until the reader arrives at line 12. Stephen Booth observes the poet activating the sense of *lines* meaning cords or ropes:

> *As he comes upon line 12, however, a reader may well understand* lines *in its root meaning,* "cords" *or* "ropes", *and take* in eternal lines *as* "bound eternally". *That meaning is sustained – though finally made less ominous – by* to time thou grow'st, *which recurs to the grafting metaphor of 15.14 ...; a graft is usually bound in place with cords until it had coalesced with the stock. Lines also suggest the threads spun by the Fates in classical mythology; the Fates decided the length of each human life and cut each man's thread accordingly.* Eternal lines *would be threads never cut; ...* [18]

In discussing Sonnet 124, Booth also notes that:

... "leash" was often spelled "lease" and the two words appear to have been pronounced alike."[19]

4 Possibly ***leash***. See comment above.
12 ***eternal lines*** may activate ***lease*** meaning ***leash*** in line 4 (see notes on previous page).

[18] Booth, *Shakespeare's Sonnets*, p. 161.
[19] Ibid., p. 423.

Appendix 3: Sonnet 134

In 2012 an independent British researcher Rosemary Warner approached us with a discovery she had made in 2003. She too had been setting Shakespeare in grids, but she was investigating the sonnets themselves rather than the Dedication.

In 2005, as a result of Brenda James's first book, Rosemary Warner became aware of Sir Henry Neville as a Shakespeare authorship candidate. She recalled having found this name in 2003, and generously shared her discovery with us.

Just as we had done in our later setting of the Dedication, Warner had removed all the punctuation, retaining only the letters. The number of columns in each of her sonnet-grids was determined by the number of letters in the first line of the sonnet.

In working through all 154 sonnets in this way she discovered that the name *NEVILLE* can be read in a reversed diagonal in Sonnet 134. It is common for short acrostic words to be generated by chance when text is laid out in a grid, but a seven-letter word is most unusual. We soon saw that by changing the number of columns in her grid from 30 to 29, *NEVILLE* would read vertically rather than diagonally, as on page 207. As noted, at the time she made this observation, Neville had not yet been proposed as a candidate author.

Warner's setting was striking but we were doubtful as to whether the author would embed code in a sonnet. Whereas the artificial phrasing of the Dedication betrays that it might be code, in contrast, the magnificence of the sonnets argues against the presence of encryption. On the other hand, the vagaries of early modern spelling would allow the insertion of an acrostic without any great intrusion.[1]

Her method of transcribing a sonnet into a grid and the omitting of punctuation is essentially identical to the method that we have found to be productive with the Dedication. In addition, the perfectly formed acrostic *NEVILLE* provides the surname which the Dedication seems to bury so deeply, and immediately below it is the potentially very meaningful *RIMER*, suggesting irony or the conflict within a poet who is both great and unknown.

---

[1] It is worth noting that the meagre 148 characters of the Dedication present a far greater challenge as a source for code.

Sonnet 134

S	O	N	O	W	I	H	A	V	E	C	O	N	F	E	S	T	T	H	A	T	H	E	I	S	T	H	I	N
E	A	N	D	I	M	Y	S	E	L	F	E	A	M	M	O	R	G	A	G	D	T	O	T	H	Y	W	I	L
L	M	Y	S	E	L	F	E	I	L	E	F	O	R	F	E	I	T	S	O	T	H	A	T	O	T	H	E	R
M	I	N	E	T	H	O	V	W	I	L	T	R	E	S	T	O	R	E	T	O	B	E	M	Y	C	O	M	F
O	R	T	S	T	I	L	L	B	V	T	T	H	O	V	W	I	L	T	N	O	T	N	O	R	H	E	W	I
L	L	N	O	T	B	E	F	R	E	E	F	O	R	T	H	O	V	A	R	T	C	O	V	E	T	O	V	S
A	N	D	H	E	I	S	K	I	N	D	E	H	E	L	E	A	R	N	D	B	V	T	S	V	R	E	T	I
E	L	I	K	E	T	O	W	R	I	T	E	F	O	R	M	E	V	N	D	E	R	T	H	A	T	B	O	N
D	T	H	A	T	H	I	M	A	S	F	A	S	T	D	O	T	H	B	I	N	D	E	T	H	E	S	T	A
T	V	T	E	O	F	T	H	Y	B	E	A	V	T	Y	T	H	O	V	W	I	L	T	T	A	K	E	T	H
O	V	V	S	V	R	E	R	T	H	A	T	P	V	T	S	T	F	O	R	T	H	A	L	L	T	O	V	S
E	A	N	D	S	V	E	A	F	R	I	E	N	D	C	A	M	E	D	E	B	T	E	R	F	O	R	M	Y
S	A	K	E	S	O	H	I	M	I	L	O	O	S	E	T	H	R	O	V	G	H	M	Y	V	N	K	I	N
D	E	A	B	V	S	E	H	I	M	H	A	V	E	I	L	O	S	T	T	H	O	V	H	A	S	T	B	O
T	H	H	I	M	A	N	D	M	E	H	E	P	A	I	E	S	T	H	E	W	H	O	L	E	A	N	D	Y
E	T	A	M	I	N	O	T	F	R	E	E																	

The 29-column setting of Sonnet 134 reveals inverted *NEVILLE*, directly below which is *RIMER*[2]

Rimer is of course a disparaging or a self-deprecating term for a poet. *Rimer* is used in just this sense in Sonnet 38 (pp. 164–5) and spelt the same way. The word *rime* also occurs in Sonnets 16, 17, 32, 55, 106, and 107.

Perhaps the most remarkable aspect of *NEVILLE/RIMER* is the sonnet in which it is found, Sonnet 134. On the surface, Sonnet 134 is confessional (*So now I have confessed* ...) and seems to speak of a love triangle. It plays on "to write for" (a legal phrase meaning to act on behalf of) to refer to an agreement where one lover takes the place of another, but it may just as easily be construed as an explicit confession of a ghost authorship. Accordingly, when he says, "*He learned but surety-like to write for me*", the true poet may be referring to the front-man.[3] *Surety* is used in the legal sense where one individual stands as guarantor for another.[4]

This sonnet is full of meaning that could be relevant to a confession of ghost authorship, and a few phrases are clustered symmetrically around the vertical NEVILLE/RIMER. We have highlighted two such phrases that may be particularly significant.[5]

We find Sonnet 134 very compelling, and like the paired Sonnets 57–58, 59–60, 67–68, 77–78, 97–98, 104–105, 113–114 (discussed in Appendix 4), and 151–152, Sonnet 134 follows on and forms a pair with Sonnet 133. As with the other paired sonnets, the result is a poem consisting of two stanzas each having the 14-line sonnet form.

---

[2] If the grid remains in 30 columns then *RIMER* occurs on the same diagonal as *NEVILLE.*
[3] The gender of the addressee of the poem is not disclosed, but the phrase *statute of thy beauty* invokes the conventional "royal" status of the beloved.
[4] Booth, *Shakespeare's Sonnets,* p. 464.
[5] The vertical message could be read as *NEVILLE IS RIMER.* Combining the first two lines together with the intersecting inverted vertical *NEVILLE* could be read as *SO NOW I HAVE CONFEST THAT I MYSELFE AM NEVILLE.*

Sonnets 133–134

Beshrew that heart that makes my heart to groane
For that deepe wound it gives my friend and me;
I'st not ynough to torture me alone,
But slave to slavery my sweet'st friend must be.
Me from my selfe thy cruell eye hath taken,
And my next selfe thou harder hath ingrossed,
Of him, my selfe, and thee I am forsaken,
A torment thrice three-fold thus to be crossed:
Prison my heart in thy steele bosomes warde,
But then my friends heart let my poore heart bale,
Who ere keeps me, let my heart be his garde,
Thou canst not then use rigor in my iale.
  And yet thou wilt, for I being pent in thee,
  Perforce am thine and all that is in me.

So, now I have confest that he is thine,
And I my selfe am morgag'd to thy will,
My selfe Ile forfeit, so that other mine
Thou wilt restore to be my comfort still:
But thou wilt not, nor he will not be free,
For thou art covetous, and he is kinde;
He learnd but suretie-like to write for me,
Under that bond that him as fast doth binde.
The statute of thy beauty thou wilt take,
Thou usurer, that put'st forth all to use,
And sue a friend, came debter for my sake;
So him I loose through my unkinde abuse.
  Him have I lost; thou hast both him and me:
  He paies the whole, and yet am I not free.

The paired Sonnets 133 and 134 can also be seen to fit the pattern of co-ordinate mappings. The number that would apply to the pairing of 133–134 is of course the first number 133 which offers the co-ordinates 13,3. These co-ordinates map to the single (apparently deliberate) blank space in the Dedication (see image of the Dedication on page 64).

Sonnet 134

	1	2	3	4	5	6	7	8	9	10	11	12	**13**	14	15
1	T	O	T	H	E	O	N	L	I	E	B	E	G	E	T
2	T	E	R	O	F	T	H	E	S	E	I	N	S	V	I
3	N	G	S	O	N	N	E	T	S	Mr	W	H		A	L
4	L	H	A	P	P	I	N	E	S	S	E	A	N	D	T
5	H	A	T	E	T	E	R	N	I	T	I	E	P	R	O
6	M	I	S	E	D	B	Y	O	V	R	E	V	E	R	-
7	L	I	V	I	N	G	P	O	E	T	W	I	S	H	E
8	T	H	T	H	E	W	E	L	L	-	W	I	S	H	I
9	N	G	A	D	V	E	N	T	V	R	E	R	I	N	S
10	E	T	T	I	N	G	F	O	R	T	H	T	T		

The sole blank space within the Dedication grid is at coordinates 13-3

It does not seem unreasonable to suggest that this blank space may well distil the very essence of this sonnet pair – the torment of an anonymous writer.

We have not examined all possible grid-settings of all 154 sonnets. Rather, we have taken a sample of the sonnets, around 20 that we regard as most suggestive in relation to authorship, and examined those in grid-settings of between 10 and 60 columns. This limited study has not generated anything else that we regard as noteworthy, although it may provide an indication of the rarity of the findings in Sonnet 134.[6] The reader will find many other acrostic words in Sonnet 134, but none that seem to convey any obvious meaning. They include *foles* ("fools" as in Sonnet 124), *very, half, have, felted, meat, tone, trio, sour.* In addition, there are words that are generated at the joining of two words, such as *skin* in row 7. We note the two instances of the word *free* in the sonnet each intersect with one of our acrostics *NEVILLE* or *RIMER.*

Sonnet 134 is highly intriguing. If the message contained within it is intentional, as seems highly likely, it would certainly support the hypothesis that Sir Henry Neville is the author of the works attributed to Shakespeare.

6 It has been argued that exponents of cryptanalysis may succumb to the temptation to seek code everywhere. Further analysis would be very valuable, either to uncover additional encryptions within the sonnets, or possibly to exclude them from further cryptanalysis. Although this might conceivably be achieved more readily via computer analysis, software algorithms would have to make sense of the vagaries of Elizabethan spelling, the use of phonetic puns and numerous other literary devices.

Appendix 4: Poison Arrow

In Chapter 7 we noted an apparent pictogram, being an arrow or a clock hand which we take to be *the hand of time* (pp. 90–101, and Appendix 5).

Sonnet 113 and 114 – *POISWN*

The *W* of *POISWN* maps to 11-3, Sonnet 113, and the vertical *EIE* maps to Sonnet 114.

	1	2	3	4	5	6	7	8	9	10	11	12	13	14	15
1	T	O	T	H	E	O	N	L	I	E	B	E	G	E	T
2	T	E	R	O	F	T	H	E	S	E	I	**N**	S	V	I
3	N	G	S	O	N	N	E	T	S	Mr	**W**	H		A	L
4	L	H	A	P	P	I	N	E	S	**S**	**E**	A	N	D	T
5	H	A	T	E	T	E	R	N	**I**	T	**I**	E	P	R	O
6	M	I	S	E	D	B	Y	**O**	V	R	**E**	V	E	R	-
7	L	I	V	I	**N**	G	**P**	O	E	T	W	I	S	H	E
8	T	H	T	H	**E**	**W**	E	L	L	-	W	I	S	H	I
9	N	G	A	D	**V**	**E**	**N**	T	V	R	E	R	I	N	S
10	E	T	T	**I**	N	G	F	O	R	T	H	T	T		

We observed the similarity of this image to the arrow in the crest of Mr. William Hunnis. We also noted that the letters along the diagonal spell out the near-word *POISWN* which has a compelling association with "arrow". In Horace's Ode 1.22, which we propose is central to the grid system, the poet has no need of "Moorish spears", nor "a quiver full of *poisoned* arrows":

> *Nec **sagittis** gravida **venenatis***
> *Fusce, pharetra.*

Poison arrows are also central to the myth of blind Cupid, the god of love who is invoked throughout the sonnets; the *bow and arrow* is Cupid's emblem. If the *hand of time* were also Cupid's *poison arrow* it would fuse the two central themes of the sonnets, *Time* and *Love.* The most common nouns in the sonnets are *Time* (79 instances) and *Love* (194 instances).

However, *POISWN* is not *POISON* and *W* is not *O*, so we must regard this as a very uncertain hypothesis. In Greek the lower-case symbol *omega*, which is equivalent to *O* in the Latin alphabet, is represented by a symbol (ω) that is similar to W. Indeed, the word *omega* means literally "large *O*" (mega O).

As noted, Sonnet 113 forms a pair with Sonnet 114, and together they may be seen to evoke each of the myth of blind Cupid, poison, and a quiet play on the letter “O”. When struck with Cupid’s arrow, the first person the victim sees becomes the object of their desire. In *A Midsummer Night’s Dream* Puck plays this role and Titania falls in love with an ass (a *monster*).

Sonnets 113–114

Since I left you, mine ***eye*** *is in my minde,*
And that which governes me to goe about,
Doth part his function, and is partly ***blind,***
Seemes ***seeing****, but effectually is out:*
For it no forme delivers to the heart
Of bird, of flowre, or shape which it doth lack,
Of his quick objects hath the minde no part,
Nor his owne ***vision*** *houlds what it doth catch:*
For if it ***see*** *the rud’st or gentlest* ***sight,***
The most sweet-favor or ***deformedst creature,***
The mountaine, or the sea, the day, or night:
The Croe, or Dove, it shapes them to your feature.
Incapable of more repleat, with you,
My most true minde thus maketh mine untrue.

Or whether doth my minde being crown'd with you
Drinke up the monarks plague this flattery?
Or whether shall I say mine ***eie*** *saith true,*
And that your love taught it this Alcumie?
To make of ***monsters****, and things indigest,*
Such ***cherubines*** *as your sweet selfe resemble,*
Creating every bad a perfect best
As fast as objects to his beames assemble:
Oh *tis the first, tis flatry in my* ***seeing,***
And my great minde most kingly drinkes it up,
Mine ***eie*** *well knowes what with his gust is greeing,*
And to his pallat doth prepare the cup.
If it be ***poison'd,*** *tis the lesser sinne,*
That mine ***eye*** *loves it and doth first beginne.*

3 ***Blind***
10 Compare with Bottom in *A Midsummer Night’s Dream.*
19 ***Monsters*** Compare with ***deformedst creature*** in Sonnet 113.
20 ***Cherubines*** may evoke the cherub *Cupid.*
23 ***Oh*** The answer to the two questions in lines 1-4 is *Oh.* This is reminiscent of Sonnet 76 in which the answer to the three *why* questions is *of you* or *your.* ***seeing***
25 ***eie*** In this sonnet pair concerned with the errant behaviour of an *eye* it may be relevant that 11-4 maps to the vertical word *EIE.*
27 Like Cupid’s arrow and the arrow motif in the grid, the *cup* is ***poisoned.***

Appendix 5: Sonnets measuring time

Love may be seen to be the primary theme of *Shakespeare's Sonnets*, but it is usually considered in relation to *Time*. The endurance of true love and the fickleness of imitation can only be measured against the passage of *Time*. The author struggles between two conflicting truths; love is eternal, yet all things change. *Time* is the common denominator[1]. Scholars are unanimous in recognising the author's debt to Ovid in this regard. The Sonnets liberally reference both specific ideas and individual passages in Book 15 of Ovid's *Metamorphoses*.

Perhaps related to this phenomenon, there is at least one other observable pattern in which the numbering of certain sonnets relates to their content; this occurs where the number of the sonnet relates to the measurement of time. In these cases, the number of the sonnet is intertwined with the subject of the sonnet.

Five sonnets seem to encompass the five primary Elizabethan and Jacobean measures of intervals of time:

Sonnet 60: Minute
Sonnet 12: Hour
Sonnet 7: Day
Sonnet 30: Month
Sonnet 52: Year

In addition, there is one other related "interval" that may be observed. This is the interval in music. More than any other art form, *Music* is mysterious because it is both time-based and it can communicate eternity. The fundamental musical interval is the octave:

Sonnet 8: Octave

It is not immediately obvious how these numerical alignments might relate to the Dedication. Although they seem incidental, we propose they enrich the exploration of the cycles of time discussed in Chapter 7.[2]

At the very least, this pattern does seem to provide further evidence that the Sonnets were not a pirated work. Rather, there is a sophisticated authorial logic at work in their sequencing that one would not expect an unauthorised compiler either to perceive or to value.

---

[1] *Time* is one of the most common nouns in the Sonnets, occurring 79 times.

[2] If there is a relationship between these time-based sonnets and the Dedication it may be found in the representation of *Mr WH*. In Chapter 7, we consider Master William Hunnis as a candidate for *Mr WH*. Both the themes of *time* and *music* may be seen to coalesce in his biography.

Time is also invoked in the Dedication to the sonnets. The word *ETERNITIE* is at the very centre of the Dedication grid and maps sequentially to Sonnet 64 (see pp. 222–3).

The clock at Hampton Court Palace, installed in 1540.
The dial is divided into 24 hours and has a single hand.[3]
Note the two positions of the numeral III on the 24-hour dial.
(See pp. 69 and 98)

[3] Photograph by Man Vyi (2009), via Wikimedia Commons. Neville's father was knighted at Hampton Court in 1551 so there can be little doubt that this clock was well-known to his son.

Sonnet 60 – Minute

Sonnet 60 is explicitly concerned with the passage of Time, measured in minutes. At the time the sonnets were published, the minute was directly associated with the number sixty because there are sixty minutes in an hour.

Like as the waves make towards the pibled shore,

So do our ***minuites*** *hasten to their end,*

Each changing place with that which goes before,

In sequent toile all forwards do contend.

Nativity once in the maine of light,

Crawles to maturity, wherewith being crown'd,

Crooked eclipses gainst his glory fight,

And ***time*** *that gave, doth now his gift confound.*

Time *doth transfixe the florish set on youth,*

And delves the paralels in beauties brow,

Feedes on the rarities of natures truth,

And nothing stands but for his sieth to mow.

And yet to ***times*** *in hope, my verse shall stand*

Praising thy worth, dispight ***his cruell hand****.*

2 ***minutes***
8 ***time***
9 ***time***
12 We note the similarity of line 12 to line 13 of Sonnet 12 which invokes the *hour: And nothing gainst Times sieth can make defence*
13 ***times***
14 Time's ***cruel hand*** may evoke an image of the ***hand*** of the clock (as discussed in Chapter 7).

Sonnet 12 – Hour

Sonnet 12 is also explicitly concerned with the passage of Time. In general, Elizabethan clocks had only one hand, the hour hand. The dial was divided into 24 hours, grouped into two twelve-hour intervals of ***day*** and ***night*** as in line 2 below.[4]

When I doe count the clock that tels the time,
And see the brave ***day*** *sunck in hidious* ***night****,*
When I behold the violet past prime,
And sable curls or silver'd ore with white:
When lofty trees I see barren of leaves,
Which erst from heat did canopie the herd
And Sommers greene all girded up in sheaves
Borne on the beare with white and bristly beard:
Then of thy beauty do I question make
That thou among the wastes of ***time*** *must goe,*
Since sweets and beauties do them-selves forsake,
And die as fast as they see others grow,
And nothing gainst ***Times*** *sieth can make defence*
Save breed to brave him, when he takes thee hence.

1 ***the clock that tells the time***
2 ***Day*** and ***night*** are the separate 12-hour intervals that add up to the 24 hours of the clock.
10 ***time***
13 ***times.*** Line 13 is very similar to line 12 of Sonnet 60 which invokes the minute: *And nothing stands but for his sieth to mow.*

[4] Kinney, A.F., *Shakespeare's Webs: Networks of Meaning in Renaissance Drama* (Routledge, New York, 2004), p. 72.

Sonnet 7 – Day

Sonnet 7 is explicit in tracing the passage of Time over one day. This Sonnet puns ideationally on ***Sun***. That is, the image of the Sun is invoked throughout to support the final words ***unless thou get a sonne***. However, the word **Sun** never appears in the sonnet. The construction of ***Sun-day*** is less obvious. There are of course seven named days, and Sunday is the 7th day. Sunday is the Sabbath, the day dedicated to worship. The imagery of Sonnet 7 revolves around worship, and the period of this Sonnet is explicitly one arc of the sun – one ***day***.

Loe in ***the Orient*** *when the gracious light,*

Lifts up his burning head, each under eye

Doth ***homage*** *to his new-appearing sight,*

Serving *with lookes his* ***sacred*** *maiesty,*

And having climb'd the steepe up ***heavenly*** *hill,*

Resembling strong youth in his middle age,

Yet mortall lookes ***adore*** *his beauty still,*

Attending on his goulden ***pilgrimage****:*

But when from high-most pich, with wery car,

Like feeble age he reeleth from the ***day****,*

The eyes (fore dutious) now converted are

From his low tract and looke another way:

So thou, thyself out-going in thy noon:

Unlok'd on diest unlesse thou get a ***sonne****.*

1 ***The Orient*** is the cradle of the Judeo-Christian tradition and the place to which pilgrims travel for worship (**pilgrimage** below).
3 ***homage***
4 ***serving, sacred***
5 ***heavenly***
7 ***adore***
8 ***pilgrimage*** (as to the ***Orient*** above)
10 ***day***
14 The word ***sun*** is invoked throughout, but never actually appears.

Sonnet 30 – Month

Sonnet 30 describes behaviour and emotions during a period of time dedicated to grieving. Then as now, the word ***Moon*** is relevant. In the Shakespeare canon, *Moon* is not only entirely interchangeable with *Month;* it is also identified with grief.

Antony and Cleopatra IV, ix:

> *O thou blessed moon...*
> ...
> *O sovereign mistress of true melancholy,*

Weeping, sighing, sorrow and woe dominate this sonnet.

Sonnet 30 seems to play on a phonetic similarity between *Moan* and *Moon* that no longer exists today. As we have seen, the author rhymes *noon* with *son* in Sonnet 7, lines 12–14. In Sonnet 149, he rhymes *moan* with *upon.* Moreover, while the author rhymes *moon* with *soon* and *noon,* he also rhymes *moon* with *done* (*Hamlet* III, ii, *Midsummer Night's Dream* V, i), and with *Biron* (*Loves Labours Lost,* IV, iii).

In this sonnet he rhymes *moan* with *foregone,* lines 9–11. Therefore we can infer that for the author there was a strong phonetic similarity between ***Moan*** and ***Moon***.

We also know that the author invoked the number 30 as a standard approximation of the number of days in a month, as in *Hamlet,* III, ii:

> *Full* ***thirty*** *times hath Phoebus' cart gone round*
> *Neptune's salt wash and Tellus' orbed ground,*
> *And* ***thirty*** *dozen moons with borrow'd sheen*
> *About the world have times twelve* ***thirties*** *been ...*

Sonnet 30 – Month

When to the Sessions of sweet silent thought
I ***sommon*** *up remembrance of things past,*
I sigh the lacke of many a thing I sought,
And with old woes new waile my deare ***times*** *waste:*
Then can I drowne an eye (un-usd to flow)
For precious friends hid in deaths dateless ***night****,*
And weepe a fresh loves long since canceld woe,
And ***mone th'****expence of many a vannisht sight.*
Then can I greeve at greevances fore-gon,
And heavily from woe to woe tell ore
The sad ***account*** *of fore-****bemoned mone****,*
Which I new pay as if not payd before.
But if the while I thinke on thee (dear friend)
All losses are restord and sorrowes end.

2 ***Summon.*** In this context of "counting a month", possibly ***sum moon*** (see note on pronunciation above).
4 ***times***
6 ***night*** (when the *moon* appears)
8 ***Moneth*** is the standard Early Modern spelling of **Month**. The conflation of *grieving* and of the *moon* is explicit in the construction ***mone th'***.
11 Possibly **account** (count) **of fore-bemooned moon** (see note on pronunciation above). A *count of moon* would be 30.

Sonnet 52 – Year

Sonnet 52 invokes special times of intimacy within ***the long year set*** (52 weeks). The special times referred to are likened to religious feasts (or festivals). In the theocracy of Elizabethan England, these festivals were central to the social and cultural rhythm of the year. Christian Feasts typically last several days. The Christian calendar is divided into 52 weeks. Each feast is celebrated on the weekly Sabbath as set out in the *Lectionary*, the book that details the rituals, vestments, decorations and foods.

So am I as the rich, whose blessed key,

Can bring him to his sweet up-locked treasure,

The which he will not ev'ry hour survay,

For blunting the fine point of seldome pleasure.

Therefore are ***feasts*** *so sollemne and so rare,*

Since sildom comming in ***the long yeare set,***

Like stones of worth they thinly placed are,

Or captaine Iewells in the carconet.

So is the ***time*** *that keepes you as my chest,*

Or as the ward-robe which the robe doth hide,

To make some speciall instant speciall blest,

By new unfoulding his imprison'd pride.

Blessed are you whose worthinesse gives skope,

Being had to triumph, being lackt to hope.

5 The ***feasts*** are the solemn religious feasts of the Christian Calendar.
6 ***The long year set*** is 52 weeks.
9 ***time***

Sonnet 8 – The Octave

Sonnet 8 associates the harmony of family, with musical harmony. The simplest harmony is the interval of 8 notes, the Octave.

More than any other art form, *Music* is mysterious because it is bound by time but it can communicate eternity. In a very real sense, time is the fabric of music; from the tempo, rhythm and repetition of phrases to the frequency of the oscillations that determine pitch and the interplay of pitch that creates polyphony.

Though Sonnet 8 encourages attention to any pleasing musical interval, the octave has a number of qualities that may be most relevant. An octave interval is a reasonable approximation of the difference in pitch between the normal register of an adult male and that of a child or female voice, as suggested in lines 6 and 11. In addition, the octave is a doubling (or halving) of the number of oscillations of a note. A higher note can be seen to contain all lower octaves; effectively a harmony of ***one note*** as suggested by lines 12 and 13.

Sonnet 8 – The Octave

Musick *to heare, why hear'st thou* ***musick*** *sadly,*
Sweets with sweets warre not, joy delights in joy:
Why lov'st thou that which thou receavst not gladly,
Or else receav'st with pleasure thine annoy?
If the ***true concord of well tuned sounds,***
By ***unions married*** *do offend thine eare,*
They do but sweetly chide thee, who confounds
In singlenesse ***the parts*** *that thou should'st beare.*
Marke how ***one string, sweet husband to an other,***
Strikes each in each by mutuall ordering;
Resembling sier, and child, and happy mother,
Who ***all in one, one pleasing note do sing:***
Whose speechlesse ***song being many, seeming one,***
Sings this to thee thou single wilt prove none.

1 ***music, music***
5 (harmony)
6 (harmony as of a male and female voice – an octave)
8 (harmony created from musical ***parts***)
10 (harmony)
11 (harmony as of a male, child and female voice – an octave)
12 The octave may be seen to be a harmony of ***one note.***
13 The octave may be seen to be a harmony of ***one*** note.

Sonnet 64 – ETERNITIE

***E**TERNITIE* maps *sequentially* to cell 64, Sonnet 64.

	1	2	3	4	5	6	7	8	9	10	11	12	13	14	15
1	T	O	T	H	E	O	N	L	I	E	B	E	G	E	T
2	T	E	R	O	F	T	H	E	S	E	I	N	S	V	I
3	N	G	S	O	N	N	E	T	S	Mr	W	H		A	L
4	L	H	A	P	P	I	N	E	S	S	E	A	N	D	T
5	H	A	T	**E**	**T**	**E**	**R**	**N**	**I**	**T**	**I**	**E**	P	R	O
6	M	I	S	E	D	B	Y	O	V	R	E	V	E	R	-
7	L	I	V	I	N	G	P	O	E	T	W	I	S	H	E
8	T	H	T	H	E	W	E	L	L	-	W	I	S	H	I
9	N	G	A	D	V	E	N	T	V	R	E	R	I	N	S
10	E	T	T	I	N	G	F	O	R	T	H	T	T		

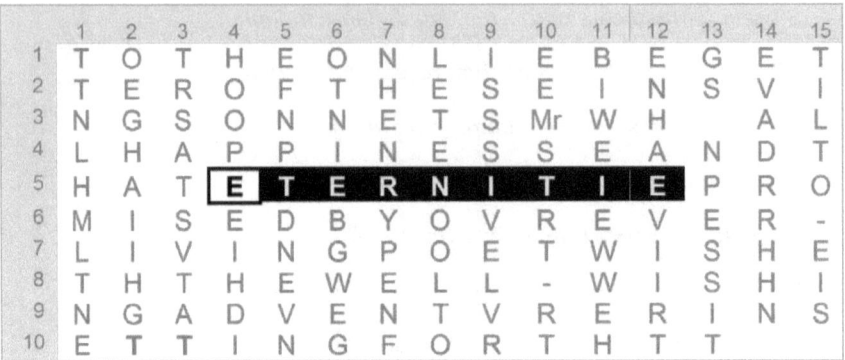

*When I have seene by **times** fell hand defaced*

*The rich proud cost of outworne buried **age**,*

When sometime loftie towers I see downe rased,

*And brasse **eternall** slave to mortall rage.*

When I have seene the hungry Ocean gaine

Advantage on the Kingdome of the shoare,

And the firme soile win of the watry maine,

Increasing store with losse, and losse with store.

When I have seene such interchange of state,

Or state it selfe confounded, to decay,

Ruine hath taught me thus to ruminate

*That **Time** will come and take my love away.*

This thought is as a death which cannot choose

But weepe to have, that which it feares to loose.

Sonnet 64 – ETERNITIE

Of all the sonnets that concern *Time*, Sonnet 64 evokes the most absolute and chilling expression of *Eternity*. This is encapsulated in line 10, where *state itself* is *confounded to decay*. Here, *state* would seem to include the entire universe, including time itself.[5]

1 ***time***
2 ***age*** Antiquity
4 ***eternal***
10 ***Or state itself confounded to decay***
12 ***Time***

---

[5] Telford Conlon interprets line 10 as follows: '... state itself confounded to decay' is a universal generalisation. Not just particular states but state in general is confounded to decay, and in fact is an early statement of what became the second law of thermodynamics which didn't appear in its scientific form for another 250 years. It led to one German scientist in the 19th century, Clausius, to express it as 'the heat death of the universe.' Conlon, Telford. "Was Shakespeare a Scientist", *The Science Show,* Australian Broadcasting Corporation, aired 29 July 2017.

Appendix 6: Neville's Letter to King James

Neville's letter to King James is taken from Jansson, M. (ed.), *Proceedings in Parliament, 1614 House of Commons* (American Philosophical Society, Philadelphia, 1988), p. 247.

An Advice touching the holding of a Parliament (Carte 77, FF.135-37v, Bodleian Library).

> *There is a question grown and much debated amongst us, whether the King should relieve himself in his great want (whereof the world taketh knowledge both at home and abroad), by a Parliament, or by some projects and devices to raise money, which may be set on foot to that purpose.*
>
> *For my part, I will not examine what these projects may be, although by experience of such as have been put in use since the dissolution of the last Parliament, I am induced to believe that either they will fail or fall short in the practice, howsoever they may appear likely in the theory; or that they will prove like some medicines, which do rather take away sense of pain for the present than cure the grief for which they were applied.*
>
> *But admit there may be other ways devised to relieve the King, yet am I clearly of opinion that there is none so fit, so honourable, and so necessary as by a Parliament. My reason is this: I consider on what terms the King and the last Parliament parted at the dissolution, full of distaste and acrimony on His Majesty's part, and not without some discontentment on theirs. I consider also that from the Parliament, the apprehensions that are taken there are spread and dispersed over the whole realm. And further, that the knowledge of these misunderstandings between His Majesty and the Parliament is not confined within this kingdom only but is flown abroad into all foreign parts that have any commerce or dealing with us.*
>
> *Now what disadvantage this opinion may breed us, and what hopes it is like to raise both in our enemies abroad and our discontented persons at home may easily be gathered. For, as there is nothing that more upholds the reputation of any Prince than the opinion of his strength at home, which consists principally in the love and concord between him and his people from whence there followeth naturally a sequence of all other duties on their part to make him strong and able to help and hurt his neighbours; so there is nothing that emboldeneth more an enemy, either open or secret, to attempt the disturbance of the peace of any State than the imagination that the Prince and people stand not in kind and loving terms together.*

And to this purpose I remember a story of Antigonus, one of the immediate and mightiest successors of Alexander, who, being solemnly set in great state to give audience to some other prince's ambassador; as he was in that solemnity, his son Demetrius came in from hunting, and being arrayed in his hunting attire, with his darts in his hand, presented himself so unto his father, and after a salutation given according to the manner of that people, sat down by him. The audience being ended, and the ambassadors retiring themselves, Antigonus called them again and willed them to report one thing more to their masters, namely, in what fashion they had seen him and his son converse together, intending that it would be taken for a great argument of his strength and a great assurance of his safety that his son and he lived in that confidence and concord. If this were true in that case between the father and the son, how much more is it verified between the Prince and the people. And hereupon I conclude: that the world being possessed with a conceit that the last Parliament ended with some sourness and distaste on the King's part, and not with the best satisfaction on theirs, there is nothing more necessary for the King's Majesty, either in regard of honour or safety, than to deface that opinion, and to make it apparent to the world that as he was received into the kingdom at his first entry, with the greatest demonstrations of the love and joy of his people that ever Prince was, so he is still rooted and established in their hearts; and that whatsoever cloud or mist might seem to have darkened or overshadowed the kind respects between them at that time, it was no other but that which happeneth often by some distemper, between a tender father and dutiful children which quickly vanish when the distemper of either side is removed.

For the effecting of this I can think of no other way but by another Parliament, for there this error grew, and there and nowhere else it must be repaired.

The harsh conclusion of the former Parliament bred that ill-conceit, and the sweet close of another must beget a better. And by this means two notable effects will be wrought together if matters be well handled; the removing of that erroneous and dangerous conceit of a misunderstanding between the King and his people, and the relieving of the King's present necessities in a sure speedy and plentiful manner; whereas that other cause of projects may haply prove slow and fail in the most, and in very few succeed according to the first design.

And for rectifying the misconceit between the King and his people there is no hope at all that way. It is rather to be feared it will do hurt, and rather aggravate than cure that malady if there be not great judgment used in the choice of the projects, and much dexterity in the managing of them. Against this opinion there are two objections. The one that the Parliament may still continue adverse and unwilling to relieve the King at all, and so no hope of making up the breach, the other that as long as it is conceived the King cannot help himself without them, they will play upon the advantage of his necessities and extort some unreasonable demands from him before they yield to do anything for him. Both these objections are grounded upon the same false foundation, namely, that whatsoever the last Parliament did in that kind, they did it out of evil affection, which I do know, and do confidently avow to be otherwise, and have before in speech delivered the true reasons of that averseness, as one that lived and conversed inwardly with the chief of them, that were noted to be most backward and know their inwardest thoughts on that business. So, I dare undertake for the most of them that the King's Majesty proceeding in a gracious course toward his people, shall find those gentlemen exceeding willing to do him service, and to give him such contentment as may sweeten all the former distastes, and leave both His Majesty and the world fully satisfied of their good intentions, and of the general affection of his subjects.

It is true (as I lately delivered unto His Majesty), that some things will be desired and expected of him by way of grace, which may both give some contentment to them that shall pay what is given, and justify the care and honest regard of them that shall give it. And, without this, I dare promise nothing ; for it is most certain that, as in private families and all other societies, where the straitest bonds of nature or election do concur to unite affections, there is almost a continual necessity of mutual offices of kindness to nourish and maintain that love, so in kingdoms, besides that great bond of protection and allegiance between the sovereign and the subject, there is a like necessary use of the frequent interchange of mutual effects of grace and love to cherish and foster that tender affection that daily is to be renewed between them. But what be the things that will be demanded or expected by the Parliament on behalf of the people will be hard for any one man to set down. Yet what I have collected out of the desires of sundry of the principal and most understanding gentlemen that were of the last Parliament, and are like to be of this, I will be bold to deliver in a memorial hereunto adjoined, whereby it shall appear that they aim not at anything unjust or unreasonable, or that may derogate from His Majesty in point of sovereignty (further than His Majesty hath already been pleased to offer in writing to the last Parliament, which no doubt will be remembered), nor in point of profit to any matter of certain and considerable value, but only at such things as being now of small moment and loss to His Majesty to depart with, because they have been sifted and ransacked to the bottom, may yet be valued to the subjects, both in opinion and truth, at a high rate, because they shall thereby enjoy a great repose and security from vexation which any of them may otherwise be subject unto.

These things being taken into His Majesty's consideration, and receiving His gracious approbation as matter not unfit to be yielded of grace unto his subjects, the next points to be thought of are the time of holding the Parliament, the things preceding to be done by way of preparation, and the manner of proceeding with the House of Commons when the Parliament is assembled. For the first, I see no cause why it should be deferred longer than Michaelmas, for after the session there must be a time proportionable for the Commissioners to sit, and for the money to be levied and brought into the Exchequer, which the sooner it is done, the sooner will the King be eased of his debts for which he payeth interest, and the sooner will his reputation be recovered and settled, which is the thing that most deserves to be respected. If the Parliament begin at Michaelmas, the Term may be adjourned to Hallowtide; or if not yet, till that time there is little business done, so as the lawyers may well attend the Parliament, whose absence will otherwise breed delay. And I do not see but in a month or five weeks this point of supplying the King and of his retribution will be easily determined if it be proposed betimes and followed close afterwards.

For the second, which concerns matter of preparation, these be the things that I would humbly offer to His Majesty's gracious consideration, to forbear to use any speech that may irritate, and to seem rather confident than diffident of their affections, casting the fault of any former error upon evil offices done on both sides, and want of true understanding rather than want of good affection. To speak graciously and benignly to the people that shall flock to see His Majesty this progress. And especially, to take notice of the principal gentlemen, and let them kiss his hand, and do them some other grace. To give order to the Archbishop to prohibit all books and invective sermons against the Parliament, so as notice may be taken of His Majesty's commandment before the meeting. To peruse the grievances exhibited the last Parliament, and if His Majesty would please to be gracious in any of them, to do it of himself before he be pressed. For a small thing in that manner will give more contentment than much more obtained with importunity. And especially, to call to mind if His Majesty promised anything to the last Parliament which is not yet performed; for upon the performance of that men will be like to ground their trust and hopes in those things which shall be offered now.

For the last point concerning the manner of proceeding, I wish that His Majesty will be pleased to make his propositions by himself or by his ministers and servants that are of their own body, and not by mediation of the Lords. For the Commons will be rather willing to make oblation of their affections themselves unto His Majesty than that any others should do it, and intercept both the merit and thanks from them. I wish also that the King should forbear to nominate any particular men to be sent unto him from the Commons to treat upon any point or occasion, but after His Majesty hath declared his own desires and made likewise known his gracious inclination to gratify his subjects with any favours and graces that with reason and moderation they can desire for them.

His Majesty may be pleased to require the House to nominate a competent number of thirty or forty or fewer which may repair unto him with their demands, and be authorized both to ask and answer such questions as the debate about them shall beget without concluding or binding the House in any point, but only to clear things and report all back to the House. This course, I conceive, will much expedite the business, avoid jealousies, and give good satisfaction to the most, when they shall see that the King shall understand their desire immediately from themselves without any interposition, or danger of misinterpretation, and that upon any point of doubt they shall be admitted to clear their own intentions and not to be subject to the construction of other.

Matters being thus prepared beforehand, and thus managed at the time, and His Majesty being pleased to be gracious to his people in the points proposed or any other of the like nature which may be thought of by the House, when they meet (for beforehand no man can precisely say these things will be demanded and no other) I have no doubt, but am very confident, that His Majesty shall receive as much contentment of this next Parliament as he received distaste of the former, and that all things will end in that sweet accord that will be both honourable and comfortable for His Majesty and happy for the whole realm. And when His Majesty hath made use of his people's affection to put him out of want, any fit projects that shall be offered may be the boldlier entertained to fill his coffers. For whatsoever shall be done in that kind will be the less subject to offence when there is a perfect renewing of affections gone before; whereas otherwise whiles dislikes continue seu bene, seu male facta premunt.

In this advice, it may evidently appear that I have proceeded with more zeal to His Majesty than caution or wariness for myself; for I am not ignorant what a hazard I run if things should fall out contrary to my expectation. But love and faith cast no perils. And I hold it a matter of that consequence both to King and people to have these misunderstandings cleared as well in truth as in opinion, that I would think my life of little value in respect of it, and had rather hazard anything that may befall me than leave such an office unattempted. Wherein if I fail, howsoever my discretion may be censured, yet I am sure the honest purpose and sincerity of my heart cannot be reproved.

Bibliography

Allen, R.H., *Star Names* (Dover, 1963), first published 1889.

Bassi, S. and Fei, A.T., *Shakespeare in Venice. Exploring the city with Shylock and Othello* (Editrice Elzeviro, Treviso, Italy, 2007).

Bate, J., *Soul of the Age* (Penguin, London, 2008).

Booth, S., *Precious Nonsense: The Gettysburg Address, Ben Jonson's Epitaphs on His Children, and Twelfth Night* (University of California Press, Berkeley, 1998).

Booth, S., *Shakespeare's Sonnets* (Yale Nota Bene, New Haven, 2000).

Boswell-Stone, W.B., *Shakespeare's Holinshed, the Chronicles and the Historical Plays Compared* (*Notes and Queries* (1st series), ii, 307; London, 1896, New York, 1966).

Bradbeer, M. and Casson, J., *Sir Henry Neville, Alias William Shakespeare: Authorship Evidence in the History Plays* (McFarland, Jefferson North Carolina, 2015).

Burgon, J.W., *The Life and Times of Sir Thomas Gresham Vol. 2* (1849).

Burrow, C. (ed.), *The Oxford Shakespeare Complete Sonnets and Poems* (Cambridge, 2002).

Burrow, C., "Life and Work in Shakespeare's Poems", *Chatterton Lecture on Poetry. Proceedings of the British Academy* 97, 15–50 (1998).

Casson, J., *Much Ado About Noting: Henry Neville and Shakespeare's Secret Source.* (Dolman Scott, 2010).

Casson, J. and Rubinstein, W.D., *Sir Henry Neville was Shakespeare: The Evidence* (Amberley Press, 2016).

Chamberlain, J., *The Letters of John Chamberlain.* Edited by N.E. McClure. 2 vols (Philadelphia: American Philosophical Society, 1939).

Conlon, Telford, *"Was Shakespeare a Scientist"*, The Science Show, Australian Broadcasting Corporation, aired 29 July 2017.

Davys, J., An Essay on the Art of Decyphering (1737), p. 42.
Cited in Tomokiyo, S., http://cryptiana.web.fc2.com/code/elizabeth.htm. Accessed 3 April 2016.

Donaldson, I., *Ben Jonson. A Life* (Oxford University Press, 2011).

Duncan, O.L., *The Political Career of Sir Henry Neville: An Elizabethan Gentleman in the Court of James I* (PhD Thesis, Ohio State University, 1974).

Duncan-Jones, K., "Was the 1609 Shake-Speares Sonnets Really Unauthorized?" *The Review of English Studies*, New Series. 34, no. 134, 151–71 (1983).

Ellis, D., *The Truth About William Shakespeare. Fact, Fiction and Modern Biographies* (Edinburgh University Press, 2012).

Falk, D., *The Science of Shakespeare. A new look at the Playwright's Universe* (Goose Lane Editions, Fredericton, New Brunswick, Canada, 2014).

Friedman, W.F. and Friedman, E.S., *The Shakespearean Ciphers Examined: An Analysis of Cryptographic Systems Used as Evidence That Some Author Other Than William Shakespeare Wrote the Plays Attributed to Him* (Cambridge University Press, 1957).

Froude, J.A., *History of England from the Fall of Wolsey to the Death of Elizabeth, Vol. III* (1856–1870).

Gayley, C., *Shakespeare and the Founders of Liberty in America* (Macmillan, NY, 1917).

Goulding, R.D., "*Savile, Sir Henry (1549–1622)*", Oxford Dictionary of National Biography, OUP, 2004; online ed., www.oxforddnb.com/view/article/24737.

Green, M., *Wriothesley's Roses in Shakespeare's Sonnets, Poems and Plays* (Clevedon Books, Baltimore, Maryland, 1993).

Hotson, L., *Mr WH* (Rupert Hart-Davis, London, 1964).

James, B., *Henry Neville and the Shakespeare Code* (Music for Strings, Bognor Regis, 2008).

James, B. and Rubinstein, W.D., *The Truth Will Out: Unmasking the Real Shakespeare* (Pearson Longman, Harlow, England, 2005).

Jansson, M. (ed.), *Proceedings in Parliament 1614: House of Commons* (American Philosophical Society, Philadelphia, 1988).

Kinney, A.F., *Shakespeare's Webs: Networks of Meaning in Renaissance Drama* (Routledge, New York, 2004).

Lesser, Z., "Mixed Government and Mixed Marriage in a King and No King: Sir Henry Neville Reads Beaumont and Fletcher", *English Literary History* 69, pp. 947–77 (2002).

Lesser, Z., *Renaissance Drama and the Politics of Publication* (Cambridge University Press, 2008).

Leyland, B. and Goding, J.W., "Authors crack the Bard's code", *The Australian*, 19 July 2006.

Long, J.H., "Shakespeare and Thomas Morley", *Modern Language Notes* 65, 17–22 (1950). Johns Hopkins University Press.

McCarthy, K., *Byrd* (Oxford University Press, 2013).

Manning, J.A., *The Lives of the Speakers of the House of Commons* (Myers and Company, 1850).

Michell, J., *Who Wrote Shakespeare?* (Thames and Hudson, London, 1996).

Miles, R., *Ben Jonson. His life and work* (Routledge and Kegan Paul, London and New York, 1986).

Nelson, A., *Monstrous Adversary: The Life of Edward De Vere, 17th Earl of Oxford* (Liverpool University Press, 2003).

Nicolson, A., *God's Secretaries. The Making of the King James Bible* (HarperCollins, New York, 2003).

Ogburn, C., *The Mystery of William Shakespeare. Foreword by Lord Vere* (Sphere Books, Penguin, London, 1988).

Price, D., *Shakespeare's Unorthodox Biography: New Evidence of an Authorship Problem* (Greenwood Press, Westport Connecticut, 2001; revised edition published by shakespeare-authorship.com/Bookmasters USA, 2012).

Roe, R.P., *The Shakespeare Guide to Italy* (Harper Perennial, New York, 2011).

Rollet, J.M., "Secrets of the Dedication to Shakespeare's Sonnets", *The Oxfordian* 5, no. 2, 60–75 (1999).

Rollins, H.E. (ed.), *The Paradise of Dainty Devices (1576–1606)* (Harvard University Press Cambridge, 1927).

Rowse, A.L., *Shakespeare's Southampton. Patron of Virginia* (Harper and Row, New York, 1965).

Sawyer, E. (ed.), Sir Ralph Winwood, *Memorials of Affairs of State in the Reigns of Queen Elizabeth and King James 1* (London, 1725).

Schlueter, J., "Drawing in a Theatre: Peacham, De Witt, and the Table-book", *Theatre Notebook* 68, pp. 69–86 (2014).

Schmidt, A., *Shakespeare Lexicon and Quotation Dictionary* (Dover, New York, 1971).

Schoenbaum, S., *Shakespeare's Lives* (Clarendon Press, Oxford, 1970).

Shapiro, J., *Contested Will. Who wrote Shakespeare?* (Simon and Schuster, London, New York and Toronto, 2010).

Stewart, A., *Shakespeare's Letters* (Oxford University Press, New York, 2008).

Stopes, C.C., *William Hunnis and the revels of the Chapel Royal: a study of his period and the influences which affected Shakespeare* (A. Uystpruyst, Louvain, 1910; reprint 2013 by Isha Books, New Delhi).

Stopes, C.C., *The Life of Henry, Third Earl of Southampton, Shakespeare's Patron* (Cambridge University Press, Cambridge and New York, 1922).

Streitberger, W.R., *Court Revels 1495–1559.* Studies in Early English Drama (University of Toronto Press, 1994).

Thomson, E. (ed.), *The Chamberlain Letters* (Capricorn, New York, 1966).

Tomokiyo, S., *Ciphers during the Reign of Queen Elizabeth I,* http://cryptiana.web.fc2.com/code/elizabeth.htm.

Vendler, H., *The Art of Shakespeare's Sonnets, Volume 1* (Harvard University Press, Cambridge, Mass., 1997)

Waldman, M., *Elizabeth and Leicester* (Collins Clear-type Press, London, 1946).

Wells, S. and Taylor, G., *William Shakespeare: A Textual Companion* (W.W. Norton, New York, 1997).

Wrixon, F.B., *Codes, Ciphers and Secret Communication* (Black Dog and Leventhal, 1992).

Index

www.ingramcontent.com/pod-product-compliance
Lightning Source LLC
Chambersburg PA
CBHW030853170426
43193CB00009BA/589
* 9 7 8 1 9 2 5 5 8 8 6 7 5 *